Amazon
TOP SELLER SECRETS

Insider Tips from Amazon's Most Successful Sellers

Brad Schepp and Debra Schepp

Technical Editor, Gary Richardson

AMACOM

American Management Association

New York • Atlanta • Brussels • Chicago • Mexico City • San Francisco
Shanghai • Tokyo • Toronto • Washington, D.C.

Special discounts on bulk quantities of AMACOM books are available to corporations, professional associations, and other organizations. For details, contact Special Sales Department, AMACOM, a division of American Management Association, 1601 Broadway, New York, NY 10019.
Tel: 212-903-8316. Fax: 212-903-8083.
E-mail: specialsls@amanet.org
Website: www.amacombooks.org/go/specialsales
To view all AMACOM titles go to: www.amacombooks.org

This publication is designed to provide accurate and authoritative information in regard to the subject matter covered. It is sold with the understanding that the publisher is not engaged in rendering legal, accounting, or other professional service. If legal advice or other expert assistance is required, the services of a competent professional person should be sought.

Various names used by companies to distinguish their software and other products can be claimed as trademarks. AMACOM uses such names throughout this book for editorial purposes only, with no intention of trademark violation. All such software or product names are in initial capital letters or ALL CAPITAL letters. Individual companies should be contacted for complete information regarding trademarks and registration.

Library of Congress Cataloging-in-Publication Data

Schepp, Brad.
  Amazon top seller secrets : insider tips from Amazon's most successful sellers / Brad Schepp and Debra Schepp.
      p. cm.
  Includes index.
  ISBN-13: 978-0-8144-1034-9 (pbk.)
  ISBN-10: 0-8144-1034-0 (pbk.)
  1. Amazon.com (Firm) 2. Electronic commerce. 3. Selling.
I. Schepp, Debra. II. Title.

HF5548.32.S277 2009
658.8'72—dc22
                                    2008053870

Printing number

10 9 8 7 6 5 4 3 2 1

In memory of Marvin J. Schepp.

Dad spent his whole working life in the retail industry.

We never knew anyone who loved shopping more.

He would so have enjoyed this new world of

e-commerce, and we would have loved

to share it with him.

B.S

D.S.

CONTENTS

ACKNOWLEDGMENTS

Writing a book can seem like such a solitary pursuit. Even between co-authors, each has assigned tasks, and much of the actual work happens in the quiet between thought and keyboard clicks. However, writing a book only seems like a solitary pursuit. When the pages are done, it's very easy to look back and see the dozens, if not hundreds, of people who made those pages possible. Here's our chance to introduce you to some of the many people who helped us and, in some small way, thank them for everything they've done.

First in line is our friend and technical editor, Gary Richardson, Goggles and Glasses. Gary was the one who actually suggested that we write this book, and he was right. He's incredibly busy running his successful e-commerce business, but that never kept him from answering our questions and offering us guidance every single time we asked. He's smart, clever, funny, and very insightful. We couldn't have asked for a better partner or friend, and we're sure, once you finish reading this book, you'll feel the same way.

Bill Gladstone and Ming Russell of Waterside, Inc. have long been reliable and loyal agents to our work. We can always count on them to represent our best interests and tell us when they think we're wrong. Thanks, once again.

To the staff at Amacom, you made our job so much better. Jacquie Flynn was a writer's dream editor. She was there when we needed her, but she also gave us the freedom to produce the book we envisioned. That's a rare combination. To our copy editor, Cheryl Ferguson; our associate editor, Erika Spelman; and our proofreader, Robin Perlow, you made us look so much smarter than we are! Thanks.

We were very fortunate to have the help and support of some wonderful Amazon staff. Kay Kinton, public relations manager, and Anthony Joseph of Amazon's Seller Central answered uncountable questions and gave us the feedback necessary to make sure we were telling the Amazon story accurately. Thank you both.

For years now, we've immersed ourselves in the world of e-commerce. During that time, we've met so many fascinating and successful sellers. In some ways, these folks are the pioneers of the twenty-first century. No, they don't set out to cross the Rockies in Conestoga wagons, but they do often chart new and unfamiliar lands in order to build better lives for themselves and their families. We'd like to list all of them here, but you'd really get annoyed if we did. Instead, we'll call out some of the ones who have consistently answered our e-mails, instead of pretending they'd been caught in spam filters. In no particular order, but with great affection, we'd like to thank the following: Kevin Boyd of preferreddiscounts.com, Stephanie Inge of stephintexas, Drew Friedman of White Mountain Trading Company, Bing Yang of Augustina Jewelry, Xavier Helgesen of Better World Books, Charise Richards of OneChicBoutique, Rene Klassen of Musicnmore, Chris Schlieter of timezone, Barry Mark of Treebeard Books, Steve Jay of wholesalelaptopbattery, Cynthia Lizana of Texcyngoods, and

Steven C. Grossberg, a hugely successful seller on Amazon and eBay and president of the Internet Merchants Association (IMA).

Consultants to the e-commerce industry and people who have built their own businesses in support of that industry represent another group to whom we will always be beholden. Special thanks go out to them. Brian Elliot, president and CEO of Alibris, gave us wonderful insight into the world of online bookstores. Debbie Leavitt, president of As Was, is always reliable in her good advice. Wes Shepherd is CEO of the software company Channel Velocity, and Robert Green of Auctiva provided plenty of great information about his company's fine product. David Yaskulka, president of Blueberry Consulting, knows more about e-commerce than any 10 of his peers. He's smart and kind and has always been a true friend to us. Mark Taylor of Redroller.com taught us a lot about shipping, and Steve Weber of Weber Books has already forgotten more than most people will ever know about online marketing. The same is true of Andy Geldman of *Auction Software Review*, except he knows everything there is to know about e-commerce automation software. Thank you to Alex McArthur of OrangeSoda and Joe Cortese, president of the Professional eBay Sellers Alliance (PeSA). Finally, a special thank you goes to Ina and David Steiner of AuctionBytes.com. They consistently publish an invaluable e-commerce newsletter, and we know just how hard that is!

We've saved a special thank you for our profiled Amazon sellers. Not only did they tolerate our endless questions, but they opened their businesses to scrutiny and shared their stories with us. We hope you'll find them inspirational as well as informative. Michael Jansma of GemAffair, Gary Richardson of Goggles and Glasses, Eric Lau of Visiondecor, Kathy Wojtczak of Element Jewelry & Accessories, Andy and Deb Mowery of debnroo, Asad Bangash and Jody Rogers of Beachcombers!, Dan Morrill of Alternating Reality, Kirk Holbert of Cosmic-King, and Tricia Records of Read_Rover_Books are all amazing. From our first e-mail exchanges, we knew we were in competent hands, and they never let us down for a moment. We owe them all a huge debt of thanks.

We'd also like to thank our family—the ones far away who haven't seen us in months, and the kids who put up with us everyday. They were so tolerant of our distractions, the endless microwaved dinners, and all the conversations that included the word *Amazon,* but had nothing to do with rainforests. Thanks for being everything you are to us. You know how endlessly we love you, Stephanie, Ethan, Andrew, and Laurel. Finally, to the beasts who warmed our desks and made us laugh, Max, Mollie, and Moe: We were never once endangered by a single mouse, and your goofy ways brightened lots of long and work-filled days.

Amazon
TOP SELLER SECRETS

Introduction

This is a book of secrets for success from some of Amazon's top sellers. They're some of the brightest entrepreneurs of this still-new century. They work for themselves, but under the smart, knowledgeable, somewhat-stern watch of the Internet's top retailer, Amazon.com. Some of these successful business owners brought their thriving businesses with them when they came to Amazon. Others set out to build e-commerce businesses that might never have existed without the Amazon platform. They all have fascinating stories to tell and a wealth of knowledge they have been willing to share with others who'd like to follow their paths to success. You can be one of them. We wrote this book to help you get there.

Along our journey together, you'll learn about people like Kathy Wojtczak of Element Jewelry & Accessories. She'd been operating a bricks-and-mortar store until she tested the Amazon waters in 2005. Now, she would never turn back. You'll meet experienced e-merchants like Michael Jansma of GemAffair and Andy Mowery of debnroo.

These two Amazon top sellers were hugely successful eBay PowerSellers first. They saw some changes at eBay that drove them to look for other, better environments for their businesses. They soon realized that Amazon fit the bill. You'll meet Dan Morrill, who never owned a store before, but set out to build a successful online bookstore of his own, with Amazon as its cornerstone.

But back to you, our reader. We'll share with you the advice these sellers offer and the knowledge base they've gained to help make your trip to a successful e-commerce business faster and more comfortable. Amazon isn't quite like its famous competitor, eBay. You can find books and seminars galore to help you build a life for yourself using that site. But Amazon hasn't received much attention of that kind, and it's not as easy to immerse yourself in a self-directed Amazon education. So picking up this book is a great first step. We've not only provided shared advice and "secrets" we've gleaned from these sellers, but we've also put those secrets within the context you need to understand them. We realize that selling on Amazon is new to many of you, so we've helped you find your way around this neighborhood and explained how it works. We've also profiled some of your most successful new neighbors at the end of each chapter. They're a fascinating lot, and we've enjoyed telling their stories, convinced that you will enjoy reading them.

Happily for us all, the sellers who worked with us were all great teachers, as well as being smart businesspeople. Anyone who's ever been to school knows what a huge difference that makes. Your teachers throughout this book will help you learn by sharing their experiences and engaging your curiosity. They might even make you smile. They've helped us sprinkle surprises throughout this book, including these great tidbits:

- Profiles, or real-life Amazon success stories, complete with pictures

- Savvy advice from experts, such as one of the world's top

shipping experts, Mark Taylor, and e-commerce marketing wizard Dale King

- Details needed for moving to other selling venues, such as your own WebStore
- Quotes and stories from some of Amazon's most successful sellers

Perhaps most important, Gary Richardson worked with us to prepare this book. Gary was Amazon's number-one seller in his category for 2007. He helped us keep things fresh and real. Gary was our sounding board, our teacher, and our cheerleader every step of the way as we prepared this book for you. We're excited to share the benefits of his experience with you as you travel through these pages.

We're convinced that you will agree with us. You made a great decision to read this book. Here's a brief rundown of the chapters that follow. We'll guide you all along the way, from sourcing products for your Amazon business to building a successful presence on the Web itself.

Chapter Summaries

Chapter 1. Amazon, and You're Done. You may think you know all about Amazon because you've bought a few things from the site, but trust us, you'll be amazed at just how far-reaching the Amazon empire has become. We'll describe that empire briefly, and throw in a little history to add some context. We devote much of this chapter to Amazon's Marketplace—a very good place to start selling on Amazon.

Chapter 2. Which Way Should I Go? It turns out that selling on Amazon's Marketplace is not your only option for making money there. You can also become a Pro Merchant. Seller

Central also fits in here. Additionally, you can sell through your own Amazon WebStore(s). Amazon gives you plenty of options for building a business, and while that can seem intimidating at first, it's ultimately what you want: choices.

Chapter 3. You Have to Buy It Before You Can Sell It. It doesn't matter whether you've set up shop on eBay, Amazon, or Main Street; if you don't have a steady stream of great products to sell, you won't be around very long. Our years of speaking to new entrepreneurs have shown us that this is the number-one question all sellers have: Where do I get more products to sell? This important chapter covers strategies for sourcing products—from finding inventory on your own shelves, to working directly with manufacturers, to buying wholesale lots on eBay for resale on Amazon. (We can tell you from personal experience that eBay can be a very good source of products for resale on Amazon.) And guess what? Amazon, too, with its millions of products, can also be a great source of inventory for you when you start selling on your own website.

Chapter 4. Creating Great Product Detail Pages. Here we provide "best practices" advice on describing, classifying, and, yes, pricing your items. You'll learn tips for creating high-performing product detail pages. And here, as in every chapter, we'll include success strategies from top Amazon sellers. Of course, you don't always have to create your own product pages if your products are already part of Amazon's vast catalog. So we'll also describe how best to piggyback on pages that already exist.

Chapter 5. Automating Your Amazon Business. Smart sellers use software tools, whether they download them from Amazon or other sources, to help them automate listings, track sales, manage inventory, and run their businesses effectively. The largest sellers work with companies such as Channel Velocity to help them move vast amounts of inventory through more than one channel. An industry insider told us the information in this chapter is difficult to find in a single place, so we were happy to compile it for you.

Chapter 6. Customer Service Without the Smile. Although your online customers can't actually see your warm smile, there's still much you can do to ensure that buying from you is a pleasant experience. Just as on eBay, your feedback score is hugely important, and is a keen measure of your success. We'll ensure that you have all the information and success strategies you need to leapfrog competitors and attain (and keep) the highest score feasible. For example, it is more important to maintain good feedback than to have large numbers of customers. Sellers must also know how to encourage feedback, since Amazon buyers are less likely to leave feedback than are other online buyers. Sellers must learn not to be shy about asking customers to reconsider unfair feedback.

Chapter 7. Marketing Your Amazon Business. Amazon has more than 1 million "third-party" sellers, yet many customers think that all Amazon sellers are the same. As a matter of fact, many of your Amazon customers won't even realize they're not purchasing directly from Amazon. So, how can you possibly distinguish yourself in such a setting? Here are true secrets for setting yourself apart from other sellers. We provide tips and tricks from branding experts that would make a marketing whiz at Coca-Cola proud. We'll show you how to win the *buy box* and build your customer base even when Amazon fulfills your orders using its own well-branded boxes. Also, we'll show you how to drive traffic to your listings through reviews, which are very powerful, yet sometimes hard to get. Finally, there's advice about using Amazon tags, your Amazon blog, and Amazon's already popular shopping features, such as recommendations and Listmania.

Chapter 8. Shipping: The Workhorse of Your Operation. *Sold! Ship now!* Those three words bring joy to the hearts of Amazon sellers worldwide. But two more words, *packing* and *shipping*—the less glamorous parts of operating e-commerce businesses—are hugely important. They're also quite time consuming. We'll share secrets for making the shipping process as inexpensive and efficient as possible. Did you know, for example, that you could outsource all of this to Amazon through its Fulfillment by Amazon service? More and more sellers are using this program, and the vast majority are glad they've signed up. Finally, you'll learn how to make the best use of packing slips, invoices, shipping materials, and return labels.

Chapter 9. Life Beyond Amazon: Selling Through Other Venues. OK, you're an Amazon success story yourself. Now what? Should you also sell on eBay? How about other media-oriented sites such as ABE or Alibris? How can you get your products on comparison shopping engines, which more and more shoppers use to ensure that they are getting the best deals? Most important of all, when should you consider creating your own e-commerce site? Finally, why not leverage all that hard-earned experience by becoming a consultant or trainer?

Appendices

A. Amazon's Associates Program. We'll show you how to earn real money by referring others to Amazon. You'll learn how the program works and how to make it work for *you*.

B. The 18 Best Resources for Researching Anything Amazon. As part of our goal to make this book indispensable, we've included a handy checklist to other sources you can use to keep your Amazon IQ at Mensa-level.

By now, you may be asking who we are, and what makes us qualified to write a book like this. Well, as much as we like tooting our own horns, we'll keep this short. We met as Rutgers College students and have been collaborators ever since. We're both into technology and popular culture and have blended these interests to write books about cutting-edge technologies and how they are changing our lives. Together, we've written 16 books, from *The Complete Passive Solar Home Book*, to *The Telecommuter's Handbook,* to *Kidnet: The Kid's Guide to Surfing through Cyberspace.* We're especially proud of *eBay PowerSeller Secrets*, which for most of its life has been among the best-selling eBay books on Amazon.

But enough about us. This book is all about *you*—your dream to run your own business. Your love and respect for Amazon have led you to buy the very book you're holding. We promise you won't be disappointed.

Please contact us at www.bradanddeb.com, as we're always interested in hearing from our readers.

CHAPTER

1

Amazon, and You're Done

Welcome to Amazon! We're thrilled to be your tour guides on this e-commerce adventure. We believe Amazon is one of the best opportunities ever available for people who want to have their own businesses. Taking your place as an Amazon third-party seller gives you the chance to build a business that reflects exactly what you want out of your entrepreneurial voyage. Sign up for the ride, and you'll instantly be the captain of the ship. Sail as far and as fast as you decide. Stock the ship with the cargo you select. Build it right, and your business will give you (and someday your employees) a livelihood of your own design. Amazon can be a business incubator rivaled by few opportunities ever available to humans. It's the best venue for online entrepreneurs since, well, eBay. Many sellers will tell you Amazon is years ahead of its famous competitor.

Surely you know the amazing opportunity that is Amazon, which is why you're here. Amazon is no longer the Internet's bookseller—not that it really was ever just that. The Seattle-based company now sells products in 42 categories. It's the Web's number-one retailer, with millions of customers. But, you don't have to believe it just because we say so. Companies that measure website traffic, such as ComScore, consistently rate Amazon the most popular shopping destination—by far. Amazon's motto and this chapter's title—Amazon and you're done—is for real. Consumers know that, and, as a seller, you may find it true, too.

OK, so you already knew Amazon is huge, and hugely popular, in the United States. But it's also strong internationally. There are Amazon sites for the United Kingdom, China, Japan, France, and Germany. Combined, these vastly popular websites bring in almost as much money as Amazon's U.S. site. In the United Kingdom, for example, college students have made Amazon's Marketplace the number-one seller of used books! These international sites are growing quickly, and soon Amazon may become one of the *world's* largest online retailers. So, there's no better time than right now to hoist anchor and set sail. Welcome aboard, Matey.

Amazon: Where It's All About the Customer

Amazon may owe its success to the goal it set for itself from the start. Way back in 1995, Amazon set out to be the most *customer-centric* company in the world. With that goal, the company then did everything it had to do to become just that. Amazon customers know the company isn't satisfied until *they* are satisfied on every score—the price was right, the product arrived on time, the purchase worked out right.

Amazon's approach is really a focus on the *customer experience*. Think about it. Amazon makes payment simple, remembers customers, offers recommendations based on previous purchases, and backs up each purchase with an *A-to-z Guarantee* of 100 percent satisfaction. It has taken the big fear some people had, and many still have, of doing business "over" the Internet, and sucked the wind right out of it. You're safe on Amazon. But, the company didn't stop there.

It may have started out as a place to buy books, but today it seems more like a city of sorts, populated by many people sharing many interests. Through tools such as reviews, Listmania, tags, and blogs, Amazon has continued growing and adapting in its quest to provide customers with the best possible shopping experience. *Reviews* help shoppers make decisions about which product might be right for them. With *Listmania* lists, fans can share opinions about books, CD, cameras, whatever. And many thousands do just that! People even create tags (quick identifiers, such as "whaling" as an obvious but accurate tag for the book *Moby Dick*) to index their favorite books and DVDs. This lets other shoppers find related products. A *blog* can allow you to share opinions on just about anything with your fellow Amazon shoppers. Just take a look at Figure 1-1 for an example of how Amazon uses its vast database of shopping data to make recommendations to you.

Amazon was creating a "Web 2.0" company, enabling all kinds of networking, before anyone knew there would be a Web 2.0. Jeff Bezos, founder and still boss, has had much to do with the company's bright reading of the market and its evolution over the years. Bezos also stands alone as the only founder of a big-name Internet company who's still running things day to day. The man is nothing if not consistent. Recently, he said Amazon's strategy is simple: "Figure out what customers want and repeat that consistently." Turns out, customers wanted four basic things:

1. A feeling that it is safe to do business on the Internet
2. Completely trustworthy, reliable customer service

3. Fast delivery

4. A great price

That's what Amazon provides. As the Internet evolved and customers began to expect to network and share, as well as shop, Amazon was already there. Setting the course for figuring out what your customers want and repeating it is a pretty good strategy for a business

Figure 1-1. Amazon has mastered the art of using its customer data to encourage additional sales.

What Do Customers Buy After Viewing This Item?

60% buy the item you viewed

15% buy this alternative

9% buy this alternative

5% buy this alternative

eBay PowerSeller Secrets, 2E Paperback by Debra Schepp, Brad Schepp

How and Where to Locate the... Paperback by Dan W. Blacharski

Three Weeks to eBay Profits: Go from... Paperback by Skip McGrath

eBay Income: How Anyone of Any Age... Paperback by Cheryl L. Russell

> View or edit your browsing history

Latest from Your Favorite Authors, Including Brad Schepp

The Online Genealogy Handbook Paperback by Brad Schepp, Debra Schepp (Why is this recommended for you?)

Berlitz Pocket Guide Italy Paperback by Jack Altman, Patricia... (Why is this recommended for you?)

Ladies of Liberty: The Women Who... Hardcover by Cokie Roberts (Why is this recommended for you?)

The Complete Idiot's Guide to eBay Paperback by Lissa McGrath, Skip McGrath (Why is this recommended for you?)

> See more recommendations

of any size, yours included. But it's not a simple course to follow. A map and some knowledgeable neighbors to guide you would get you there much faster. That's what we hope you've found here with us.

First, a Little More History

Let's start back in 1995—a monumental year in Web history. That's when both eBay and Amazon (see Figure 1-2), now two of the Internet's biggest companies, were founded. For years, things proceeded along just fine between the two pioneering Net merchants. Each had its niche: Amazon specialized in new stuff such as books, videos, and then electronics and much more. Customers bought these things at a fixed price with no waiting for an auction to end. Sellers on eBay sold mainly used stuff—collectibles, antiques, musical instruments, you name it—mostly through auctions. Over the years, there's been some overlap, of course. Amazon has its Amazon Auctions area, which is a pebble next to eBay's boulder. And eBay has its fixed-price listings (a success), and for a time even a whole marketplace—eBay Express—where only new items were sold. However, each giant still presided over a particular corner of the market. Everything was fine.

This is not to say that Amazon hasn't weathered any storms. Surely you've heard of the great Internet implosion of 2000. Amazon survived, obviously, but for a time the company's high-flying stock dropped like a rock. Still, even with the added pressure this brought to the bottom line, the company didn't worry about profits. Amazon had actually operated in the red for years when it was launching the business, but while it did, it built an infrastructure that supports the company you know today. Of course, today's success wasn't guaranteed during those difficult days. Lots of folks worried about Amazon. Stock analysts at times called the company "Amazon.toast," or

Figure 1-2. Amazon's home page has changed considerably since it first appeared on the Web in 1995.

Welcome to Amazon.com Books!

One million titles, consistently low prices.

(If you explore just one thing, make it our personal notification service. We think it's very cool!)

SPOTLIGHT! -- AUGUST 16TH

These are the books we love, offered at Amazon.com low prices. The spotlight moves **EVERY** day so please come often.

ONE MILLION TITLES

Search Amazon.com's million title catalog by author, subject, title, keyword, and more... Or take a look at the books we recommend in over 20 categories... Check out our customer reviews and the award winners from the Hugo and Nebula to the Pulitzer and Nobel... and bestsellers are 30% off the publishers list...

EYES & EDITORS, A PERSONAL NOTIFICATION SERVICE

Like to know when that book you want comes out in paperback or when your favorite author releases a new title? Eyes, our tireless, automated search agent, will send you mail. Meanwhile, our human editors are busy previewing galleys and reading advance reviews. They can let you know when especially wonderful works are published in particular genres or subject areas. Come in, meet Eyes, and have it all explained.

YOUR ACCOUNT

Check the status of your orders or change the email address and password you have on file with us. Please note that you **do not** need an account to use the store. The first time you place an order, you will be given the opportunity to create an account.

"Amazon.bomb" (both plays on Amazon.com), feeling that, with no profits on the books, failure was inevitable. Today, Amazon.com is a Fortune 500 company with more than 17,000 full-time employees in operations covering 12 million square feet (see Figure 1-3).

Figure 1-3. Amazon's current headquarters building is in Seattle.

As the two giant Internet merchants made their way out of the rubble of the burst dot-com bubble, Amazon and eBay each respected the other's strengths. Neither one tried to change things, until 2006. That was when Amazon started courting eBay's largest and most successful sellers. Amazon executives started showing up at trade shows. They began calling some of eBay's biggest PowerSellers, doing whatever it took to get them to come over and set up shop on Amazon.

As part of its mission to add such successful merchants to its base of third-party sellers, Amazon went beyond eBay. It also approached sellers who sold only through their own websites, and even those who just sold through regular old bricks-and-mortar stores! These were people without websites at all. Amazon invited them in and helped them all to set up e-commerce businesses.

We've asked many of those same successful pioneers to help you. You'll hear from them many times throughout this book.

Amazon: A River of Opportunity for Third-Party Sellers

Since 2006, when Amazon started to actively court major-league third-party sellers, it has gone on the record praising the efforts and the successes of its third-party sellers. Third-party sellers represent everyone selling on Amazon except Amazon itself (see box). These sellers now sell about 30 percent of everything sold through the Amazon site. Ready to join them?

Why Are We Third to the Party?

You may be asking yourself a reasonable question: "If I'm a 'third party,' who are the 'first party' and the 'second party'?" The customer, of course, is the first party. Remember that goal to be the most customer-centric business on earth? Then, Amazon is the second party, there to meet every customer's needs. You get to join as the third party, a partner with Amazon in providing customers with more choice, more opportunities for savings, and plenty of excellent customer experiences.

The most recent count of Amazon's third-party sellers found 1.3 million businesses. These include everything from giants like the Bose Corporation (see Figure 1-4), to college students selling last semester's books. We asked long-time Amazon seller and expert Steve Weber how he thought that 1.3 million figure broke down. He thinks that as many as 70 percent of the people selling on Amazon right now are selling items from their closets or bookshelves. Many are people like Deb and I, who sell books and DVDs we no longer need. But that still leaves a huge number of people operating full-blown businesses on Amazon, and we know lots of them. There's no reason why you can't join them to build a business that supports your family and employees.

The opportunity for you to start or expand your business on Amazon is there, because Amazon has spent years and plenty of money to create a website that represents a highly efficient, yet massive, online shopping site. Over time, the company has added services such as Super Saver (free shipping on orders over $25) and Amazon Prime (two-day shipping for a flat yearly rate). These have become tremendously popular (even if they hurt Amazon's bottom line a bit). Amazon continues to innovate by selling digital music, movies, and TV shows, as well as e-books. Hop aboard the Amazon ship, and you'll become true business partners. Sure, you've got plenty to gain from associating with Amazon, but the company also stands to benefit from your success. That can make for a very rewarding partnership, indeed.

Need more encouragement? We're ready for you:

● **It's simple to start selling on Amazon.** If you've already bought things on the site, you have an Amazon account. That means you can start selling stuff in minutes. Just click on the *Sell yours here* button in the More Buying Choices box that appears on many Amazon pages (see Figure 1-5).

● **Amazon wants you to set up shop and profit on its site.** If you profit, Amazon profits. As long as you follow the rules, Amazon stays by your side. If you need help, Amazon will

Figure 1-4. The Bose Corporation is considered a third-party Amazon seller, just like you would be.

provide it. The site is loaded with FAQs and help files, and support is just a mouse click away. Through its click-to-call feature, you need only click the *Call Me* button under the *Phone* tab in the Contact Us box, appearing on many seller-related pages. An Amazonian will call you right away. You'll get immediate live help to solve the trouble and get you back to work.

- **Niches remain.** Although competition grows every day, there are still many opportunities to create a thriving business for yourself, as you'll find out. It may seem that with all the millions of online sellers, all the good ideas have been taken— that there's nothing new under the sun. Well, we've been following "the online industry" since 1984, and e-commerce specifically since 1997, and you take can take our word for it—opportunities abound. If you couple a good idea with smart sourcing and superb customer service, you'll be well on your way to success.

Make Money on Amazon Right Now

You must be eager to test the waters if you've never sold anything on Amazon. So go to Amazon's home page and look for the Features & Services box along the left-hand side of the screen (see Figure 1-6). Click on the *Sell Your Stuff* link that appears under Selling on Amazon. The screen shown in Figure 1-7 then appears. Enter the title or a keyword describing the item, click the *Start selling* button, and you're on your way. Many people start with items they have laying around the house. You can, too. Now that you've watched your DVD collection of the *X Files*, or *Little House on the Prairie*, do you really have to keep it for all posterity, or could you use the 15 bucks or so it could fetch on Amazon? We thought so. Get busy selling.

Figure 1-5. Click the Sell yours here *button in the More Buying Choices box to list your own item.*

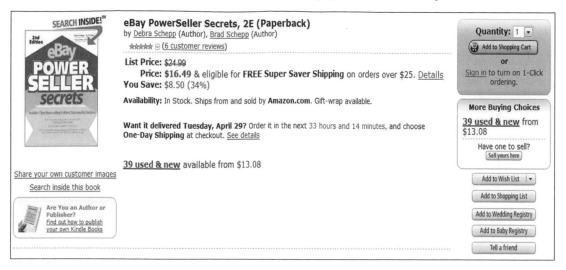

Figure 1-6. The best way to learn about selling on Amazon is to click on the Sell Your Stuff *link in the Features & Services box.*

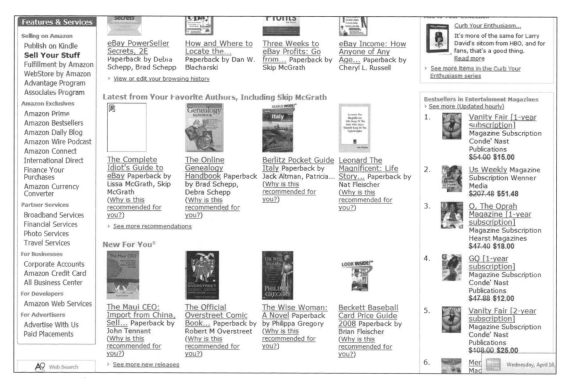

Figure 1-7. This is the screen that appears when you click on the Sell Your Stuff link.

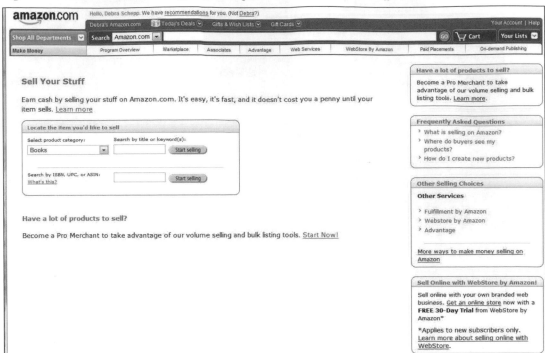

Getting Started

You've already seen how easy it is to get started selling on Amazon's Marketplace, and this is definitely the place for you to begin. For those just starting out without deep pockets for marketing, "Amazon is by far the best online marketplace for small businesses who do not have a big advertising budget," says Bing Yang of Augustina Jewelry. If you're already selling in an online market, you will be delighted to see how simple it is to move business to Amazon. But, even if you've never sold anything on the Internet, you'll be on your way in no time.

No Up-Front Fees Encourages Experimentation

For a new seller, you can't beat the fact that listing your items for sale on Amazon is free. That's right, you don't pay a thing unless your item sells. Whether you list a single item or start out with dozens, your only cost will be in commissions when your items sell. Then you'll pay Amazon a flat 15 percent commission on the sales price. Amazon will charge your customers a set fee for shipping and handling, and if you buy your supplies carefully (much more on that in Chapter 8), that allowance usually more than covers your costs. The items you put up for sale on Amazon remain listed for 60 days (unless they're purchased, of course). After this 60-day period, Amazon sends you an e-mail inviting you to relist for another 60-day period if the item doesn't sell.

Because you don't have to pay to list, you can easily test out new items for your product line as you get started. If you think you've come across a good item, go ahead—list it and see. You'll know soon enough whether you've found a winner, and you won't risk much as you lower the sails and look around.

Charise Richards of OneChicBoutique thinks Amazon is the best online selling venue, partly for that very reason. Amazon has just "one price to list as many items as you want, with only a final fee on sales only! Great system," she says.

No Need to Time Listings to Catch Sellers

Another seller, who sells books from his location in the southeast, told us he likes Amazon because he doesn't have to bother timing his listings to carefully catch potential buyers when they're most likely to be looking for what he's selling. On Amazon he can set his prices higher, because the item stays until the right buyer shows up.

Be Prepared: Bring Your A Game

Amazon customers have been sold on the Amazon philosophy that the customer comes first and that a guarantee is behind every purchase. You should know before you go any further that your customer will expect the very same from you. This philosophy empowers customers and forces sellers to bring their A games when they come to Amazon. Andy Mowery of debnroo has heard people suggest: "I'm an Amazon buyer, so don't mess with me." Amazon's A-to-z Guarantee is virtually bulletproof, Andy says. For Amazon buyers, "It's like they have a club in their hands." So be prepared to shield yourself with excellent products, prices, and customer service. If you can't make this promise to yourself and your customers, you simply won't thrive on Amazon.

Be a Buyer, Too

There's no question that the best, and most risk-free, way to learn how to sell on Amazon is by buying a few things from third-party sellers. Note how they describe their products, how quickly they ship, how they pack their items, and the overall feel you get from the transaction. "As a buyer you'll see what you expect, and then you'll know what your buyers can expect from you," says Rene Klassen of Musicnmore.

The A-to-z Guarantee

Behind all those high customer expectations is the knowledge that Amazon offers an ironclad guarantee. Here's how Amazon describes its A-to-z Guarantee program to customers:

> We want you to buy with confidence anytime you purchase products on Amazon.com. That is why we guarantee purchases from Amazon Marketplace, Auctions, and Merchant sellers when payment is made via the

Amazon.com website. The condition of the item you buy and its timely delivery are guaranteed under the Amazon.com A-to-z Guarantee.

....

No wonder some Amazon customers feel they have a club to protect them! But this guarantee also helps sellers by making buyers more comfortable with doing business on the site.

As long as you're prepared to meet the standards, you'll find yourself offering your items to serious and dedicated customers. They'll trust you, because you're on Amazon, and you can trust that they simply want to make their purchases and move on. The levels of buyer fraud are greatly reduced when this type of trust is built into the marketplace.

The A-to-z Guarantee Is Your Friend

For proof that this guarantee is actually putting more money in their pockets, listen to what these sellers have had to say:

David Yaskulka, who sold jewelry at the time, said his profit on Amazon "was 10 times what it was on eBay. That's because on eBay there's a 'trust discount.'"

Steve Grossberg, a video game seller, notes that the program has not created a lot of red tape for him. He gets very few claims. Last year on Amazon, out of 25,000 orders he processed, he had 27 claims.

Eric Lau of Visiondecor feels that the A-to-z program "actually helps us catch things we missed most of the time." Now that's the right attitude to have!

Feedback

Any discussion of customer empowerment must mention feedback. On Amazon, the feedback that buyers leave for sellers is even more important than it is on eBay. The big challenge on Amazon is that buyers are a lot less likely to even leave feedback. Some sellers say only 10 percent of transactions result in feedback, although Amazon is working to raise this percentage. Feedback is extremely important to your success, however, so we'll be spending a lot of time on it throughout this book.

Keeping Your Head Above Water on Amazon

We wouldn't be doing our jobs if we didn't point you toward other great sources of information. You simply must stay on top of all the latest developments. You'll also have many questions about how to do things (list products in bulk, find relevant reports, become a Featured Merchant). We'll introduce you to some great learning tools and opportunities, both on Amazon and off.

Seller Support on Amazon

Any Amazon Marketplace seller has access to tremendous resources that are right on the Amazon site. Asking Amazon for help is "a great place to start. The Amazon staff is extremely helpful. They take a no-nonsense approach," says Andy of debnroo. Asad Bangash of Beachcombers! is another fan of the help that's available on the site. "There is so much information on how to become successful on Amazon that 99 percent of what I need is on Amazon," he says. "The most useful resources have been the Amazon FAQ and help guides." Figure 1-8 provides just a glimpse of what awaits you, should you need help.

Figure 1-8. On Amazon, a wealth of help is available.

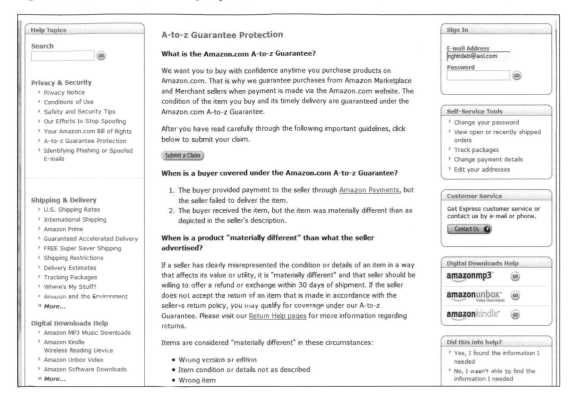

Amazon's Seller Central

Once you move up the seller ranks, you'll find that a lot of the information you need is consolidated in one place: Seller Central. Seller Central is Amazon's web dashboard, which you use to manage your business, from uploading inventory to tracking payments. Kathy Wojtczak of Element Jewelry & Accessories likes Seller Central because "it provides seller-related news and an in-depth Help section." Seller Central's homepage has regular announcements and headlines that keep sellers informed on selling tips, account changes, scheduled maintenance, and so on. The Help section has every topic imaginable, and even provides tutorial videos for some issues.

Amazon's Tech Support

If you can't find what you need on the site, help is just a phone call or e-mail away. Amazon's tech support is highly responsive. You've already seen that you can request a phone call from an Amazon support person with a mouse click, but there's more. "If I can't get my question answered using the Help section," says Kathy of Element Jewelry & Accessories. "I'll e-mail or call the Technical Account Management team. There is a Get Technical Support link on the bottom of each page in Seller Central that sends an e-mail straight from my account to the support team. If I need immediate help, they provide a toll-free number I can call."

Amazon's Discussion Boards

Amazon is a huge marketplace, and much of your time as an Amazon seller will be spent alone with your computer. But, Amazon has also grown into a community of sorts, and Amazon's discussion boards are tremendously popular. Warning—they can also be a tremendous time sink! Long-time e-commerce success story David Yaskulka feels that the boards are dominated by the media sellers (those selling books, music, DVDs, and videocassettes), which may or may not be to your advantage. Rene of Musicnmore confided that he finds it easier to get answers to his questions through eBay's discussion boards than through Amazon's, but when he does get an answer through other Amazon sellers, it is usually fast and to the point. He likes the professionalism of the Amazon boards.

Some sellers recommend that new sellers check the boards every day, as it can take a long time to figure things out. One experienced media seller told us, "You learn about things there. You get the benefits of possible input from hundreds of thousands of sellers." For example, he learned about things like shipping and postage.

Help Outside of Amazon

There is so much to do and explore on Amazon that it's quite easy to narrow your focus only to the sources of information available on the site. However, Amazon doesn't exist in a vacuum, and you'll find that many of the problems and challenges you face are also being faced by e-commerce merchants all over the Internet. It's a good idea to see what others are doing. That's the way to keep your perspective broad enough to thrive and grow wherever you set up shop.

Trade Groups

The Internet Merchants Association (IMA) and the Professional eBay Sellers Alliance (PeSA) are just two of the e-commerce trade

Figure 1-9. Trade groups like the Internet Merchants Association can provide the contacts and information you need to give your business a jump-start.

groups you can join. They are both great sources of support and information. Kirk Holbert of Cosmic-King is just one of many sellers who think it's important to join a group like IMA (see Figure 1-9 on the previous page), which he says is a "group with personal integrity." Through IMA, he can get news and information about future products and trends. He can also learn best practices from more experienced sellers. Steve Grossberg, the president of the IMA and a successful seller himself, estimates that more than two-thirds of all IMA members now sell on Amazon. That number is quite likely to be higher by the time you read this!

Join a Support Group

Your life as an e-commerce merchant will be a lonely one. Again, you'll spend most of your time sitting in front of your computer or preparing your packages for delivery. It's very easy to narrow your focus and make your world as small as your home office. However, isolating yourself isn't just unhealthy for you as a human, it's also detrimental to the growth of your business. Without a network, you'll miss important trends and news. You'll also spend way too much time solving problems alone that others have already solved. The members of these groups become friends and business associates. Kirk Holbert told us he had never met another PowerSeller until he went to the eBay Live! show. His life got much more connected and interesting once he did.

AuctionBytes

AuctionBytes is an online newsletter devoted to all things e-commerce. Operated by Ina and David Steiner, it's a source of well-researched and carefully written information you can rely on. (We're a little prejudiced since we write for the newsletter frequently and think the world of the Steiners.) "The only website I pay attention to anymore is *AuctionBytes*," says Steve Jay of wholesalelaptopbattery. "They seem to pick up on all the news and you can read it all in one place." He's far from the only fan. *AuctionBytes* is, hands-down, the best and most respected Internet source for information about online auctions and the e-commerce world in general. Just about all the sellers we know, us included, regularly read *AuctionBytes* for the latest news, feature articles, how-to articles, and original surveys and product reviews.

Bookthinker

If you're planning to sell books on Amazon, *Bookthinker* is a "must-read" for you. This weekly online newsletter is for people who both sell and read books. It's a great example of the kind of specialized, market-specific information now available. There are feature articles (one recent article discussed how to grade books that you want to sell online). Even the classified ads are worth your time, as you will find ads for software products such as AMan Pro, which can help you automate your business. Steve Weber is one of *Bookthinker*'s regular contributors, and he knows more about selling books online, and especially on Amazon, than anyone we know.

Internet Retailer

Internet Retailer is an e-commerce trade magazine and more. Every article that's ever appeared in the magazine's paper version or online version (that's 24,000 news stories, magazine articles, and press releases) is searchable through its website. One of its biggest fans is Rene of Musicnmore, who gets his daily Internet news from internetretailer .com. Since you're setting up shop on the Internet, you might as well make it a habit to read the neighborhood news! *Internet Retailer*'s trade shows are huge and feature only the best speakers.

Pace Yourself

Now that you've gotten some background, you're probably eager to get started selling on Amazon. We understand completely. But be careful—give yourself the time you need to do things right. "People get in over their head when they start out in their own business," warns Eric of Visiondecor. "They fail to realize that taking things one step at a time can help them in the long term, which is what really matters in business. Gaining an extra sale here and there will make no difference if your business can't service their customers in the long term and stand the test of time." So, by all means, get to it and get busy selling, but don't overextend yourself by listing more than you can process or by buying more equipment than you can afford. A year from now, you'll look back in awe at how much you've learned, but give yourself the time you'll need to do the learning.

Oh, the Challenges You'll Face

Nothing is perfect, alas. You'll find you have your share of issues and challenges to address as an Amazon seller. Did you ever have a relationship that was completely perfect in every respect? We didn't think so. This one won't be different, but at least you'll have advice from the others who have found success before you. Throughout this book's pages, you'll meet many who have found success before you. You don't have to forge the path yourself, which is good. But coming into the game after others who are thriving has disadvantages as well as advantages.

Since so many sellers already have caught on to the tremendous opportunity that is Amazon, you're facing growing competition. As Kirk Holbert of Cosmic-King puts it, it's "an overcrowded marketplace." He says, "Your margins will shrink—that is inevitable. But Internet commerce continues to grow. If you keep your feedback rating high, ship quickly, have affordable prices, and provide personal contact where possible, you'll be fine."

As you read through this book, you'll see that it's hard to make a name for yourself on Amazon, or "brand" your business. Amazon prefers that buyers see the site as one big marketplace instead of a mall with many different sellers. Thus, many of your buyers will think they're buying from Amazon directly and not from the business you've worked hard to establish. There's no doubt that on Amazon you have less control than you may be used to from selling on other venues. "Make sure you're comfortable with that," says Chris Schlieter of timezone. "If so, be a chameleon so that you blend in with the Amazon way of doing business."

Some sellers worry that Amazon will use all the data it can gather from the sales its third-party sellers make to assess opportunities, and one day put them out of business. So far, the folks at Amazon have used their powers only for good, but once you've invested your time, sweat, and money into building your own business, such worries can seem reasonable.

Again, remember that your aim is to become an e-merchant and not just an Amazon seller. For example, Drew Friedman of White Mountain Trading Company says this:

· ·

Amazon just happens to be one of the places where I'm selling. I'm a firm believer that I have to be knowledgeable about it before I do it. The Internet is maturing in many ways, and the ignorant need not apply…. The challenge for me is to have a better understanding of the site. How do I navigate the site better? I feel like I still don't know exactly how it works. Customers are finding us by shopping a category or shopping by brand. That's the only way they can be since I'm not yet doing the other things, like AdWords, blogs, Listmanias, or such.

· ·

We hope you will be doing some of those "other things" to increase traffic to your listings, and the ensuing chapters will explain just how.

Use Your Strengths

One of the most successful e-merchants we've encountered, Eric Lau of Visiondecor, had some wise advice that we're going to leave you with: "Do what you do best and understand the most. Don't sell things you have no experience and passion for. Because the midnight oil will be burning, and you better not mind packing and shipping the things yourself until things take off. Without the understanding and passion of what you are selling/doing, you will not last long in selling on Amazon, let alone establishing a business."

Looking Ahead

We hope we've introduced you to the wonders of the Amazon.com market. We certainly are enthusiastic believers in the site's ability to change the lives of its third-party sellers for the better. With this overview in mind, it's time for us to move on to show you the many different paths you can take as you go about the business of building your thriving Amazon presence. You have some great choices ahead. Chapter 2 will help you to determine the best way to set up shop.

An Amazon Success Story

Michael Jansma had been operating his thriving jewelry business, GemAffair, on Amazon for nearly three years when we spoke. Michael has more than 13 years in the fine jewelry business, and 8 of those have included an online presence. That makes Michael an online veteran, a wise seller willing to share his experience. When we first asked Michael to share how he is building his business on Amazon, he asked us, "Why do you think I'd want to actually build a business there?" The question really gave us pause. "My goal is to have a successful business," Michael explained. Whether he had that business on Amazon or not depended on how successful he found the Amazon platform to be. If it helped his business grow, then putting his business on Amazon would make sense. When we spoke, Michael had a very strong presence on Amazon. But he also sold on eBay, Overstock, and through his own successful website, www.gemaffair.com.

Michael is an experienced Amazon merchant in a closed category (jewelry). He also operates a WebStore by Amazon. Michael met his Amazon contacts through his membership in PeSA, and today he has his own account representative. Over the years of his association, Michael has found Amazon to be a reliable and trustworthy business partner.

His comfortable alignment with the Amazon way of life was simple in that Amazon's and Michael's principles of operation agreed at the core. Both business partners believed in providing the best customer experience possible. Michael had already built his business both offline and online based on those philosophies. That made for an easy blending onto the Amazon Marketplace, where he knew he'd feel at home. As we write this, Michael enjoys a 100 percent positive feedback rating on the site. Because of his long standing in the online marketplace, Michael has seen the evolution of Internet shopping. "In the beginning, online shoppers were looking for bargains," Michael explained. "But that only represents 6 to 8 percent of the population.

In the first five to seven years, Internet shoppers were made up of this group. Now the other 90 plus percent of people are online." Michael knows that he doesn't have to depend strictly on bargain hunters anymore. He can bring fine-quality goods to the online marketplace and expect to be paid fairly for his products and his exceptional customer service.

His years in the jewelry business have allowed Michael to source jewelry directly from manufacturers around the world. He can offer his customers discounts from 50 to 75 percent of retail prices. His product listing pages and his WebStore all prove him to be an online professional. With their first visit, customers can quickly see that they've found a reliable and knowledgeable jeweler. With 100 percent customer satisfaction guaranteed on all purchases, no matter which venue, there's simply no reason for a customer to decide not to buy. "Every venue we've ever gone to, we've been successful by offering products, making good sales, and gaining long-term customers," explained Michael. "It makes people loyal to us, because they know they're going to be satisfied and not have to take a risk."

Michael's business offline and online, on Amazon or beyond, was built for success. You'll see how you can learn from his ways to build your own Amazon success story throughout the chapters that follow.

CHAPTER

2

Which Way Should I Go?

We met Gary Richardson when he was a hugely successful and quite fascinating eBay PowerSeller. Today, not only is he our friend and technical adviser for this book, but he is also a hugely successful and quite fascinating Amazon seller. You'll find him as Goggles and Glasses. As a matter of fact, Gary made the Amazon Best of 2007 list in the Apparel & Accessories category for his product line: sunglasses, goggles, and such. Now, success is always an achievement, but Gary reached this particular mark after selling on Amazon for only one year! Perhaps you're beginning to see the potential of selling on Amazon.

We are proud of our friend's achievement, but what will matter to you is that he had a successful start. Because of that great start, we'll be sharing Gary's story with you throughout this chapter—indeed, throughout the book. Many sellers have built successful eBay businesses over the years, but how many have then branched into a whole new venue and achieved star status this quickly? Luckily for all of us, Gary's also a willing and patient teacher.

Selling on Amazon isn't the same as selling on eBay. In some ways, it may seem the same, but you're stepping into a new neighborhood, and like any new neighbor, it will take you some time to settle in. A trusted guide will be a real asset.

It's pretty hard to find someone with access to a computer and the Internet who has never been on Amazon's Marketplace. It's where you land when you click to Amazon.com (Figure 2-1). Sure, years ago, you'd go there for books, music, and videos, but now you can also go there for music downloads or diapers or linens or lawn mowers—we could keep going through Amazon's 42 different categories of offerings, but you get the point. Whereas it once called itself "the world's biggest bookstore" (you bring the coffee), today it's much more like the Internet's Mall of America. And yes, you can buy the coffee there, but you'll still have to brew it for yourself.

For a seller looking to place items within any of those 42 categories, you enjoy the opportunity to reach millions of Amazon shoppers from around the globe. The numbers are easily massaged, but Amazon does keep an actual count of "active" customers who have ordered from the site within the last year. At last count, that number was over 65 million. So, as you can see, Amazon.com is a very good place to build a business.

Join the Amazon (Third) Party!

More than six years ago, the folks at Amazon had a radical, but highly successful, idea. Once they'd built their huge infrastructure to allow easy and reliable shopping on their site, why not open it up to other people who also wanted to sell? At first it seems a little nutty. Why invite your competitors into your store to sell many of the same things you're already selling? Well, for one, it's that old Amazon philosophy of finding out what customers want and giving it to them. Amazon figured, for example, if some of its customers would rather

Figure 2-1. Amazon's home page, showing the online retailer's breadth of products.

buy a gently used book than a brand new one, why not let them come to Amazon to do that? Second, of course, was the prospect of the company earning a piece of every sale through the site, no mat‐ter who was sponsoring it. So, yes, you may actually buy that book from the guy in the next county over, but it's still going to come through Amazon.com, and a little profit of that sale will fall into Amazon's accounts on the way. You get the book you wanted at a satisfying price, the guy in the next county makes a bit of a profit, and Amazon takes a little share, too. It may not be much, but multi‐ply it out through the 42 Amazon categories and across millions of active customers, and you'll see why everyone is so impressed by the ingenious idea of opening the site to third-party sellers. Now you're poised to become one of them.

As you saw in Chapter 1, getting started selling an item on Amazon couldn't possibly be simpler, but it's not quite that easy to actually build your business there from scratch. Selling on Amazon can be broken down into three different choices. As an individual seller, you will operate on the Amazon Marketplace. As your business grows, you'll be likely to join the Pro Merchant program, a subscription-based service that is like a business membership. And when you've reached the top as a Pro Merchant, other options open up to you. "The way we look at it is, we have different tiers of sellers," Amazon Director of Business Solutions Matt Williams recently said in *AuctionBytes*. "You have the individual, you have the Pro Merchant, and then you have what we call the Gold- or Platinum-level seller. So, you as an individual seller, or you as a small business, or even a large multibillion-dollar enterprise can partner with Amazon to sell your products on the website." As you build your business, you may also consider two of Amazon's other services available to sellers: WebStore by Amazon and Fulfillment by Amazon. We'll cover Fulfillment by Amazon in detail in Chapter 8. For now, let's look at all of your other choices together.

Amazon Marketplace

This is surely the first place you'll come to test Amazon's selling waters. Many of you have already sold an item or two through the site, simply by clicking the *Sell yours here* button we told you about in Chapter 1. We've sold our kids' used textbooks, books we've had laying dormant on bookshelves for years, and DVDs that we realized we need to see only once. If you have done the same, you may want to skim over the next few paragraphs. If you're completely new to selling on Amazon, we'll step you through the simple process to get you started. First, let's find the item you want to sell. It's likely that a product page for it already exists on Amazon, and if so, you can add your own listing to that page. Say that we're selling a Tickle Me Elmo doll (it's OK for us to do this, since we're not selling during the holiday season, when the Toy & Games category closes to all but preapproved sellers.) The TMX Special Edition Elmo pops right up, and there we see the list of all possible choices (see Figure 2-2). The first one on the list is exactly like ours, so we'll click on it to get to the product page. If you look to the right of the product page, you'll find the More Buying Choices box (see Figure 2-3). The last button in that box says *Sell yours here*. Click that, and you're ready to go. The next screen asks you to note the item's condition and add any comments you think might be relevant. Be completely honest with yourself and your customers at this point. If the item is brand new, never opened, select that one. It would also be a wise idea to highlight the "never been opened" status in the comments box.

Figure 2-2. A search for Tickle Me Elmo doll brings up results like these.

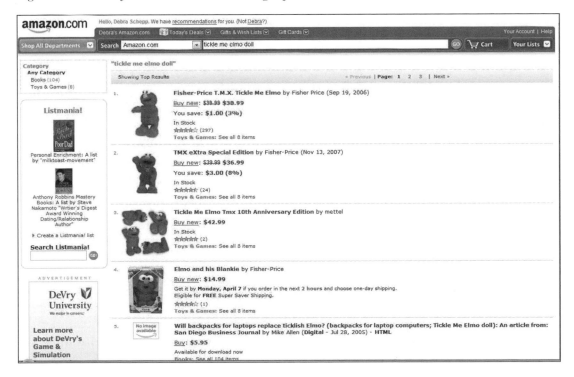

Figure 2-3. Notice the More Buying Choices box along the right margin.

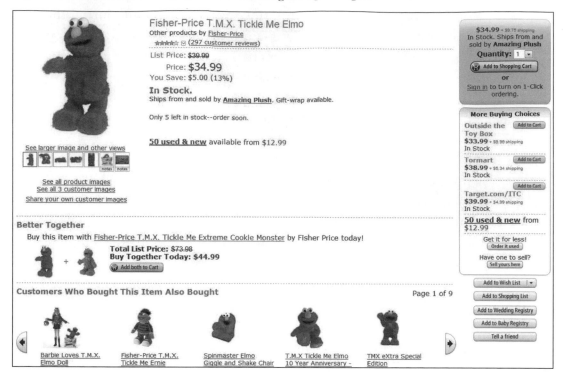

The Comments box (see Figure 2-4) is where you have a chance to distinguish yourself from other sellers by choosing friendly wording that suggests you are as concerned about your customers' satisfaction as they are! So if your item is gently used, be honest about that. It's a very good idea to grade your item slightly below that which you really believe it to be. Your goal is a customer who is delighted by the product, not one who is disappointed that this doll was billed as "like new" when it had obviously been enjoyed by a toddler. There are many more grabbers you could include in that box, having to do with your shipping, return guarantee, and so on. We'll bring those opportunities up in later chapters.

Once you've completed this screen, click *Continue* and move on to the pricing page. Here, you'll list your desired price, the quantity

Figure 2-4. The Comments area of a product listing is where you can distinguish yourself from other third-party sellers.

$5.45 + $3.99 shipping	Used – Good	**Seller:** MCKENZIEBOOKS **Rating:** ★★★★★ 99% positive over the past 12 months (33430 ratings.) 57609 lifetime ratings. **Shipping:** In Stock. Ships from OR, United States Expedited shipping available International shipping available See shipping rates **Comments:** Softcover. Has some writing in the margins. Some underlining. Slight cover wear. Ships the next business day, with tracking a... (» more)	Add to Cart or Sign in to turn on 1-Click ordering.
$5.50 + $3.99 shipping	Used – Good	**Seller:** LIZS_QUALITY_USED_BOOKS **Rating:** ★★★★★ 97% positive over the past 12 months (500 ratings.) 2931 lifetime ratings. **Shipping:** In Stock. Ships from WA, United States See shipping rates **Comments:** some bookshelf wear to cover & edges; v good reading condition/ DELIVERY CONFIRMATION FREE	Add to Cart or Sign in to turn on 1-Click ordering.
$5.64 + $3.99 shipping	Used – Good	**Seller:** RIVER-CITY-BOOKS **Rating:** ★★★★★ 96% positive over the past 12 months (22756 ratings.) 49111 lifetime ratings. **Shipping:** In Stock. Ships from WA, United States Expedited shipping available International shipping available See shipping rates **Comments:** GOOD with average wear. We ship quickly and work hard to earn your confidence. Orders are generally shipped no later than nex... (» more)	Add to Cart or Sign in to turn on 1-Click ordering.
$5.65 + $3.99 shipping	Used – Like New	**Seller:** ATHENA_BOOKS **Rating:** ★★★★★ 96% positive over the past 12 months (7340 ratings.) 28528 lifetime ratings. **Shipping:** In Stock. Ships from NY, United States Expedited shipping available International shipping available See shipping rates **Comments:** Ships Within 24 Hours - Never Read!	Add to Cart or Sign in to turn on 1-Click ordering.
$5.66 + $3.99 shipping	Used – Very Good	**Seller:** BOOK_SELLER223 **Rating:** ★★★★★ 96% positive over the past 12 months (680 ratings.) 779 lifetime ratings. **Shipping:** In Stock. Ships from CA, United States Expedited shipping available See shipping rates **Comments:** INTERNATIONAL SHIPPING AVAILBLE PLEASE ASK FOR MORE INFO. May show signs of shelf wear. Choose EXPEDITED shipping, receive in... (» more)	Add to Cart or Sign in to turn on 1-Click ordering.
$5.70 + $3.99 shipping	Used – Like New	**Seller:** CAROLBOOKS1 **Rating:** ★★★★★ 96% positive over the past 12 months (57 ratings.) 57 lifetime ratings. **Shipping:** In Stock. Ships from MA, United States Expedited shipping available International shipping available See shipping rates **Comments:** like new copy with no markings. cover clean and intact. fast shipping	Add to Cart or Sign in to turn on 1-Click ordering.
$5.70 + $3.99 shipping	Used – Like New	**Seller:** CARGOLARGO **Rating:** ★★★★★ 96% positive over the past 12 months (23380 ratings.) 74412 lifetime ratings. **Shipping:** In Stock. Ships from MO, United States Expedited shipping available See shipping rates **Comments:** UNREAD PAPERBACK.	...

of the item you own, and the shipping options you are willing to offer. Notice the box to the right of the screen shown in Figure 2-3. This will give you valuable information as you decide what to charge for your toy. The price at the top of the box is the Amazon price for the item, in this case, $34.99. Look beneath this price, and you'll get a quick glimpse of the item as it is currently being offered on Amazon. The other dolls in new condition range in price from $33.99 to $39.99. Also, note there are 50 used and new from $12.99. Now, based on what the competition has done, you'll have to set a realistic price for your own doll.

Selecting the correct price can be a bit tricky when listing on Amazon. You, of course, have to consider your acquisition cost for the item, but if you're not careful, you could easily end up selling the doll at a loss rather than a profit. Now is the time to carefully calculate what your fees will be for the item you're selling. You won't actually be collecting money directly from your customer, who will instead be paying Amazon. Amazon will then deduct its fees and apply the shipping charges before you ever see a penny of your customer's money. That's why it's so important that you are clear about the fees Amazon will charge before you set your item price. These fees begin with a transaction fee of $0.99, waived for a Pro Merchant, but charged to us in this instance, since we are simply selling an individual item on the Marketplace. After the transaction fee, you will also have to pay a commission rate. These rates vary with the type of item you are selling. In our example, the commission rate is 15 percent of the price. Finally, there will be a *variable closing fee*. That also differs, depending on the type of item you're selling. In our case, it will be $0.45 plus $0.05 per pound. If we ultimately sell our doll for $30.00, we'll owe:

- $0.99 (transaction fee)
- $4.50 (commission)
- $0.60 (variable closing fee for a 3-pound item)

Now we know that our total fees to Amazon will be $6.09 for selling this doll on the site. Still, we'll have to arrange for shipping. If we only offer standard shipping without expediting it, for a "toy or baby item" Amazon will charge your customer a shipping charge of $4.49 plus $0.50. Note that the shipping fees that Amazon charges vary with the item (for books it's typically $3.99, as another example). This fee is your shipping credit, which Amazon adds to your price. The credit should usually cover your costs, as long as you ship the item via standard shipping (usually media mail for books, for example). If your customer wants to receive the item more quickly than the standard fee would allow, the customer would need to pay for expedited shipping. In any case, it's your responsibility to ensure that the shipping credit covers your cost, so you'll need to buy mailing and packing supplies at the best rates you can. For more on shipping, see amazon.com/gp/help/customer/display.html.

TIP *Set Your Price with the Marketplace in Mind*

Setting your price on Amazon isn't quite the gamble that it can be on other sites. Your item will be offered at a fixed price rather than being up for auction, so there's really no point in setting a price that will put you way ahead of your competition. As a matter of fact, lowballing is something Amazon sellers complain a lot about on the Seller Boards. Amazon seller Treebeard, who specializes in books, told us that on Amazon his prices can actually be higher than on eBay, because his item will stay up on the site for sale until the right buyer comes along. He has no need to try to time his sale in order to "catch" the right buyer. Experienced sellers agree that competing on price alone is not the way to build profits on Amazon. We'll go into more detail on pricing and pricing strategies in Chapter 4.

With our price set and our shipping options chosen, we'll sit back and wait for the right buyer to come along and purchase our doll. Our listing will stay up on the site for 60 days. If no one buys it within that time, Amazon will send an e-mail warning us that the listing is about to expire. That will give us the chance to take a fresh look at our item and decide if we need to change the price or perhaps the wording in the comments section to better grab customers. Still, we won't be charged a cent when we renew the listing for another 60 days, regardless of whether we make any changes to it.

Select Your Nickname Carefully

Selecting your seller's nickname is very important on Amazon. Once you've pleased your customers, it's difficult for them to find you again among the mass of listings on Amazon. If you choose your name carelessly, it will become even more difficult. If you choose your name carefully, but don't consider the realities of search engines, you'll still be stuck.

When you register as a seller, you'll be asked to supply a nickname that identifies you to your buyers. Choose something that will be easy to remember and representative of the products you plan to sell. Gary, for example, uses Goggles and Glasses. That not only has a nice alliterative ring to it, it also clearly identifies the type of products he sells. He then purchased a URL— www.motoglasses.com—to easily redirect people to his Amazon store. We think Visiondecor, a seller specializing in home furnishings, also chose a great nickname. Anyone who is satisfied with a purchase from this seller can easily find him again by searching Amazon for his nickname.

As you select your nickname, be sure you don't create one that violates Amazon's rules. You are prohibited from including anything in your nickname that will divert an Amazon customer to another website. Specifically, you can't use domain names, URLs, e-mail symbols, or even words that spell out those symbols. Here's a brief list, just to give you an idea of what you shouldn't include in your nickname:

- Com, ca, or net
- www or @
- dotcom, dtcom, or atdotnet

So, if you stop and think it over, avoid prohibited words and phrases, and carefully evaluate how you want to represent your business, how can you still make a mistake? Consider what will happen if you choose a nickname that can easily be applied to search terms on the Amazon website. For our example, let's use Evolution Toys. Now, you may be thinking you're planning to carry the latest and coolest toys in your product line, and the name describes those perfectly. But, if customers type Evolution Toys in the search box, they'll get back more than 1,000 responses. Some of these are for books about the evolution of particular kinds of toys. Some of them are toys that transform from one thing to another. But, your business name is not likely to be right at the top of the list, which is where you want customers to find it.

As long as you're listing individual items, one at a time, the Marketplace is the spot for you to sell as you build your business. But, ultimately, you'll need to move beyond the boundaries of the Marketplace to see real growth. Once you get to about 40 sales per month, it's time to upgrade your operation and either sign on for Seller Central or become a Pro Merchant.

Seller Central

Signing on to Seller Central (SC) gives you advantages, both financial and strategic. Once you're processing enough orders to justify the $39.95 per month fee, you'll save the cost of that $0.99 transaction fee. (You'll still pay the 6 to 15 percent commission and the variable closing fee, however.) You'll also have access to a *dashboard* from which you can upload your inventory, manage orders and payments, and view a variety of Web analytics that will help you to evaluate your business, profitability, and growth. Figure 2-5 shows you just what your tools will look like as a Seller Central merchant. We'll go into the specifics of working with Seller Central in great detail in Chapter 5, but we wanted you to know something about this option for running your Amazon business now.

Figure 2-5. The main Seller Central page directs you to many business tools.

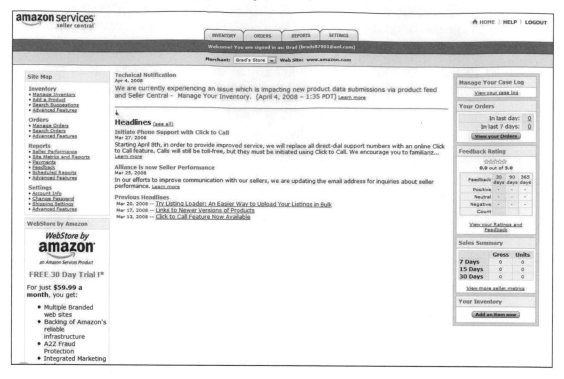

Seller Central is the way to operate your business if you are planning to sell nonmedia items. It is not yet available to media sellers who handle books, DVDs, and CDs. If you are basing your business plan on those commodities, join the Pro Merchant program instead, but do it outside of the SC program. Note that when you sign up for Seller Central, you are also then eligible to become a Featured Merchant, which is the goal of any serious Amazon seller. You'll find out later what being a Featured Merchant entails.

Once you are signed up with Seller Central, you'll be able to take advantage of promotions and merchandising campaigns through Amazon. You'll be able to set your own shipping costs, enabling you to offer your customers special shipping rates for multiple purchases, for example. You'll also be able to offer gift wrapping and personalized messages to your customers if you'd like.

With the Web tools available through Seller Central, you'll be able to analyze your operation to calculate the percentage of items that are selling—your *sell-through rate*—and how quickly your inventory is moving. You can also set different access levels for your Seller Central information so your employees can access the account information they need to do their jobs. For example, you may enable your shipping clerk to go onto your account only to view orders, print labels, and manage packing slips. For your partner, by contrast, you can set the software so he or she can view your sales data to help you track inventory decisions.

"Everything I need to manage is contained within Amazon's Seller Central," says Kathy Wojtczak, of Element Jewelry & Accessories. "I can securely log in and check my sales, print out shipping labels and packing slips, make design changes to my WebStores, download and print reports, etc. When sales occur or when I upload new product information or inventory changes, Seller Central automatically updates my listing on Amazon as well as on all my WebStores simultaneously, so my listings are always up to date."

In addition to the functional advantages of using Seller Central, signing on actually gives you the opportunity to sell in product areas not available to individual Marketplace sellers. One example is the Health and Personal Care area. Only Seller Central merchants can operate within this product line. One further advantage of Seller Central is the availability of the offline listing and inventory management tool, Amazon Seller Desktop.

Amazon Pro Merchant

If you're planning to be strictly a media seller, you'll want to become a Pro Merchant as soon as you've built your volume to the recommended level. And as your business grows, you may become eligible for Gold or Platinum Pro Merchant status. Signing up for a Pro

Merchant account is simple. Amazon will automatically convert your current listings to your new status, and then you're ready to take advantage of volume seller discounts. Just like Seller Central merchants, Pro Merchants pay $39.95 per month, and in exchange, no longer incur the $0.99 per sale transaction fee. You'll gain access to a variety of Amazon's software tools that help you list and manage your inventory. For example, you'll be able to create bulk listings and upload your inventory seamlessly and download inventory reports, too. Watch for special offers. Members of the Internet Merchants Association (IMA) or the Professional eBay Sellers Alliance (PeSA) are often eligible for discounted fees to start. Amazon also frequently runs an offer allowing you to sign up as a Pro Merchant for a fee of $39.95 for your first two months, giving you a month as a free trial.

With Pro Merchant status, you'll also be able to create your own storefront featuring only your inventory items. You'll be permitted to add items to the Amazon Marketplace that aren't currently sold on the site by creating your own product detail pages, which we'll discuss in detail in Chapter 4. Finally, your listings won't expire after 60 days as they do on the Marketplace.

Go for the Gold (or Platinum)

Pro Merchant sellers can also work toward Gold or Platinum status. These levels are based on monthly sales, and the specific criteria for them are not publicly disclosed. Amazon will automatically notify sellers as they qualify for the next level of Pro Merchant, according to Steve Grossberg, a Pro Merchant selling video games. "We certainly do reach out to specific merchants," Amazon executive Matt Williams reported to *AuctionBytes*. But, Matt also told the publication that sellers can apply for Gold or Platinum status, and their applications will be reviewed. Moving up the scale of Pro Merchant accounts makes you eligible to sell products that are restricted to preapproved sellers. Yes, it's true, unlike other online venues, Amazon restricts the number of sellers able to operate within certain inventory areas. As of this writing, selling in the following categories of items was restricted to Gold- or Platinum-level Pro Merchants:

- Computers
- Cell phones (without service) and wireless accessories
- Gourmet food
- Jewelry
- Watches
- Apparel
- Shoes
- Computer and video games
- Electronics
- Software

Additionally, these items are strictly banned from Amazon:

- Adult toys
- Gift cards and certificates
- Guns and ammunition
- Prescription medication
- Tobacco and alcohol

Aside from the obvious issues involved in allowing sellers to deal in items such as tobacco, alcohol, and prescription drugs, Amazon restricts areas of sale to ensure a positive customer experience. For example, apparel is restricted to proven professional sellers, because Amazon wants to make sure customers don't receive damaged or badly worn clothing. Likewise, during certain times of the year, toys and games are restricted to ensure that customers will be buying their items only from sellers who have proven their worth in terms of quality products and excellent customer service. As you decide what you'll sell on Amazon, keep in mind that you may need to work for a period of time to prove yourself worthy of selling the items you most want to deal in.

Featured Merchant

Your business will increase dramatically when you become a Featured Merchant on Amazon. What's a Featured Merchant? Bear with us here, because this is one of the most important tips in this book! Featured Merchants occupy a prime location on the product description page of items they list. If, for example, Amazon offers a Canon PowerShot camera for sale and you also sell the item, as a Featured Merchant, your listing is eligible to appear in the *buy box* (where it says More Buying Choices, to the right of Amazon's own listing page—see Figure 2-6). The buy box is where you want to be, because shoppers will be most likely to click on a link in that box and bypass your competitors who are selling the same item.

Using the example of the Canon camera, it's clear to see that with 52 other identical items listed on Amazon, a customer probably wouldn't bother to page through all those listings when you're offering a good deal just one click away. Only Featured Merchants can "own the buy box," but being a Featured Merchant alone will not guarantee your placement there. "Whether or not you actually get that buy box depends on price," says Kirk Holbert of Cosmic-King, a toy seller. "You need to have the lowest price. If another Featured Merchant undercuts my price and has better feedback, they'll appear in the buy box," he added.

Featured Merchants operate with the assurance that Amazon has

Figure 2-6. Featured Merchants are those appearing in the More Buying Choices box.

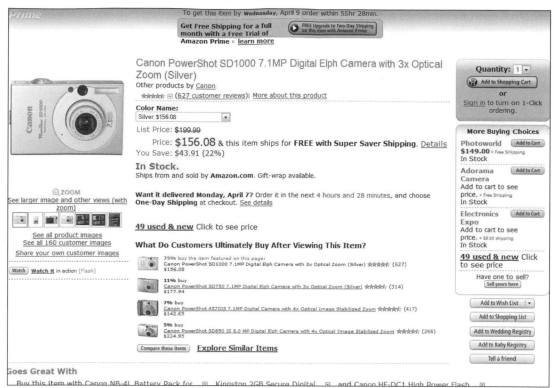

investigated and vetted them as reliable and dependable sellers offering extraordinary service and support for their products. "The flood gates opened after we became Featured Merchants," reports Andy Mowery of debnroo. "Nobody really knows exactly how you become one," Andy continued. "It's an algorithm, a closely guarded secret. Amazon is judging you. It has to do with your feedback, the number of products you have, your rate of sales, your pricing, and the number of A-to-z complaints filed against you."

So, if we're saying that you should strive to become a Featured Merchant, but that no one outside of Amazon corporate can tell you the secrets of becoming one, what should you do? "I think the most important thing is to be able to ship and process the amount of orders and volume received from Amazon to prove that you are ready to be a Featured Merchant," recommends Visiondecor's Eric Lau. That's the part we can help you with as you work your way through this book!

You Can Become a Featured Merchant After 30 Days

The one way you can be assured of becoming a Featured Merchant is to sign up for Seller Central. According to Amazon, once you do, after 30 days, as long as there are no "performance issues" against you, you will automatically become a Featured Merchant. That can make your first 30 days on Amazon the hardest of all. Here's how Gary managed that first month:

I would suggest that you just launch a few items and ride your first 30 days out. We shipped twice a day, 6 days a week, and triple inspected every shipment to ensure 100 percent perfection. Give yourself a learning period of at least 30 days. Amazon is unlike selling on any other venue, it has its own little quirks. Getting a perfect record and becoming a Featured Merchant should be your first goal, and this is automatic if you have a good performance record at the end of 30 days.

One of our friends launched 10,000 items on his first day. Due to listing errors, he had 50 percent negative feedback by the second week. His account was shut down and his funds frozen. Everything that could go wrong for him, did go wrong. The customers were brutal in their feedback. Eventually, he was able to get his account reinstated after submitting a comprehensive plan to bring up his service level and fix all the mistakes. His negative feedback from this period still remains. It will haunt his account for at least one year, and then it will stay on his lifetime feedback record.

··

WebStore by Amazon

If your own e-commerce site is one of your business goals (and no e-commerce merchant should ignore this goal), then Amazon can help you here, too. Fortunately, Amazon.com has made that easy for you with its WebStore by Amazon program. Now you can have your own website with the power of Amazon standing right behind you.

Open More than One Amazon WebStore

For a monthly fee of $59.95, plus a 7 percent commission on sales, you can create as many WebStores on Amazon as you'd like. Kathy of Element Jewelry & Accessories had three when we spoke. "WebStore by Amazon provides my business with as many freestanding branded websites as I want," she explained, "all powered by Amazon. I am able to choose from several design templates and completely customize my websites from there to fit my business needs. Customers complete their orders by logging into their existing Amazon accounts, and since most customers keep their credit card numbers and shipping addresses on file, their information is available for quick checkout."

Andy Mowery of debnroo agrees. "It's brilliant!," he exclaimed. "You can create as many of these as you want. My store, automatic-litterbox.com (see Figure 2-7) features products that I don't even carry myself. I plan to have a whole host of these sites."

Figure 2-7. One of Andy Mowery's Amazon WebStores is automatic-litterbox.com.

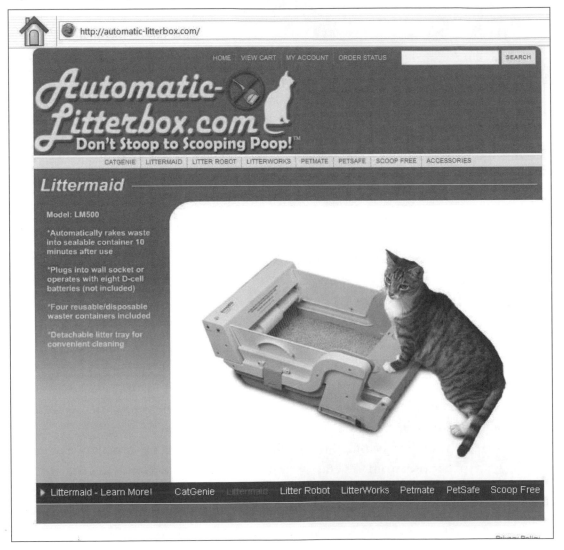

Carry Amazon Inventory as Well as Your Own

Yes, it's true, once you have a WebStore by Amazon, you can add products to your store that you don't source or own yourself. You can take items from Amazon's catalog and add them to your inventory. Suppose you sell digital cameras, for example, but you don't want to deal in the batteries or memory cards that go along with them. You can list those accessories from Amazon's inventory, and when they sell, you'll receive a referral fee from Amazon.

All of your store management features are available through your Seller Central account. Amazon handles all payment processing, so you don't need a separate merchant credit card account, and you also get the fraud protection of working under the Amazon umbrella. Of course, your items are all covered by the Amazon A-to-z Guarantee program. As an added benefit, Amazon will actually help to promote your store through search engines such as Google.

Amazon Auctions

Amazon has dipped its giant toe into the Web auction business. And why not? With its amazing reputation for customer service and trust, you'd think auction lovers would flock to Amazon to place their bids. Amazon's description of its auction services refers to Amazon.com auctions as "the most trusted auction site on the Web." Amazon's giant status among Internet retailers, however, has not translated well to the Internet auction business. *AuctionBytes*, the leading online newsletter for e-commerce types, recently surveyed its members about the auction sites they used. They found that of the 700+ respondents, 92 percent sold items through eBay, while only 4 percent sold through Amazon Auctions. So it makes sense that none of the Amazon merchants we spoke with mentioned using Amazon Auctions to sell merchandise.

We looked at a couple of categories to see what was going on for ourselves. Once interested in collecting coins, we thought we'd check out the *U.S. cents* category. On Amazon there were 681 separate listings. On eBay there were five separate subcategories for cents, but under *small cents* alone there were more than 12,000 listings! We tried another category, one that we thought might favor Amazon: *picture books*. On eBay there were 1,466 picture books up for auction. On Amazon—166. You get the idea. Auctions are not where the action is on Amazon!

Other Amazon Choices

Although it seems that Amazon has never been able to quite break into the online auction business, the company continues to seek new ways of serving both the customers who come to shop and the merchants who come to sell. Fulfillment by Amazon (FBA) was introduced in early 2007 as a way to allow sellers to offload the warehousing, packing, and shipping process to Amazon. Sellers simply box up and ship their inventories to Amazon fulfillment centers (see Chapter 8), where Amazon staff will pick, pack, and ship their items as the orders come in. You can bundle your packages and include your own correspondence to your customers, but when Amazon receives your merchandise, it must be ready to go in complete bundles.

That can make it challenging for you to prepare your items to be shipped as you, personally, would want them to go out to your customers. But your efforts there will be rewarded. When you participate in FBA, your items become eligible for both Amazon Prime shipping (which gives buyers two-day shipping for a flat $79 per year) and Amazon Super Saving shipping (free standard shipping on all orders

$25 and over). This may give you a tremendous competitive edge over your competitors, as these programs are hugely popular. There's no doubt that some buyers are likely to select the products that offer this reduced shipping, ignoring those that don't. We'll look at how this works in more detail later on in the book.

For the occasional seller, and we're thinking that's not your goal, you can also use EasySell. Amazon introduced EasySell in 2007 for sellers of media products. EasySell merchants must also use FBA, sending their media items to Amazon, where they will be stored and shipped as they sell. Their listings appear right alongside Amazon's products on the main Marketplace. Because this program is geared only to casual sellers, we won't go into too much detail on it here.

Looking Ahead

Now it's on to the number-one question on all sellers' minds. Where will you find your product sources so that you can keep your inventory fresh and moving? How will you identify the hot commodities, and where will you locate them once you do? No business can operate for very long without inventory, and yours is no different. Chapter 3 will address ways to buy the items you plan to sell!

An Amazon Success Story

When we first met Gary Richardson, he was operating a successful business on eBay selling sunglasses. His username, Harleyglasses, not only represented a successful e-commerce merchant, but reflected his interest in both sunglasses and motorcycles! Today, Gary defines himself as a "multichannel merchant," quite a bit removed from his first tentative tiptoes onto eBay. Before

that, Gary says, "I avoided eBay like the plague." At first, he feared online scammers were all who awaited him there. But, like so many others, he sold a few of his family's things there, and then explored developing a business for himself based on a lifelong fascination with sunglasses.

Today, Gary still sells on eBay, but his main focus has expanded to include Amazon, his own website, www.goggles and glasses.com, neweggmall.com, Mailcar store, and Talkmarket, to name just a few channels. "I wished I'd had a picture for multichannel selling when I was just starting out," Gary told us. Selling on so many different venues gives Gary a unique view of the Amazon seller.

"I really don't know much about my Amazon customers," he said, "because I hardly ever hear from them. They don't ask questions. They seem to be very confident and trusting in their purchases." Gary reports that on Amazon he doesn't get questions like, "Are the new sunglasses really new?" "Our Amazon customers seem to be willing to pay for service and product," he noted. "Shoppers definitely trust Amazon.com."

That trust has made Gary even more intent on making sure he provides extraordinary customer service. He offers his customers quick e-mail responses to their inquiries and a toll-free phone number so they can speak directly to him, although he noted that customers rarely use it. He includes printed communications in all of his packages, so every shipment contains his own personal touch. "Amazon has legendary customer service," he noted. "How do I do it better than they do?" That is the goal Gary strives to achieve.

One way Gary makes sure his customers are happy is to provide a very easy return process. "If customers find it difficult to return items, they may skip the process and go directly to leaving you negative feedback." Since feedback on Amazon is a one-way process, "buyers don't hold back when things go wrong." His advice is to do whatever you can to maintain perfect feedback, and that includes attempting to resolve every customer dispute.

Going into the future, Gary enthusiastically embraces the changes he sees coming. "I want to find a way to make returns fun and profitable," he said. "I am always into new marketing methods. I really like video for selling products, and I like that Amazon allows me to think and become the marketer I am!" Check out Gary's video of folding reading glasses at https://www.talkmarket.com/video/product/433/. We think it's impressive, but as you have already guessed, we're a couple of Gary's biggest fans!

CHAPTER

3

You Have to Buy It Before You Can Sell It

People operating successful e-commerce businesses have many issues to consider. You'll have shipping issues, customer service policies to develop, and employees to hire, just to name a few. But, of all the subjects most likely to haunt a budding e-commerce entrepreneur, the subject of where to locate the items you'll sell is the gold standard of worries. You simply can't build your business until you've got a stable of reliable suppliers behind your operation. Nothing makes a business falter faster than running out of product and leaving a stream of disappointed customers behind. So, perhaps this chapter is the one that will really set you on your way. We can't, of course, tell you exactly where you'll find your sources of products. Nobody can. Sellers guard those secrets like the keys to Fort Knox. And if all those companies selling directories of wholesalers and distributors really knew the can't-miss sources, they'd be using them themselves. But, what we can offer you are *proven facts and strategies* about sourcing your products and great bits of advice from the successful Amazon sellers we've worked with.

The first thing to remember in sourcing your products is that the work is never finished. It's kind of like being a parent. You'll be paying careful attention to the details no matter how successful and independent your operation seems to grow. You're going to have to stay open minded and keep your sourcing options fluid. To do that, you'll need to get very good at research. Research is the skeleton on which you'll build your business. You can't add the muscle if you don't have solid research at the core. We'll help you to see how to effectively do that research, but you're going to have to make the commitment to stick with it until it becomes a routine part of your business day. Lots of sellers enjoy this part of their jobs the most.

Once you've identified some reliable sources and built a well-rounded product line, you'll be able to use your own sales data to track how your suppliers are working for you and which parts of your inventory are performing to expectations. Sourcing for an online business means you have to stay a step ahead of the curve. Even after you've found your niche, you simply can't concentrate all your attention on items that are profitable now—you need to keep your eyes on what's about to become popular, too. That way, when the inventory you're currently earning a nice profit from begins to falter, and it's likely that it will, you'll have something new in the wings waiting to take its place.

If all of this sounds a bit like juggling, you've got the right idea! You're going to have to stay open to change and be flexible if your goal is to stay profitable. You'll have to reach a point beyond accepting change; you'll have to learn to enjoy it. Those characteristics are hallmarks of successful e-commerce merchants. Moving your attention away from a product line that is still earning you money can be incredibly difficult, but trends surge and fade, and you don't want to get stuck basing your income and profits on an item that is losing market share. "Eventually the price of an item will drop like a lead weight," notes a successful Amazon bookseller who asked not to be named. "You need to make a highly educated guess of what the demand will be over the next few months," he added. Fortunately, we have lots of advice to help you do just that.

Let's Put the Horse Before the Cart

Before you get yourself all ready to open up that checkbook and start buying inventory, there are a few basics you'll need to address. As tempting as it might be to rev your engines, charting your course first will make the trip much more successful. If you're going to take this ride, make sure you've got a reliable plan in sight before you set out.

Get a Tax ID Number

If you don't already have a tax ID number, you'll need to get that before you proceed. As long as you live in a state that collects sales tax, and most of them do, you'll need this ID number to legitimately sell your items, even to people ordering from you online. You'll also need this number before you can place orders with the many manufacturers and wholesalers who will require it. Fortunately, getting a tax ID number, or resale certificate as it may also be called, is relatively simple. (We want to strongly encourage getting *resale certificates* to be 100 percent in compliance with the law.) Begin by typing into any search engine, the search term "Tax ID Number (*your state*)." This will at least provide you with information about the tax ID program for your location and, at best, may actually direct you to the forms you need to process your ID number. As an alternative, you can go to mtc.gov/Resources.aspx?id=272&ItemId=272, shown in Figure 3-1. Here you'll find links to information about obtaining your tax ID number for most of the states and the District of Columbia. The link for our location actually took us directly to the forms we needed.

Don't delay in getting this number. If we sound like we're harping on the subject, that's because it is just that important. You can't be legitimately in business until you're in compliance with the tax laws of your location (and that means make sure you understand what your local county and municipal requirements are, too). The process can take several weeks to complete, so starting it now is only smart. By the time you've got the rest of your research in place, you want to be able to start buying inventory, and overlooking this detail now can easily hold you up when you really want to get moving.

You'll also need to stay on top of where this issue stands with Congress. Periodically, Congress considers whether Internet sales, as

Figure 3-1. The Multistate Tax Commission site provides links to the tax forms you may need.

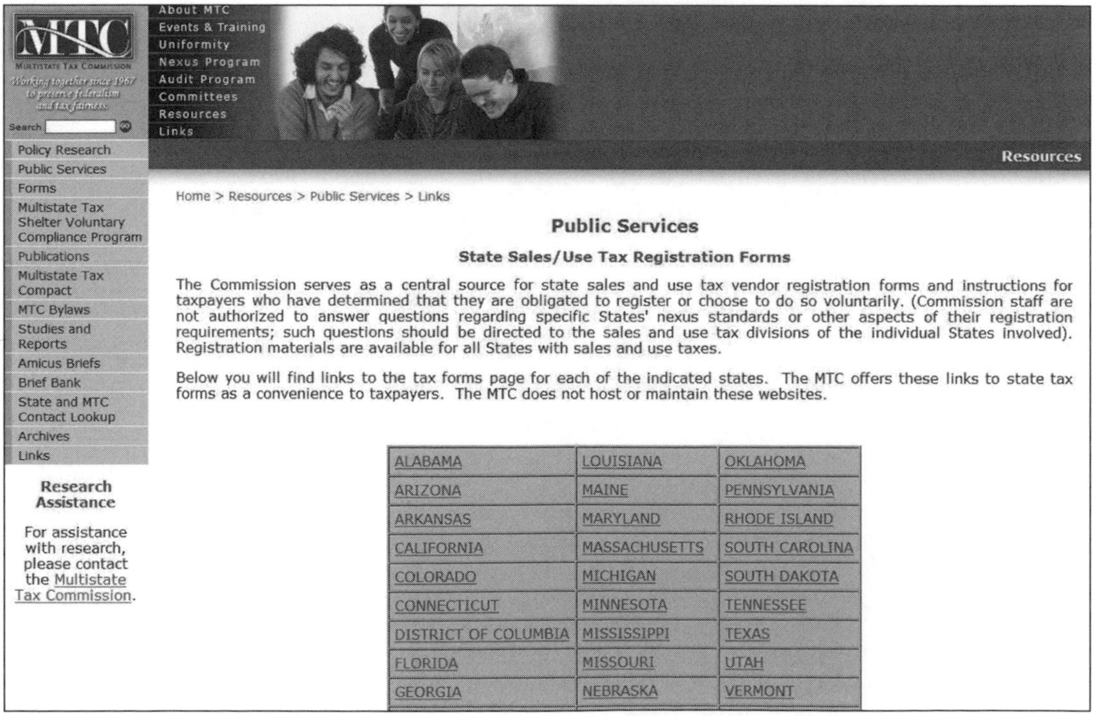

a whole, should be taxed. Joining an organization such as PeSA or the IMA (see Chapter 1) can help you stay abreast of what's going on, and give you an action plan should it seem things might change.

Where Will You Store It, and How Will You Ship It?

As you're considering the items you want to sell, also consider the practical limitations you may have for storing those items and shipping them. Unless you plan to exclusively use Fulfillment by Amazon (discussed at length in Chapter 8), you'll need a clean, safe, dry place to house your inventory, and you'll need to have a plan for handling fulfillment and shipping your orders. These are considerations best made *before* box after box of inventory begins to arrive. Do some reality checking now!

You should have a very clear idea of how you will ship an item before you purchase it for resale online, because shipping your items is a constant in your business. You can get a great bargain on a particular item, only to find that shipping that item is unwieldy or cost-prohibitive. That changes the whole equation about whether the item belongs in your inventory. Lucky online retailers handle items that are all the same size and weight. That way, not only do they avoid having to calculate shipping expenses over and over again, they can also bulk-order shipping supplies in advance and have everything stored, just waiting for order fulfillment. You may not complete your product line along this model, and that's fine, too. There are plenty of opportunities for fulfilling orders of varying size and weight efficiently. It's just something you have to prepare for and plan for as you're considering what your inventory will be. Amazon knows that shipping is a great place to make some customer service points. That's why it offers programs like Amazon Prime (see Figure 3-2) and free shipping. As we've said, you too can offer those rates to your customers if Amazon fulfills your orders. They can make or break a sale.

Figure 3-2. The popular Amazon Prime service enables customers to receive items within two days, for a flat yearly fee.

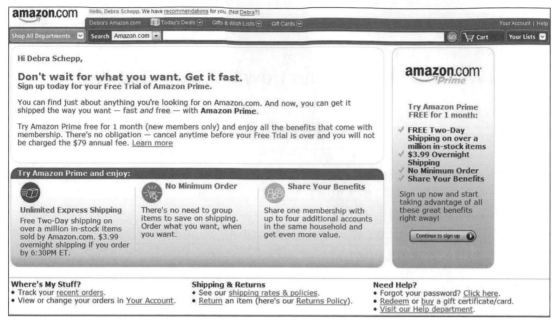

Calculate Your Budget

Once you know where you'll store your inventory and how you'll ship your items to your customer, create a clear budget for what you can afford to invest in inventory. Don't forget to set aside part of that budget for shipping supplies. If you know exactly how much you're comfortable spending, you will avoid the downfall of spending too much on one type of item or forgetting to calculate the cost of shipping supplies. For example, we use a lot of Jiffy envelopes for mailing. We've found they range in price from $0.40 to $1.29 or more each. That's such a huge range that it can easily spell the difference between a sale that's profitable and one that's taken at a loss.

Your budget, with hard work and good luck, will certainly increase as you build your business, but spending too much at the outset only adds stress. As you begin to source your inventory, always be sure you're shopping with a calculator. Eventually, you'll be experienced enough to eyeball a bargain, but not in the beginning. Carefully calculating the cost of your inventory, especially now, is a great way to build your experience without crashing your budget.

What Have You Got Going for You?

With the practical issues tucked away, let's turn our attention to the question, "What can you bring to the market?" Each one of us has that something that no other can offer. The products you'll be selling will become the stuff of which you build your life. You'll be spending countless hours researching, evaluating, comparing, considering, acquiring, and processing whatever it is you are now deciding about. Why not make all that work as enjoyable as possible? Give some thought to the hobbies you love, the passions you pursue, and the stuff that really spins your motor. Then figure out which part of that you can profitably bring to this market. Not only will knowing something about your products from the beginning boost your confidence, but it will also help you to make smart sourcing choices. Because you already know a lot about value, you'll have a real feel for how profitable a sourcing decision is. You'll also add value to all your communication with your customers. You'll know how to speak their language.

"We read that a bookseller should focus on products that they know a lot about, either through a hobby or through experience," explained Dan Morrill of bookseller Alternating Reality. "We chose science fiction, because that has been our major lifestyle choice. We love everything to do with science fiction," he added. "We can discuss it intelligently, and we want to share cool things we know. That's why we chose the niche we did."

If you don't seem to have anything drawing you in a particular direction, look around your own backyard for a profitable source of products. Is there a local manufacturer you might approach? Can you identify items local to you that other people would find desirable, if they knew about them? Once you start thinking about what might make for profitable sales, you'll start seeing everything for its earning potential. As long as you're looking in your own neighborhood, reach out to the non-Internet merchants, too. They may have inventory they'd be happy to see you move online for them.

Your local librarian might be able to help you research and locate local businesses and manufacturers. Call in advance to arrange a time when your librarian can be free to help guide you in the right direction. Librarians are professional researchers. Helping people find information is how they earn their livings, and many are experts in their own particular fields and the communities they serve. We've never found a single one who didn't enjoy helping people find the information they need. Since they're already working on your behalf, don't hesitate to ask them for exactly the information you want.

Obvious Solutions and Good Advice

You're bound to find dozens of offers to buy lists of wholesalers, manufacturers, and liquidators. It's pretty hard to miss these offers once you start researching. Now, we're not saying that no one ever found a valuable source of products this way. We're just saying it's not likely to be worth the money you'll spend if you do. Think about it. If these folks really had great information about reliable sources of profitable online products to sell, do you really think they'd earn their livings selling you these lists? It sounds too good to be true, because it is. Instead of investing in rehashed sourcing information, devote your energy to finding the real thing and your money toward testing your products' profitability.

You Profit When You Buy

We know that we're talking now about sourcing your product line, but this old business adage is as true on the Internet as it was for the wandering peddler. You don't make your profit when you sell your item. You make the profit when you buy it at a price that will allow you to sell and earn a profit. It takes a lot of work to find the right sources of the right products for the right price, but it's essential to your success.

Ferret Out New Old Stock (NOS)

"We found some dead-stock sunglasses that were made in the 1980s and had been sitting on the warehouse shelves for 20 years," Gary of Goggles and Glasses told us. "We visited one of our suppliers, and we happened to ask if they had anything that was not in their catalog. We bought everything they had at 1980 prices. They were glad to get rid of it, and we were happy to have a product that was unavailable anywhere (see Figure 3-3). Our customers are happy, because they can find the genuine and unopened 1980s product (NOS) at a good price, and we are happy, because we can sell them at a really good price compared to the small amount we paid for them!"

Find Wholesalers

It won't be too hard to find wholesalers willing to sell products to you. But, don't forget that the wholesaler is earning a profit from you that will come from whatever you earn on the selling end. You'll never get the lowest possible price for your inventory if you're paying a wholesaler to bring it to you from the manufacturer. You may

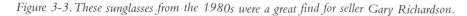

Figure 3-3. These sunglasses from the 1980s were a great find for seller Gary Richardson.

have to start by working with wholesalers, however, because manufacturers use them to move inventory. Plus, often, a wholesaler will sell to you in the smaller quantities you'll need as you get started. But, your ultimate goal is to get as close to the originator of your products as possible. Avoid the stop in the middle that scoops a piece of your income out each time you buy. Your ultimate goal is the manufacturer.

Consider Liquidators

As with wholesalers, liquidators earn a profit from finding you the products you'll sell. The difference is that liquidators buy from manufacturers in large quantities and pass the savings on to you. The sad reality, though, is that liquidators don't buy the first-run perfect merchandise you're hoping to find. Sure, some of what you can get through a liquidator will be just fine. But, much of it will be damaged, seconds, or in some way imperfect. By the time you sort through your purchase, factor in the time it takes you to locate saleable merchandise, and dispose of those items not fit for sale, liquidators can be more trouble and less profitable than you'd like.

Amazon seller Kirk Holbert, who operates Cosmic-King, which specializes in toys and action figures, does turn to liquidators with some success. "With liquidators, you can place smaller orders (say $500 to $1,000), unlike what manufacturers require (like $10,000)." Kirk finds liquidators on the Internet, but he describes his efforts as "searching and searching on the Internet for hours." So, although you can find opportunities here, know that those opportunities will require a great deal of effort, and until you locate the best ones for you, you may find that some of the time and money you invest are going to be educational expenses as you learn about your best sourcing options.

TIP *Search Safely*

While you're building your business, checking out wholesalers, liquidators, and manufacturers, remember to protect yourself every step of the way. For example, before you do business with any wholesalers, make sure they have an actual street address rather than a post office box number. You want to be sure you're doing business with an actual company and not someone who is operating a scam business through a post office box. Get a phone number for the company, and make sure to speak with a human there. Best of all, a receptionist should answer, proving that the business is substantial enough to require one. But, at least connect with a human. Don't be satisfied leaving a message on voicemail to be answered later. That's also too easy to fake. If you can't verify authenticity, keep moving along with your research until you find a company that can be verified.

Once you locate some likely resources, find out how those companies do business and how well they stack up against others in their fields. Do they belong to their trade associations? If not, find out why. There may be a logical reason, but you'll what to know what it is.

Find out if there are any strikes against them with the Better Business Bureau. A clean record here won't guarantee that you're in safe hands, but at least it will alert you if the company has a history of dissatisfied customers. Finally, look for companies that have the backing of credit-checking services, such as VeriSign, Hoover, or Dunn & Bradstreet. This type of accreditation tells you that the company has proven itself able to meet certain standards of business operations.

Are You Planning to Be a Bookseller?

In most cases, you can't expect to come to Amazon and sell second-hand items. That's not what the Amazon Marketplace is meant for. Asad Bangash of Beachcombers! says that Amazon is more like the Internet's mall than the Internet's flea market, and we agree. One exception, of course, is when it comes to selling books. Many people come to Amazon to sell books, and if that's your intention, too, then your sourcing issues will vary from those of merchants coming to sell other commodities. It may come as no surprise, but if you're planning to sell books on Amazon, you'll need to educate yourself about the value of used books in general. You can't very well come to this specific marketplace without any experience in the used books business and expect to succeed just because you list online.

You have many advantages in selling books on Amazon—the broad customer base, the easy listing, the simple payment structure your customers enjoy, just to name a few. But, surprisingly, you also have one of the world's best databases on the subject of books, and it's just waiting there for you to tap its research potential. As a bookseller, this database alone is a valuable tool for your business. Let's count some of the ways.

First of all, Amazon's book database makes it so simple to create your listings. Just about any title you want to sell most likely has a product listing page already on the site. That will make it quick and efficient for you to add your inventory to the Amazon Marketplace. Second, because so many titles are listed as both *new* through Amazon and *new* and *used* by third-party sellers, you have accurate and current information on what any one particular title is likely to bring. It really helps take the guess work out of determining your price. Third, Amazon's results page for each book lists the Amazon rank of every book, so you can quickly see how popular your item is. Figure 3-4 shows the page for the number-four ranked book at the time of this search: *Hungry Girl: Recipes and Survival Strategies for Guilt-Free Eating in the Real World*. Of course, these rankings are a moving target,

Figure 3-4. With Amazon, you can preorder a book before it is released. This page shows the number-four bestselling book on Amazon as of this writing.

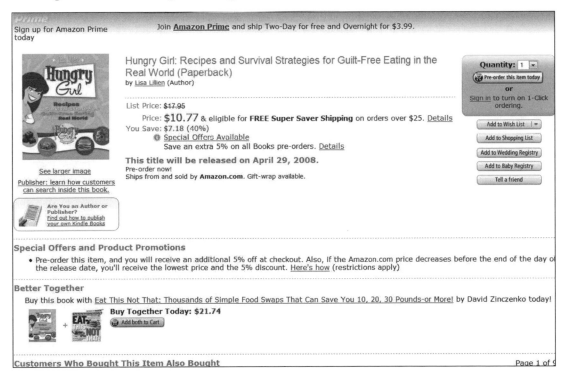

changing hourly. Popular books are usually carried by many vendors, so you'll need to price very competitively.

You can spend days working with the Amazon database to see which titles are selling, which are bringing great returns, and which titles may be in short supply. Don't overlook the site as a research bonanza, free for you to explore. Most important, since you can sort any of your search results by *bestselling*, you have tremendous marketing intelligence before you any time of day and updated on the hour. Remember, though, that Amazon, even after all this time, seems to sell more computers and business books than its share, and booksellers may find their results skewed because of that. That's where other sites such as Barnes and Noble's bn.com come in handy as a check.

As Dan Morrill of Alternating Reality did, many booksellers start with a genre they know and love. If you've been a bibliophile for years, you no doubt have a corner of the publishing field that interests you best, too. Most of the booksellers we spoke with told us that they started out with the books they loved, but they all agreed that a niche was important. "Books you love" is only one market category to explore. You can also branch out to first editions or decide to stick with bestsellers. That's not to say that, ultimately, you won't diversify your inventory to include all kinds of profitable titles, but in the beginning, it helps to focus on a niche.

Brad, for example, has always liked book about collectibles, so he keeps an eye out for these kinds of titles. When he found that Collector's Press was selling out some of its inventory of nostalgia titles on eBay, he bought all he could. He then turned around and resold those books to Amazon customers, keeping just one copy of each book for his own collection! Now, if Brad had not been zeroing in on books like that to start with, he never would have found the eBay inventory.

Build Relationships with Others Who Handle Used Books

Used books can be sourced in any number of places, from the local library sale to the Goodwill store. Since you'll be competing against other used-book sellers, it's important for you to build your relationships with any and all sources of product in your area. Start by introducing yourself to the managers of all your local thrift shops. Of course, that includes Goodwill (currently selling their own books on Amazon!), but it can also mean the local hospital thrift shop, or any of the other charity drop-off locations near you. Many people consider used books to be more nuisance than value. Something about a book can make it hard to just throw away, but at the same time, books rank pretty high on the "clutter" scale most folks like to control. They often end up donated.

The local library will be your next stop. Most libraries accept donations of books, videos, DVDs, and CDs. Some of those items actually get put into the library's collection. Surprisingly, most of them do not. They get bundled up to be sold, with the proceeds going to support the library. That can mean regularly scheduled "library sales." Library sales may be held quarterly or only annually, but they are always a great source of good, used books. Some libraries even have a display of used books for sale in the building all the time. Those are not the books the library found to be substandard for its collection, either. Often, the library simply doesn't need another copy. Or, circulation numbers may indicate that current copies are adequate. The books placed for sale in the library have all been reviewed for their condition and determined to be saleable, by people who deal with books every day. So, get to know the staff at your library, too. They'll be happy to keep you in mind when they see an especially interesting donation arrive. Better yet, join your local "Friends of the Library" to gain a real inside track on the library sales, since these service organizations generally operate them.

Share the Wealth

To keep these relationships moving along, Xavier Helgesen of Better World Books recommends offering your suppliers a portion of your earnings. If, for example, the local Goodwill store proves to be a valuable source for you, "build a relationship with them, and let them share in your success on the upside," he recommends. Going back to that Goodwill store to give a donation based on the sales of the books is bound to help them remember you next time a shipment of books arrives.

Once you have your business moving along, you can branch out to local independent bookstores. "Get them online," suggests Xavier. It's true that the Internet has made survival even tougher for the small independent bookstore. If you can offer to help them build an online presence profitable to both parties, it will be a relationship that brings hard cold cash returns.

At the very least, you can build the value of your relationships with your local suppliers by using your knowledge to help them identify particularly valuable books that come their way. Instead of scooping up *every* profitable title, point some of them out to your suppliers. Help them to learn more about their donations, and even offer them the greater profit you can deliver by selling it online on their behalf. That's bound to build loyalty to you as a business partner.

All of the contacts you make as you go about building your inventory will make your sourcing prospects expand. Building the relationship should go beyond scooping up an extra box or two of books. "Interesting things happen to you if you have lots of contacts," noted a bookseller from the southeast. After building his connections for years, he now has accounts with all the major publishers that allow him to buy his inventory direct. That may be a far-off goal to you now, but continue building your connections and relationships with suppliers, and it's likely to be an attainable one for you, too.

Know the Publishing Industry

The more you learn about books, the more you'll know about the publishing industry as a whole. By the time you're ready to buy directly from the publisher, you'll be a veritable insider. Use this insider status to give yourself strategic advantages. For example, track the careers of famous and popular writers. As their newest works become available, you'll often see a spike in well-loved older works, too. "As long as a book is well-bought, it will sell," noted this same Sunbelt bookseller. As just one example, he had an overabundant supply of *The Lovely Bones* by Alice Seybold. When her next book came out, demand for the earlier work boomed, and he sold all he had. If you follow the industry, you'll know what key writers are working on, and you'll be in a position to build your inventory with previously successful books from those authors to match the debut of a new title. Even if the new release is a dud, its release will still stir up some action for the earlier successes. One of our favorite online newsletters about the book publishing industry is PublishersMarketplace at http://www.publishersmarketplace.com/ (shown in Figure 3-5).

Figure 3-5. PublishersMarketplace is a tremendous resource for insider information on the book publishing industry.

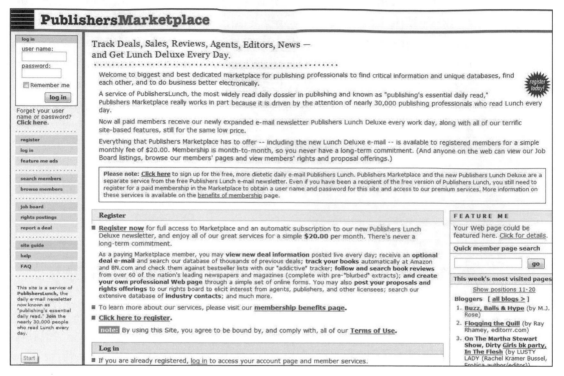

 ## *Use Technology*

Fortunately, you don't have to face the prospect of carting home bag after bag of books, only to glean the few valuable ones from the mass you plug into your computer one at a time! Sounds dreadful, we agree. Here's where modern technology allows you to use a scanner and a smart phone, which really helps booksellers. As you shop, you can scan the ISBNs directly into your smart phone and then search Amazon for their rankings and price ranges. You'll know before you even have to flex a muscle whether the potential for profit is there.

Plus, you won't be left at home with bags of books that aren't terribly saleable to cart back to your donation center on your next trip! In Chapter 5 we'll discuss these scouting tools and software in greater length.

Are You Planning to Sell Anything Else Besides Media?

If you're planning to build your Amazon business on commodity items other than books, CDs, DVDs, and videos, then your sourcing strategies and techniques are bound to be different. Still, you can apply some of the same considerations to this type of business, too. After all, determining the strengths you can bring to the market and building strong relationships with your suppliers are sound practices for any retailer.

Research, Research, Research

As you work to determine your strengths, do it with solid research to define which of your strengths are relevant to a larger audience and which are more specific to you personally. Research will be a crucial part of your everyday life, from the first moment you set out to become an e-commerce retailer. If you don't love it now, you'll have to learn to. It's simply never going to go away. Of course, researching things that interest you makes researching much more fun!

You'll be researching markets, trends, suppliers, and eventually your own operation with an eye toward filling a gap and bringing a popular item to the marketplace. How you do your research will, of course, vary, depending on what you plan to sell, but some constant rules of researching will apply across all product areas. If you are going to be selling jewelry, for example, you'll need to stay current with fashion trends. "I am constantly looking at market trends in fashion magazines, TV, industry websites, and trade shows," says Kathy Wojtczak of Element Jewelry & Accessories. "I also try to attend as many local craft fairs and markets as possible to look for unique items offered by local designers."

You can't very well make good decisions about accessories when you have no idea what the fashion industry is featuring for next season. If computer accessories are right for you, you'll have to be tech savvy from the beginning and know where you can search to keep up with the latest developments. Of course, if you're working in an area that already speaks to you you'll have a leg up on this type of research. You're probably already tracking your interests in the media, and in places that less passionate hobbyists haven't even discovered.

The great thing about researching is that the more you do it, the more tuned in you can become to it. You may start out thinking of selling toys. Then as you spend time with your children at the library, or wait for them at soccer practice, or sit in the dentist's office for their appointment, you'll notice what other kids and parents are talking about and playing with. Some of your best hints may just come from those random moments when you overhear a conversation that sparks an idea. Just a warning: Eavesdrop discreetly. It's still socially frowned upon, even if it is the best of fun! Believing that your skills will be honed as you make your way through this project is empowering. A year from now, you'll be surprised at how much more you know about your product area, even if today you are selecting something you feel confident in knowing a good deal about!

Research Your Ideas On and Off Amazon

Fortunately, once again, the amazing database that is Amazon.com can help you search out good new inventory items to pursue. Just to get started, you can sort any of your search results by *bestselling*, allowing you to quickly view what is moving on the site. "I like to research the top 100 popular items and the Movers & Shakers list in each category on Amazon.com," says Gary of Goggles and Glasses. "I can get a pulse on what the platform has its mind on each week, month, or season." You can find the Movers & Shakers list that Gary refers to at http://www.amazon.com/gp/movers-and-shakers/ (see Figure 3-6). You'll find items here that have moved up substantially in the Amazon rankings over the previous 24-hour period. If it starts to zoom, you'll find it on this list. Now, it's not likely that you'll be able to directly identify specific products and their reliable sources through this list. This list actually represents work that has already taken place in the past as other sellers have found good sources of these items. But, the list will certainly help you develop a "feel" for the market and gain insights into what is currently doing well. That's bound to help you hone your sourcing skills.

Likewise, you can use shopping aggregators to get a larger view of the Web in general. Sites such as Shopping.com and Froogle will help you see what other people are searching for. This research can help you see which items are building in momentum and which items are beginning to falter. "I also like to search for the product on Google products and use comparison shopping engines and other marketplaces to determine where it is in its product life cycle," says Gary. All of these research activities will improve your knowledge base, build your research skills, and help you make identifying potentially profitable products second nature to your workday life.

Figure 3-6. Amazon provides a wealth of market data. Here's just a part of its Movers & Shakers list.

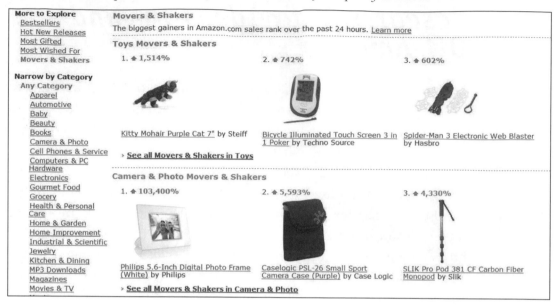

 TIP

Research Your Competition

One of the best places to get started with your research is right on Amazon. Once you've decided on a product, go to Amazon and see how others are doing with that product. "Research on Amazon is really based on its own market," explained Eric Lau of Visiondecor. "As much as we like to assume that the Internet is homogenous, each market such as Amazon has its own customers that desire specific items at specific prices." What a perfect way to test your product idea. If you come to Amazon and find the item is doing well, then you can turn your attention to acquiring inventory at a good price point to allow you to take your place on the market. If you find the market is flooded with this particular item, and that none of them seem to be moving quickly, then you know you need to go back and search some more.

Researching your competition is another way for you to see if you can sell your products at a profitable price. You have no reason to believe that buyers will pay you more for the item than they are already paying other sellers on Amazon. You have no advantage in an overcrowded market, especially as a new seller. Now, that doesn't mean you can't enter a competitive field, but you are going to have to figure a niche of that field that you are well suited to fill and go after that corner instead of running straight into the middle of the field.

We mentioned this before, but it bears repeating. Amazon has a simple, but often overlooked, tool to help you research your potential inventory. "Amazon has a certain degree of transparency," notes e-commerce consultant David Yaskulka. "You can search for items and then sort them by *bestselling*." Now, not only do you see what your competition is offering on Amazon, but you can also see which among these items is proving to be most profitable. When we asked if this wasn't information everyone hoping to sell on Amazon could access, David reminded us that just because everyone can doesn't mean that everyone will, and the ones who do will surely have the advantage.

Of course, Amazon isn't the only place for you to do your research. As long as you're sitting in front of your computer, spread your efforts across the Web. And, don't forget to stop by eBay to see what those products are selling for on a site where people expect a discount. "We do a lot of research on products, and we check pricing all over the Net," said Steve Jay of wholesalelaptopbattery. "We usually price items on eBay, and if we can buy them in bulk for half the eBay price, then we go for it. Just remember, "If you see 60 pages of the same item sold, then it is not a good idea to buy that product for resale," Steve advised.

Go to the Trade Shows

Every industry has its trade show, and many of them have more than one. Select the trade show most closely related to the product line you're interested in and prepare to travel. Before you even arrive, you should have already identified some likely business partners through your online research. Make a list of the manufacturers who seem to carry the products you're after, and visit them first. But, don't be so rigid in your plan that you don't allow for a little serendipity when the right opportunity comes along. Kirk Holbert of Cosmic-King first started sourcing his line at the Associated Surplus Dealers/ Associated Merchandise Dealers trade show. "I found that a lot of those manufacturers didn't have much of an Internet presence, and that was surprising," he told us. Now he places orders with them twice a year when he attends the show. The ASD/AMD trade show is sponsored by the Associated Surplus Dealers/Associated Merchandise Dealers and is the largest merchandising show in the country (see http://www.asdamdshows.com). Just have your budget clearly defined and your tax ID number on hand. (You *have* already done that, right? If not, put the book down and go fill out the forms!) Arrive at the show ready to do business. Take a laptop computer or a smart phone with you so that you can quickly hop online and check out the current prices for the products you're considering. That way, right on the spot, you'll be able to know if you can buy at a price that will allow you to profit. "I tend to go to conventions where I look for easy-to-ship and always-in-stock items," explained Rene Klassen of Musicnmore. "Then I search on Amazon. I type in the bar codes to see what the competition is doing and if I can fit it in."

Personalize Your Product Line

Chances are, if you're reading this book, you have been interested in buying and selling online for some time. You probably know more about the process than you're currently giving yourself credit for knowing. What have you bought online that has been valuable to you? What have you bought that has disappointed you? As you answer these questions, your sourcing options begin to open to you, and you can become a guide to customers who will shop with you to gain your advice, as well as good customer service. "People need help in knowing whether something they are going to buy is right for them," notes Andy Mowery of debnroo. Andy has been an e-commerce success for the better part of 10 years, so his advice can go straight to the heart. "A lot of products we carry are those things we found and used ourselves," Andy says. He can then tell his customers to see his blog and learn about how he got involved in selling that particular item. When Andy and his wife, Deb, moved to a new house, he let his customers come along. He blogged extensively about the decision process involved in buying patio furniture. He lets his customers see how he comes to recommend a product. Not only does that allow his customers to feel a personal connection to Andy and his business, but it allows them to see the reasoning and philosophy he brings to his life and his work. That can be especially important when all of your customer interaction is virtual. "Customers then build a bond with us as people," remarked Andy, "not just as debnroo."

Poll Your Customers

Once you have your business moving along, keep a careful eye on the feedback your customers are providing and the questions they are asking. This is research data coming to you directly from your most important source, the customers you're trying hard to please. "Now we find that much of our research stems from feedback from our customers," explained Asad Bangash of Beachcombers! Asad and his partner, Jody Rogers, sell ethnic women's fashions, shoes, and accessories. "Since we have been in business for a few years and have a following, many of our customers give us great feedback on what we could do to improve our business and what products they would like to see us sell," he said. "For example, we started selling insoles for our shoes to help compensate for half sizing of shoes. We would find that we were missing a key product to complete a part of our offerings, so we would find a supplier to fill the need."

Now, you won't be in a position to take advantage of your customers' feedback comments until you have some experience under your belt. But when you do, remember that every time you listen to a customer you have the opportunity to improve your business. Even the criticism will help you refine your line and watch your quality control. But, you can make use of customer feedback only if you keep an open mind and resist the urge to be defensive about your products or your work. Weigh all your feedback to see how you can improve. View each one as an opportunity only you have to improve your business.

Research Yourself

As you gain inventory and experience, you'll be able to analyze your own sales to see what is proving to be profitable and where the disappointments are. "Right through Seller Central I can see reports and information about my own sales," says Kirk of Cosmic-King. Kathy of Element Jewelry & Accessories agrees (see Figure 3-7). "I spend a lot of time analyzing product sales," she reports. "If a product isn't selling, it needs to be put on sale. This may make the product itself less profitable, but it allows me to then add new top-selling products (based on current sales), which will add to the overall profitability of the entire line," she explained. So, listening to your customers—along with the empirical proof of what your customers are buying—will help you refine and polish your product line.

Diversify Your Product Line

Look for ways to diversify what you sell. It's the same wise investment advice you've heard before: *Diversifying can help protect your holdings and lessen your risks.* Maintaining diversity in your product line can help you balance your earnings and build sales. "Diversification within your actual inventory is just as important," says Tricia Records of Read_Rover_Books. "I feel most secure stocking a mix of items that turn over quickly as well as investment-grade items that hold their value for longer periods of time, but also bring in significantly higher revenues. The investment-grade items may take months or even years to find the right buyer."

Figure 3-7. You can track your progress for several metrics by clicking on Seller Central's Reports tab.

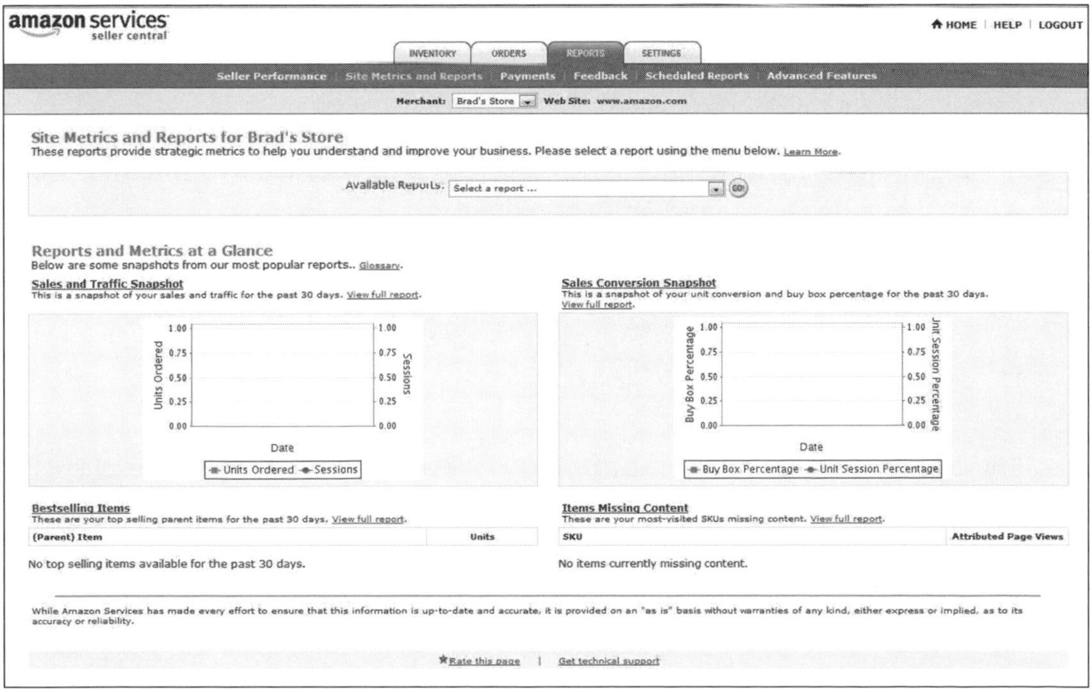

Keeping a well-balanced product line not only helps buffer your business and keep it steady, but it can also directly boost your sales. "If we notice that customers are buying more living room pieces," explained Eric Lau of Visiondecor, a furniture and accessories seller, "we will begin to offer and source more accessories relevant to the living room. We added floor lamps, table lamps, footstools, magazine holders, etc." Selling these smaller, less expensive items helps encourage sales for Eric's furniture, too. "If you were to buy a sofa or bedroom set online," explained Eric, "you would want to buy something smaller first from the seller to test our service and quality." His product line wouldn't be complete with just the larger, more expensive items he sells.

Looking Ahead

Now that you have started to clarify your ideas about what you'll sell and where you'll find it, it's time to start thinking about the face you'll be showing to your Amazon customers. Chapter 4 will help you create your virtual image so that your customers will recognize you on Amazon and every time you have contact with them. Gather your inventory, and let's get selling!

An Amazon Success Story

Eric Lau, of Visiondecor, was already a pioneer online merchant when he began selling on Amazon more than three years ago. An Amazon representative actually approached him and invited him to be one of the first home and garden category sellers on the site to sell and fulfill orders for furniture and home goods. At the time, according to Eric, Amazon was developing its merchant seller platform and looking for current sellers on competing sales channels, such as eBay, or home and garden category sellers who had their own websites. "We fit both criteria," noted Eric. Eventually, Eric signed a three-year contract with Amazon based on Visiondecor's continued sales history, growth, and performance on the site.

Today, Eric has a staff of 20 people creating the listings for his Amazon business. He is a big believer in doing each listing individually, and turns away from the tools others might use for bulk listing products. "I have thousands of items where my team of people has spent countless hours of review and research time to launch, adjust, and maintain descriptions and pricing. It's not easy for a programmer to create software that replaces all that hard work. With automation you can run into problems like picking up bad data, which results in an item incorrectly priced," noted Eric. That's very hard to find, he told us, unless someone buys it. "When you have to spend time checking the errors, you might as well sit down and do it the right way the first time around," he said.

Eric maintains a well-balanced inventory of decorative items, ranging from children's accessories such as a wall easel to entire suites of living room furniture. With this balanced selection, Eric allows his customers to test his

services on the smaller items while contemplating larger purchases in the future. Knowing that it takes a leap of faith to purchase expensive furniture online, Eric does everything he can to reassure his customers that their needs will be his biggest concern. In terms of product sourcing, that means searching for quality items that may not be the lowest-priced items in their categories. "A lot of sellers blindly price their items to just gain the sale," he explained. "They can only do so if they sourced lower-quality products." Eric doesn't take that approach. "If the first experience is a bad one, then we can pretty much expect the customer to not want to buy a sofa from us," he said. "We're not perfect ourselves, as we have had customers give us feedback on some bad-quality items we launched before, but we immediately take those comments into consideration and discontinue the bad-quality items. We minimize bad service impact to our customers that will impact the long term."

So as you see, Eric closes our chapter about sourcing products with good, practical, and well-tested advice. You can't think only of what you'll sell, where you'll find it, and how you'll ship it. You also have to consider how your customer will feel about it. You have to make sure you're offering items for sale that will likely build a following for you among your customer base, instead of just a quick return on a single sale that won't build customer loyalty. We told you in the beginning of this chapter this was going to be a bit like juggling!

CHAPTER 4

Creating Great Product Detail Pages

For the sake of this chapter, we'll imagine that everyone reading is currently a Pro Merchant. Of course, being a Pro Merchant is not necessary to qualify for further reading, but, you will need to be one before you can create your own product detail pages, and that's why you're all getting a temporary promotion. Don't despair—although becoming a Pro Merchant will require more than the turn of just one page, we'll help you get there sooner through this chapter. Learning about the ins and outs of great product pages is bound to help you sell more effectively as you build your business's volume and look toward signing up for a Pro Merchant subscription. By the time you do that, you'll be able to hit the ground running and create great product pages right away! Your products will present themselves to Amazon's Marketplace with professionalism bound to lead to success.

Amazon's Existing Product Database

It may surprise you, but it's possible to operate a successful business on Amazon without ever creating your own product detail pages. Thanks to Amazon's huge catalog of items already listed for sale on the site, many of the things you'll consider selling already have Amazon pages. The database is that extensive. Certainly, if you sell in some of the very popular categories, you'll go a long way before you come across something so original that no one else has ever listed it on the site. Think about it. With all the millions of video game sellers on Amazon, for example, where would you find a game no one else is selling? It's possible, we suppose, but definitely not too likely. Other types of products will require that you create many of your own pages. Jewelry (a restricted area, but one that you can request access to sell in) is just one example. Each piece of jewelry is slightly different. Unless you buy a whole inventory of identical products, you'll need to showplace your pieces in the greatest detail possible to tempt your browsers into becoming buyers. Operating in a niche market can also result in your creating lots of pages. Drew Friedman of White Mountain Trading Company sells fine-quality writing instruments and wooden cases for storing them. He actually creates pages for *all* the items he sells.

Whether your products are going to join the crowd or stand out on their own, considering all the parts of a product detail page and clearly understanding all its elements will make you a stronger, more knowledgeable and more confident Amazon merchant. It won't matter if you don't actually create your own pages for months to come. The understanding you will gain by carefully studying Amazon pages will help you to better understand your product line, your customers, and the marketplace. You'll learn to evaluate other sellers' listings, build on their strengths, and spotlight the special features you can bring to the market. Thinking carefully about how you will present your merchandise is bound to make your business stronger.

Ultimately, the theories behind creating product pages may be the most important thing for you to focus on. Amazon makes it so simple to fill in the forms on its site, you'll hardly need help. Plus, tools and images change so quickly on the Internet that some aspects of doing all this are quite likely to have changed by the time you read these words. The tools and forms may look different, but the practical advice and strategy behind the solid decisions that successful sellers have made about their pages will still ring true. Before we can delve into the theories, let's look at a couple of practical tips you can use to list items on pages that already exist.

Climb onto That Piggy's Back

A piggyback ride is always a treat. As you start selling on Amazon, treat yourself as often as possible. Since there's no need to create your own page unless your product is unique, enjoy the boost you'll get from riding that piggy. "Piggybacking is the easiest way to get lots of products listed quickly," said Andy Mowery of Debnroo. "It's not uncommon on Amazon to find five or six different pages for the same product," he noted. (As we write this, Amazon is working to reduce duplicate pages.) If your sleuthing has found a page for your product already on the site, Andy suggests you piggyback off of it.

Chris Schlieter of timezone agrees. "Do not create new or additional catalog pages for identical items that are already listed on Amazon. If the item already exists, find the fastest and easiest way to add your 'offer' to the existing page. This should be the first thing you focus on as you get your presence established quickly. Once you've managed the low-hanging fruit, go back and list your unique items." As you saw in Chapter 1, to use an existing listing all you have to do is click on the *Sell yours here* button in the More Buying Choices box. Then fill in data about your item, such as price and condition, and you're off and running.

As quick and easy as this is, piggybacking is just one strategy you can use. It isn't the perfect solution, because other sellers, and even Amazon itself, may not get all the facts straight in their listings. As the seller, you're on the firing line if an important detail is missing or listed incorrectly, resulting in an unhappy customer. You'll want the control that creating your own product detail pages will provide you once you've zoomed in on your product line and are building your own Amazon business. Ultimately, you'll want to combine piggybacking with maintaining your position as master of your own product listings.

Learn from the Pros

Whether you're piggybacking or starting from scratch, the first part of listing your item will always be the same. Search Amazon for competing products, then sort your search results by *bestselling*. If it turns out there are listings for similar items, examine them to see how your top competitors are presenting them. Not only will this force you to take a close look at your most successful competitors, but it will also let you examine their pages for great ideas you can learn from. We're talking about a free education here! Which pages seem especially compelling? Who captivates you with their prose and makes the mundane sparkle? What keywords have these sellers used? Look around and take some notes.

Nuts and Bolts of Creating Product Detail Pages

Each time you create your own Amazon product page, you'll be faced with three main tasks:

1. Classify the item properly so people can find it.
2. Describe the item clearly and with enough finesse to make your customer want to buy it from you.
3. Show your customers images of the item that make them want to close the sale immediately.

Within each of these tasks, you'll have decisions to make and choices to consider, so we'll look at each one individually. In addition to these three main areas, you'll have to decide on a realistic price for your item.

But first, let's look at the ground rules for adding product detail pages. You can't just create a page for any old item and add it to Amazon's site. First, as we mentioned, you have to sign up for a Pro Merchant subscription. As a Pro Merchant, you can sell in the following categories:

- Automotive
- Baby
- Camera and photo
- Electronics
- Health and personal care
- Home and garden
- Musical instruments
- Office products
- Software
- Sports and outdoors
- Tools and hardware
- Toys and games
- Video games
- Everything else

By *everything else*, Amazon means items that don't currently fit into one of its existing categories, such as "stamps, posters, or similar products." The following categories are restricted, and you must request authorization to sell in them (Amazon considers these requests on a case-by-case basis):

- Apparel and accessories
- Beauty, cell phones and plans
- Gourmet food
- Jewelry and watches
- Personal computers

Now we're ready to consider the whole process together. We'll be using Seller Central for this exercise. We don't intend to step you through each field on a product listing form. You don't need us to do that, and it makes writing this book very boring. We're instead going to share with you the strategies that successful sellers have used to create their own successful pages, and let you work out the details on your own.

Product Classification

Classifying the product accurately is important. Suppose you have an item you believe is unique and may not already be on the Amazon site. On Seller Central, for example, you just click on the *Add a product* link under the *Inventory* heading of the main Seller Central dashboard. From the next page, you can enter some search terms to look for the product in Amazon's mammoth catalog (see Figure 4-1). Amazon recommends using the product name, UPC, EAN, ISBN, or ASIN.

I'll Use the Codes, but Can You Tell Me What They Mean?

Okay, so most of us know about ISBNs and UPCs. It's hard to shop without getting an education in those little fields that get scanned at checkout. But, how do you use them in your own business? Let's take a look at each one, and then you won't have to wonder where they came from or what they're for any longer.

- **UPC:** The Universal Product Code (UPC) is a bar code widely used to identify and track trade items in stores throughout the United States and Canada. The 12 digits of the code are all numeric and identify things like whether the item needs to be weighed for sale (think produce and meat) and what category of item the product occupies, like over-the-counter medicines.

- **EAN:** The European Article Number (EAN) is a bar-coding standard that is a subset of the original UPC from North America. This 13-digit number can also be called the Japanese Article Number.

- **ISBN:** The International Standard Book Number (ISBN) originated as a 9-digit number in the United Kingdom during the 1960s. It was then known as the Standard Book Number (SBN). In 1970, an additional digit was added and the code became the International SBN. It was developed by the International Organization for Standardization. As of January 1, 2007, there is also a 13-digit ISBN. A similar code, the International Standard Serial Number (ISSN), is for periodicals.

- **ASIN:** The Amazon Standard Identification Number (ASIN), unlike its companions, has no meaning outside of Amazon itself. It is a number issued by Amazon as an internal control number within the Amazon site. In the case of books, the ISBN is also the ASIN.

Figure 4-1. The Add a product *link is under Seller Central's* Inventory *heading.*

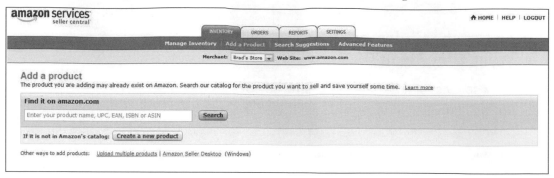

Of course, since not every product has all of those numbers, you might need to search by whatever keywords you think are likely to pull up your product. At this point you'd click on the *Create a new product* button.

Determine Search Terms

If your customers can't find your item, *buying* it will be impossible. Thanks to search engines like Google, most of us have become familiar with creating and using search terms. That's exactly what you'll be doing for your product as we place it in the correct category. OK, put your thinking cap on. You'll need to choose the best descriptors for your item. By *best*, we mean the ones that your customers are likely to put into that Amazon search box when they want to find what you have. You can do that in one of two ways. You can browse Amazon's listings to find items like yours, or you can search for items like yours by entering a term in the search box (see Figure 4-1). As a way to familiarize yourself with the site, browsing can prove valuable. By browsing categories, you get to see what the different "neighborhoods" on Amazon offer, and how they're organized. Then you can decide where your item is most likely to fit in. For example, if we start at Home and Garden, we can select *Home Improvement*. From there we'll be offered everything from tools to plumbing fixtures, from sanders to snow blowers. Each time you select one of these smaller categories, you refine your selection even further. Eventually, you'll browse your way to specific product pages, and with each click of your mouse, you will better understand how the category is structured.

Of course, browsing is not the fastest and most efficient way to find the best place for your item. Once you've learned your way around Amazon's categories, you'll search for your items by keywords. When you begin creating product listings, you'll be assigning search terms to your particular item. Don't think about the item itself, but rather, about how *your customers will describe the item* when they come online to buy it. "I think about how the customer will search for the product and build the page from that," advises Michael Jansma of GemAffair. Put yourself in your customer's shoes: What terms would *you* use to search for the products?

Use Tags for Search Term Ideas

Amazon allows customers to add their own keywords (called *tags*) to any product-listing page. These tags can be terribly important to you as you define the best search terms possible for your item. Say you're into solar energy and you find a great book about solar greenhouses. You could add the tag "solar greenhouse" (see Figure 4-2) to that book's page. By then clicking on your new tag, you can see what items others have tagged in a similar way. Steve Jay of wholesalelaptopbattery says these tags can be a source of ideas for you when you're trying to create keywords for your own products. So, that should send you scurrying off to check out the tags on your competitor's pages. You may just turn up some excellent keywords that you hadn't already considered.

Figure 4-2. If a product has tags associated with it, the tags can provide keyword ideas for similar products.

Tags Customers Associate with This Product (What's this?)
Click on a tag to find related items, discussions, and people.

Search Products Tagged with

Check the boxes next to the tags you consider relevant or enter your own tags in the field below
☐ energy conservation (1)   ☐ solar energy (1)
☐ photovoltaics (1)   › See all 5 tags...

> See most
> popular Tags

Your tags: solar greenhouse [   ] (Add) (Edit)
(Press the 'T' key twice to quickly access the "Tag this product" window.)

Help others find this product - tag it for Amazon search
Deb and Brad Schepp suggested this product show on searches for "solar houses". What do you suggest?

Product Description

After you've classified your product and you're ready to place it in the correct category, you need to determine ways to identify it. There are a lot of ways you could identify an item, including a model number and part number. Not all of these will apply to your product, but depending on your item's classification, Amazon requires you to complete mandatory fields such as UPC, product name, and manufacturer. The UPC and manufacturer are not areas you can be creative with, but the product name may be, and you should put some thought behind that one.

Always Create Descriptive Titles

Kathy Wojtczak of Element Jewelry & Accessories has been selling on Amazon for more than three years, which almost makes her a veteran. She recommends that when you create your product page titles, you be as *descriptive and specific* as possible. For example, instead of listing your item as "diamond earrings," Kathy recommends that you name them "1.3 carat princess-cut diamond stud earrings set in 14k white gold." Now your customers know something about your earrings before they ever click on the page to see them. Shoppers will be more enticed by the specifics, because they'll already know something about what to expect by opening your product page. Not every category will allow for creativity, of course. But even if you're selling cameras or software, be sure your title includes the manufacturer's full name for the product, its part number, or any other distinguishing characteristic that might be a term your customer would use to identify exactly what you've got.

Provide Product Details

Now you're ready to add the bulk of the information about your product, and you'll do that through the *Add Details* page. It's here that you can add more product information, create bullet points, add search terms, and also upload images (see Figure 4-3). The *Product Description* box, in particular, is your opportunity to really shine. Think of it as the outside packaging you'd want for a product you were placing on display in your store. You'd want that toy to be enticing and that packaged dinner to look delicious.

Amazon suggests you add as much detail to your pages as you can, and the sellers we spoke with agree. "Product listing pages represent an opportunity to showcase your inventory," said Tricia Records of Read_Rover_Books. "If you're going to take the time to create one, do yourself a favor and include as much information as you can, including a detailed description of the contents."

Read Reviews for Help with Descriptions

"I read reviews on products and find what buyers express to be valuable in building realistic descriptions that don't over-hype an item," notes Gary of Goggles and Glasses. "Also note you have 255 characters to build a title, but be aware if you put things like 'free shipping,' 'choice,' or anything else that interferes with other sellers who may list on that ASIN you could find yourself in trouble with the powers that be at Amazon."

TIP *Describe It with Passion*

Not everyone loves writing advertising copy, and there's a temptation just to use whatever information is already at hand. However, your description is a way to persuade your browser to become a buyer, and you shouldn't let that opportunity slip away without using it to its most tempting possibilities. Remember that you're selling this item because you're passionate about the product you've selected. So don't hesitate to share that passion. Kathy of Element Jewelry & Accessories

Figure 4-3. Seller Central lets you fill in a product detail page.

amazon services™
seller central

①   ②   ③   ④
CLASSIFY   IDENTIFY   ADD DETAILS   SELL

Kitty Express Pooper Scooper
ASIN: B0017CV1OE
Manufacturer: Kitty Central
Quantity: 1

Please fill out as much product information with as much detail as possible.
Add to Amazon's product details by sharing your own information. The information you provide here may appear on the product detail page and will be used to help customers find this product in search results. Please supply as much specific detail as possible.   Your content may or may not show up on the website depending on other contributions. All submissions and their sources may be reviewed at any time for accuracy and adherence to Amazon.com's policies. Learn More

⊞ **Your Product Identification**
Product identification is the information that you provided on the previous page for us to find and create the product. If you would like to change the information such as title you may expand this section.

⊟ **Your Product Details: Recommended**

Image:	Upload image(s)
	Note: Once an image is submitted, there may be a delay of up to 24 hours before it appears on the website.
Product Description: (The description you provide should pertain to the product in general, not your particular item. There is a 2,000 character maximum.)	This is a one of a kind pooper scooper designed to give you and your cats years of enjoyment.
	Example: This ham has been smoked for 12 hours...
Key Product Features: (Max. 100 characters per line. Use these to highlight some of the product's most important qualities. Each line will be displayed as a separate bullet point above the product description.)	Solid Plastic Construction
	Large Enough to Keep Bacteria at Bay
	Designed to work with Most Litter Boxes
	Money-Back Guarantee
	Example: Delicious honey-apricot glaze
Shipping Weight: (Weight of the product when packaged to ship)	1 Pounds
	Example: 2.0
Search Terms: (Provide specific search terms to help customers find your product.)	cats
	litter
	scoopers

says that when writing about your product, you should "try to create a mood." Even just an extra line or two may do it. Here's an example she gave us: "These earrings will go from the office to the Oscars seamlessly." Now, wouldn't that get your attention?

Craft Bullet Points that Help Customers Buy

Bullet points get our attention. It's just that simple. That's why you'll find them in magazine articles, newspapers, and even that boring PowerPoint presentation your boss has shown a dozen times. The Amazon form allows sellers to list "Key Product Features." These features are limited to 100 characters, but they'll show up as bullet points on your product detail page. That means they'll pop from the page, and they may be among the first thing the customer notices. So how should you handle these? Visiondecor's Eric Lau suggests that you include information that helps the customer make a purchasing decision. "Customers can tell if you put heart into making those bullet points clear and the description simple. A lot of sellers say too much and obfuscate things for the buyer, and when [buyers] get confused as to what they are buying or when they are getting it, they leave the item listing."

Here are some examples of bullet points we liked taken from actual Amazon listings:

- Simple 10-minute installation (hammock)
- Accessories Included: strings, guitar cable, gig bag, amplifier, cable, digital electronic tuner, shoulder strap (electric guitar)
- Dishwasher-safe; heat-resistant to 500 degrees F; FDA-approved (mixing bowls)

- Flowers arrive in our specially designed gift box to guarantee freshness (cut flowers)
- Padded arm rests are height adjustable for extra comfort (booster seat)
- High-precision tip; 10-ounce water tank; self-cleaning system (iron)
- Comments: Ships fast! 100 percent satisfaction guaranteed!

Now you may think a lot of this is common sense, and perhaps it is. However, it's surprising how many Amazon pages don't even include bullet points, and for those that do include them, how short or mind-numbing some of the bullet points are!

Images

What's a Web page without an image? Every online seller we've ever spoken with, whether it was a beginning Amazon seller or an eBay Titanium PowerSeller, stressed the importance of images. When you have only a two-dimensional Web page to sell an item to a customer images are essential. And not just any images, but clear images, and perhaps multiple images so customers have a very good idea of what they'll find inside that box. When you're creating a product detail page Amazon allows you to add up to eight images, so don't be stingy here.

Kirk of Cosmic-King, for example, includes as many photos as possible. Kathy from Element Jewelry & Accessories uploads multiple images and product angles. Tricia of Read_Rover_Books knows from experience that "pictures sell." While you're preparing your images, don't forget to show items from all angles. You'll want your customers to feel as though they were "holding" your item and turning it in their hands. Also, be sure to spotlight any special features such as markings or other details. Whatever you think makes your item especially appealing should be among the images that you show your prospective customers.

The specifics of creating good Web images and choosing file formats and the like are beyond the scope of this book. Luckily, Amazon has all the information and details you might need right on its site. Here are Amazon's general guidelines for images:

- Images must not have borders.
- There should not be any text within the image.
- The images must be in either .tiff or .jpg format.
- Images shouldn't be larger than 50 kb.
- If possible take the item out of any packaging. (Don't destroy the shrink-wrapping, however.)
- The product should take up at least 80 percent of the image area. This should go without saying, but the image must be clear and taken at an attractive angle, all with the aim of getting that browser to buy.
- Be sure the product is in focus and well lit.

So get out that digital camera and get busy! Once you've got those images uploaded, you'll have all the elements in place for your completed product detail page.

Mandatory Details

Before you're ready to post your listing, you'll have to provide a few mandatory details. Of the three mandatory pieces of information required, only one of them is simple: quantity. Go on ahead and list the number of items you currently have available for sale. The other two details—condition and pricing—require more thought.

Determine Condition

Is your item brand new, slightly used, or just acceptable? When you're determining the condition of anything less than brand-new items, always claim your item to be slightly less perfect than you really think it is. Condition is a subjective matter on anything that's not brand new. If you err on the side of caution and call your item slightly less perfect than you believe it to be, your customer is bound to be pleased. That's your goal. You want that customer to open the box and think that it's a great deal. Assuming the customer has bought on Amazon before, there is an expectation of feeling great about the things ordered through the site. You can set up that happy scenario before you even list your item by carefully considering the condition you claim for it.

Speak Up About Condition

"Why just say *new* when you can brag about it in your own way?" asks Gary of Goggles and Glasses. Say something like "new, 100% money-back guarantee." That, says Gary, "helps you to stand out from other merchants with just 'new' in their condition statement." Gary recommends adding a brag line about your quick shipping or customer service to the condition note, too.

Price It Right

We introduced pricing in Chapter 2. Now we're ready to delve into the subject more completely and share some specific tips about this most complex and important aspect of listing your items for sale on Amazon. Given how competitive Amazon is, the issue of pricing is far from simple. Sellers disagree about the best strategies. Some, like Kirk of Cosmic-King, say you shouldn't worry that much about pricing;

your product will eventually find its buyer. When people undercut him on price, Kirk just waits them out.

Wait Out Lowball Sellers

As in any large marketplace, sellers come and go on Amazon. Inexperienced sellers sometimes just assume that if they regularly price their products below the competition, they'll build a sustainable business. They feel that, as one seller told us, "On Amazon, it's all about price." But we feel that depends largely on the category. Obviously, the media categories are the most competitive. But what strategy should you bring to other categories such as jewelry or house and garden supplies? In those cases, some experienced sellers like Andy Mowery of debnroo believe you should just wait out these lowball sellers. Although initially these sellers may get sales because of their lower prices, you shouldn't then "follow them down to the lowest sustainable level. Who blinks first, when you can't even cover costs?" he asks.

Again, other sellers feel that pricing is an area where you can gain a competitive edge, and some even use automated programs (see Chapter 5) that adjust the price of their products automatically as the competition dictates. Rene Klassen of Musicnmore sells some limited-edition records, exclusively vinyl. "I check the prices every time I upload a new listing to see if certain items are within reach of allowing me to be the lowest-priced seller," he told us.

The middle ground is best exemplified by Kathy of Element Jewelry & Accessories, who says you should price competitively—overpriced products will not sell. Competition is ruthless—just take a look at all the booksellers pricing some books at $.01. Sellers who take this approach often use other aspects of their businesses to gain the competitive advantage. Eric Lau of Visiondecor recommends that you focus on doing what it is that you do better than your competition. "We focus on shipping faster and getting good customer feedback," he told us. Eric reasons, "If we do that, the customers are smart enough to figure out and choose us over our competitors." See Figures 4-4 and 4-5 for examples of finished product detail pages.

Tips for Pricing Books

Because there are so many booksellers on Amazon, we thought we'd share with you some pricing tips from Dan Morrill of Alternating Reality, who sells science fiction titles. Of course, many of these strategies can easily be applied to selling other items, too.

1. **Aim for the bell curve in prices.** If a book is clustered on $9.99, and you come in at $8.99, just a tad under the median price, you will sell.

2. **Some prices are never going to be matched out.** One cent or $99 books are outliers statistically. You cannot compete with that; don't even try. Most of those are caused by automated selling programs, and are usually run by people who suffer quality issues when it comes to customer service.

3. **Usually, you will find you have only four or five real competitors in the same price range.** Get to know them, check their inventory, read their comments and responses, read their websites if they have one, keep them in mind when pricing.

Figure 4-4. Element Jewelry & Accessories created this product page.

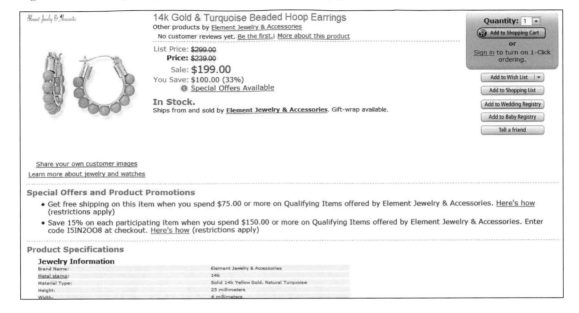

Figure 4-5. Visiondecor created this product page.

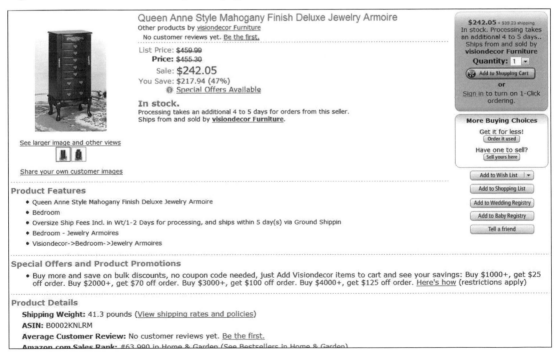

As with many other things, when it comes to price, we agree with Dan that it's smart to keep an eye on what your competitors are doing. Kathy of Element Jewelry & Accessories also does frequent product searches and looks at the price and selection of her competition. Ultimately, you'll know your products and category well enough to decide which of the pricing strategies feels right to you.

Here's one more philosophy to consider. Just focus on your business 100 percent, as Michael Jansma of GemAffair does, and don't compete. "Someone told me a long time ago, 'If you want to be a follower start watching what others are doing, but if you want to be a leader, figure what the next right thing is to do and do it,'" Michael said.

Making the Most of Your Product Detail Pages

Now we'll look at some strategies for making the most of all the pages you create. You can use the product detail page to add information that can help boost your sales and even make your operation more efficient. These tidbits can help you spotlight services you're able to offer your customers, add specific notes about the condition or value of your item, and help you create systems for managing your inventory. We'll also share with you ways you can refine your keywords by using Amazon's *tag* tool.

Add Details to Stand Out

The form you use to create your product detail page includes optional fields that you can use to your best advantage. That's especially true if you're planning to compete not strictly on the basis of the lowest price. You will want to do everything else you can to make your customers see you as the best possible source of the items you sell, so put this optional information to work for you. If, for example, you're willing to include gift wrapping and messaging, be sure to say so. Your handling time, another optional tidbit, can be a real competitive boost. Are you willing to ship within 24 hours of purchase? If so, you'll stand out from the others who don't make this offer.

You can also add notes and embellish the condition category you've already selected. This is especially helpful if you follow our advice and grade your items slightly below what you really think they are. For example, suppose you have a brand-new Lenox china Christmas tree ornament, but you don't have the box it came in. Being fair, you can't actually call it new without the box. But, you can say that the sticker is still attached and it's never been used.

Finally, you can create a personal seller SKU. That's different from the other codes we've already discussed in that it's strictly for your own internal use. You can use the digits of this code to identify where you store specific items while you wait for them to sell. For example, you can designate several digits to represent your spare room, several more to designate a specific shelving unit, and several more to indicate which shelf the item occupies. The code won't mean a thing to anyone else but you, but it will be very helpful as your inventory grows and you work hard to meet your shipping deadlines.

Let Your Customers Change Your Pages

Well, not literally. What we mean is that once you have some feedback from customers, you can use it to reword, alter the price, add pictures, or do whatever is necessary to boost your success rate.

Asad Bangash of Beachcombers! said that when he first started selling on Amazon he "spent many hours researching all the tips and tricks that Amazon had available on their FAQ and help pages. We followed 99 percent of their recommendations and built our listings based on their best practices," he told us. Asad added that "as sales started to come in and patterns of buying appeared, we then made changes to our listings to maximize our exposure."

The Page You Create May Not Stay Your Own

Remember how we talked about piggybacking onto another product description? Well, that works two ways. Other sellers can piggyback on your product pages as well. Moreover, on Amazon, product detail pages are not cast in stone. Unlike other online selling venues where the listing you created is exclusively yours, sellers can hop onto each other's pages, adding information, deleting information, and otherwise changing the way the information appears.

Sometimes that's not a bad thing. For example, when you piggyback your item on the listing of a competitor, it's a good thing. You may not actually alter the first listing, but you should definitely use the *Sell yours here* form to include bullet points and refine the details specific to your product and business. Now your page is linked to someone else's but it reflects your business.

But, just as you take advantage of other sellers' listings, other sellers will take advantage of yours, and sometimes that can create a problem. If another seller adds a listing to yours, and has a higher ranking, that seller can alter the text and pictures you use to describe your item. Having a higher status means that those changes are likely to stick, even if what the other seller has added makes your description less appealing in your opinion, or even less accurate.

Seller ranking could be based on the age of the account, total feed-back, feedback percentage account status Silver or Gold, or even your conversion rate of listings into actual sales.

It's not only other sellers who can edit your product detail pages. Amazon can do it, too. If Amazon starts to carry the item you've list-ed, it might alter your page, and those alterations may create problems for you. There's no guarantee that Amazon will get the details of your specific product exactly right, and you may have some customer service issues. Here's an example of what happened to Drew Friedman of White Mountain Trading Company in two instances. We offer it to you as a heads up:

A customer contacted us to complain that the item he bought from us on Amazon was not accurately described and he wanted to return it for a refund. When I logged onto my Amazon Seller Central account and went into Inventory Management, I clicked on *Edit the Item Description,* which allows me to see our own product description on Amazon. Our description is not the same description that a buyer sees when shopping on Amazon. According to Amazon's policy, it can add, delete, or alter a description as it sees fit to make for an improved buyer experience. Pretty ironic, eh?

Amazon's title: Gerstner 20-Inch Oak Hardwood Chest with Brass Hardware #GI-530

Our title: Gerstner International GI-530 Red Oak Tool Chest Nickel Plated Hardware FULLY WARRANTED

> Aside from these obvious differences, Amazon added an entire paragraph to the item description that we cannot edit, delete, or alter in any way. It's a full paragraph of incorrect information, I might add. I would never have picked up on this policy discrepancy until the customer e-mailed us to complain about the Gerstner International GI-530 last night. (We offered to accept the item in return for a full refund, of course.)

So, what can we learn from Drew's experience? Be sure to keep careful watch over your listings once you have them up and running. You may not be able to correct changes that make your listings less than accurate, but at least you'll be prepared to deal with the customer service issues that may likely arise once your customers receive something different from what they expected you were sending them. That can go a long way toward providing the quick and courteous refunds that will keep your feedback rating where you want it to be. For an example of a listing from White Mountain Trading Company, see Figure 4-6. Note that the branding is Amazon's only. It's not until you click the *these sellers* hyperlink that White Mountain Trading even appears.

Looking Ahead

This chapter focused on the theories and practical considerations you need to understand as you go about creating your product detail pages. But, you have other options for creating pages in addition to

Figure 4-6. White Mountain Trading Company created this product page.

what we've already described. For example, through Seller Central, you can enter data from a spreadsheet that you just upload. And should your business grow to the point where you're working with an auction management company, such as ChannelAdvisor, you'll find its product offerings will streamline this process for you, too. Chapter 5 will give you plenty of information about the automation options available to support you as your business grows. Now you can move on with a solid foundation of good practices for creating great Amazon pages.

An Amazon Success Story

Kathy Wojtczak operates Element Jewelry & Accessories. She'd been selling on Amazon for nearly three years when we met, and operating a WebStore by Amazon, too. You'll find her store at www.elementjewelry.com. "I received a phone call about three years ago from an Amazon representative who'd found my website while searching online," explained Kathy. "At that time, my site was not e-commerce enabled, and I was only selling through my physical location. They offered me the opportunity to sell on Amazon's Marketplace, and I signed up right away."

Kathy uses Seller Central and finds it to be a complete solution for operating her business. "Everything I need to manage both sales channels," is how she describes it. "I can securely log in and check my sales, print out shipping labels and packing slips, make design changes to my WebStore, and download and print reports," she explained. When Kathy makes a sale, adds new products, or otherwise changes her inventory, all changes happen simultaneously on both the Marketplace and her WebStore, so her listings are always up to the minute.

Kathy operates her business in a highly competitive category. Because competition in jewelry is so steep, she spends a great deal of time researching various manufacturers, distributors, importers, and designers to find the highest-quality items at the best possible prices. How is she able to keep her prices competitive? "The overhead and operating costs associated with selling products online, as opposed to selling in a physical store," is her answer. "I am able to pass those savings on to my customers while still maintaining a good profit margin." And that simple statement has actually changed Kathy's whole life. Before she came to Amazon, she'd operated a bricks-and-mortar store for several years. "I worked nine hours a day, six days a week, 52 weeks

a year. In-store traffic was unpredictable, advertising was expensive, and store-related overhead was outrageous," she remembers. She started on Amazon slowly and, for about a year, she didn't see much profit there. She was busy focusing on trying to keep her physical store growing.

In June of 2005, she uploaded about 100 items and started to watch the sales come in. She had two sales in June, so she added more inventory. She had 39 sales in September and kept going. In December she had over 200 sales! "Within six months, I knew that the growth potential from Amazon far exceeded the growth potential for my physical store," she recounted. When the store's lease was up in July 2007, she decided to leave the world of physical retail behind. "Now I manage my business from home. Customers can shop 24 hours a day, 365 days a year, while I have the freedom to work when I want from where I want," Kathy said. "I have been able to spend more time with my family and even take a few vacations!"

CHAPTER 5

Automating Your Amazon Business

Not long ago, an editor asked us if we were interested in compiling a book of forms e-commerce sellers might need in their day-to-day work. The workbook she described would have forms for tracking inventory, sales, customers, and so forth. Although we hesitate to turn down assignments, we turned this one down, and fast. One of the reasons is that we believe it's generally best for e-commerce merchants to use *software* for tracking these things, rather than paper and pencil.

Our years of writing about e-commerce have shown us that the most successful sellers almost always use software programs to help them automate their businesses—from inventory management, to shipping, and on to marketing through e-mail. Once you get beyond the hobbyist stage—say, listing more than 15 items per week—you just can't readily track everything you should without a computer.

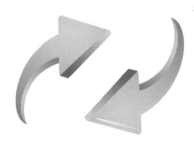

The idea of learning new software programs doesn't exactly thrill most people. Before you get too concerned about all this, please realize that Amazon's own Seller Central can provide you with all the automation help you need. If you are on Seller Central, you can start with the software that's right on the site. But many of the Amazon sellers we spoke with use software from other sources. *Auction Software Review* (www.auctionsoftwarereview.com) describes many useful software tools for e-commerce (see Figure 5-1), and we'll have a lot more to say about this great Internet resource soon.

Before we go any further, let's set some parameters. The software we'll describe covers a range of programs, from those with very simple user interfaces, which are appropriate for sellers with smaller

Figure 5-1. Auction Software Review is eBay-oriented. However, the site also has a lot of information about Amazon-related products.

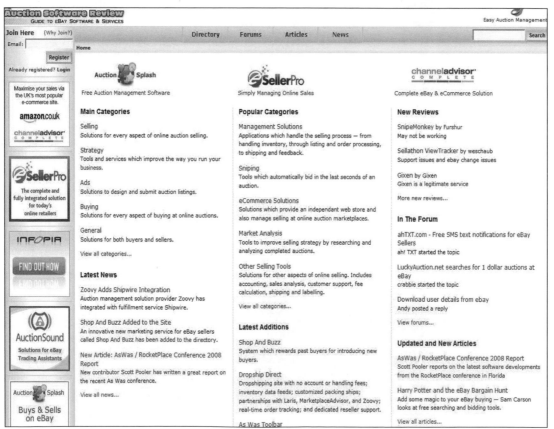

inventories, to "desktop and feed tools" for sellers with much larger product catalogs. Still other sellers use the services of companies such as ChannelAdvisor. These companies are geared to very large sellers selling on more than one marketplace, including not only Amazon, but also eBay or even their own websites. Regardless, those on our hand-picked list of great software solutions all come recommended by at least one (and usually more) of Amazon's top sellers.

Automation Should Not Be Automatic

Some sellers will tell you that nothing beats the simplest tools of all, paper and pencil. We know this goes against what we just said—that successful sellers usually use software to help them run their businesses. And we, too, wonder why in a world of megafunction calculators that handle statistics, trigonometry, graphing, and a whole lot more would some people resort to slide rules?

We were surprised to learn that even some relatively large companies, such as Visiondecor, prefer "doing things by hand." President Eric Lau just feels that this is "a good traditional way to get hands-on knowledge with each product." He finds that listing too many items at once (bulk listing) results in listings that are too general. "We have a team of 20 people contributing to the information so that we can manually manage the updating of products for stock, pricing, images, and descriptions to best represent items to customers."

We were intrigued by Eric's thinking here, so we asked him to elaborate a bit on what went behind it:

> Automated programs are not recommended, because they are always third-party and never completely accurate. I have thousands of items where my team of people has spent countless hours of review and research to launch, adjust, and maintain descriptions and pricing. It is not easy for a program developer to create a program that replaces all that hard work.

Automation runs into problems like picking up bad data, resulting in an item incorrectly priced (and very hard to find out if no one buys it) or an item that needs to be checked manually because the automation erred out. And when you have to spend time checking the errors, which takes a lot of people hours as well, you might as well sit down and do it the right way the first time around and come up with a process that does not depend on automation. One downfall to automation is that sellers (usually the few people starting the business) get in over their heads because it allows them to "do more" in less time, but the real question lies in: can they handle the "more" when it actually arrives with only the few people they have?

It's helpful to remember that Visiondecor specializes in furniture, not books, for example, and it's more cost-effective to spend more time listing bedroom sets than that latest Nora Roberts paperback. Dan Morrill, of bookseller Alternating Reality, can provide some further insights here. He's tried at least one software program to manage his business, "but so far, nothing is better than the simple inventory spreadsheet," he said.

Try the Tools Amazon Gives You

If you are going to use software (and with all due respect to Visiondecor, most sellers eventually do), you should first consider the tools right there for you on Amazon. As we've mentioned previously, Amazon's Seller Central includes software that enables you to view orders, track inventory, calculate your sell-through rate, print out labels and packing slips, and create custom reports. For those of us who may find new software intimidating, it definitely helps that Seller Central uses the familiar Amazon color scheme and page layout. As you can see in Figure 5-2, tabs at the top of the Seller Central home page let you quickly navigate the site. While you're there you can also get a quick fix on important statistics like your current orders, feedback rating, and a summary of your sales, just by check-

Figure 5-2. These tabs along the top of the Seller Central home page let you quickly find what you need.

ing the box along the right of the page. So Seller Central users get a quick snapshot of their accounts every time they log on to the site.

Amazon's tools for managing your business are mostly online, as you would expect. A big exception is Amazon Seller Desktop, a part of Seller Central. Seller Desktop (see Figure 5-3) is a free offline (or desktop-based) inventory and listing management tool. It enables you to add new products, match your products to those already in Amazon's catalog, and create variations. Some sellers prefer using tools like Seller Desktop because they don't require them to log on to the Internet. As a result they feel a greater sense of control, and don't have to worry about broadband service interruptions, power outages, or software glitches.

Kirk Holbert of Cosmic-King finds that Seller Desktop enables him to list products on Amazon faster, whether they are variations of existing products or new products entirely. There are links to Seller Desktop from the main Seller Central help page. You can download the application right from the site and then customize it to suit your own needs. Kathy Wojtczak of Element Jewelry & Accessories says she's been using Amazon's Seller Desktop software to upload bulk listings. Another fan is Chris Schlieter of timezone, who recommends Seller Desktop over a strictly online approach. "It's more stable than Internet pages, especially when you're in a learning mode," he noted. Although "it takes you longer to learn the details," he added, "it's easier to go back and forth between pages and make sure everything is right." Seller Desktop is Windows-based, so for now, you Mac fans will need to find another solution.

Figure 5-3. Amazon's Seller Desktop is a free Windows-based program for managing your inventory.

It's OK to Get Help

Two of the most experienced e-commerce merchants we know are Andy and Deb Mowery of debnroo. They've sold home, garden, and pet products online since 1999, so they're quite familiar with listing software and the like. When we asked Andy about tools he used to help him with his Amazon business, we were surprised by what he had to say.

"Amazon has some clunkiness," the refreshingly unfiltered Andy told us. "They didn't build the slickest interface." Andy realizes his talents lay in strategizing, acquiring products, and looking at the big picture. So to help him upload his merchandise to Amazon, he hired a college student who majors in computer science. Originally, Andy had hired this student to pack boxes. Then he happened to mention one day that he needed someone who understood Web design, coding, and spreadsheets. His "packer" mentioned he was a computer science major. And from there, you can fill in the rest of the story! A tip within a tip, however: A lot of kids may say they are computer literate, Andy noted, "because they know how to create MySpace pages, or post an ad to craigslist. So you have to make sure they can actually do what you need them to do (coding, Web design, etc.)."

Visit Amazon's Developer Connection

One good place to start investigating Amazon's own software products, as well as those from third-party sources, is Amazon's Developer Connection site (http://developer.amazonwebservices.com). It's here (Figure 5-4) where some of the programmers who create the types of applications we're discussing in this chapter hang out. From this site, you can pull up a list of programs for sellers (click on the *Solutions Catalog* link), and then sort them by a number of ways including "best" or "worst" (see Figure 5-5).

Please note that the reviews used to rank the programs can be skewed by competitors looking to disparage, or employees looking to promote. Also, it's not just developers who can leave reviews—anyone can. So when you see a ranking you need to consider its value—not just by the total number of stars, but also by the number of people who have rated the product.

As you can see from Figure 5-6 the descriptions provide a hyperlink to the manufacturer's website, an e-mail address for inquiries,

Figure Figure 5-4. Amazon's Developer Connection site isn't just a resource for programmers!

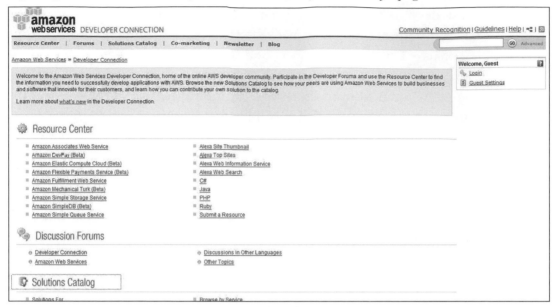

Figure 5-5. Amazon's Solutions Catalog describes and includes ratings for many seller programs.

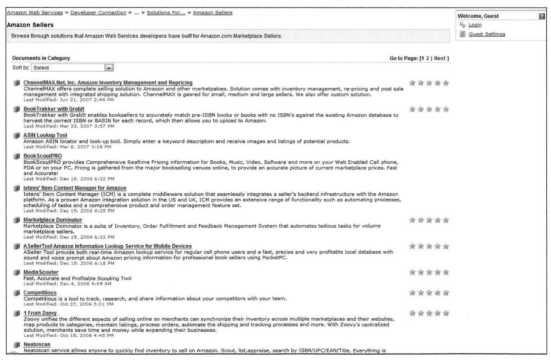

details on pricing, and the audience for the product. Of course, there's also a description of the product. Then there are those reviews we told you about.

Third-Party Management Tools

And you thought only sellers could be "third parties" as far as Amazon is concerned! A scan of the Developer Connection site (available through the Amazon Web Services hyperlink on the home page) shows how more and more programmers are creating software for Amazon sellers, to make running their businesses easier and more profitable. And most of them don't work for Amazon. Some programs, such as Monsoon, are full featured and handle fulfillment, list-

Figure 5-6. The AMan Pro program description from Amazon's Solutions Catalog is shown here.

ing, inventory management, and so on, while others handle specific tasks such as soliciting feedback.

Again, researching these various programs can seem very intimidating, which is one reason we list some of the most recommended programs later in this chapter. But if you enjoy doing your own research, or you just want to make sure everything we've said is still the same, you should check out the *Auction Software Review* site. We've recommended this website in every e-commerce book we've written and have always been glad we did. Here's a link to ASR's software reviews for Amazon: http://www.auctionsoftwarereview.com/amazon. We asked the site's owner, Andy Geldman, for tips in choosing software to help you run your Amazon business.

Choosing Software to Run Your Amazon Business

The important features for Amazon software are different from those for eBay software, mainly because the Amazon system is more tightly controlled. Amazon selling is mostly based upon cataloged products, listing fees are zero or negligible, high visibility is given to price comparison, all payments go through Amazon, and there are clear rules and set prices for shipping. Important software features are:

- Quick listing of large product catalogs by ISBN or UPC
- Automatic price adjustment to stay near the top of the list
- Post-sales order processing

You get some products that just handle Amazon or specialize in cataloged product selling, such as AMan Pro, FillZ, and Indaba. Of those, FillZ is clearly being actively developed, and has the well-established AbeBooks.com marketplace behind it.

Recommended Software

Here is some of the best software out there for keeping track of your business on Amazon.

AMan Pro (http://www.spaceware.com)

Many Amazon sellers highly recommend AMan Pro. Steve Jay of wholesalelaptopbattery uses AMan Pro to automate his company's shipping and to send e-mails out. "We also use it to send customers follow-up e-mails about 20 days after the transaction takes place," he said.

In addition to what Steve mentioned, AMan Pro handles listing, order management, and pricing. You can use it whether you sell books, electronics, "or any other category of product." As we write this, the software was intended just for those selling on the Amazon Marketplace, but the company had a version for Seller Central in development. You can download a fully functional version of the program to try for 21 days. AMan Pro costs $49.99 per month, or $499 per year.

FillZ (http://www.fillz.com/)

Just as highly recommended is FillZ (see Figure 5-7), software that handles order management, and inventory management for sellers of media products, which the company defines as books, music, movies, and games. FillZ is especially strong in automated pricing, allowing you to adjust your pricing to meet or beat your competition. This is quite important for sellers in the competitive media area. Three versions of FillZ are available: standard, premium, and customized. You can try it "risk-free" for 30 days. Pricing is based either on a percentage of your revenues or your inventory, whichever works out to be greater. The minimum charge is $50 per month. FillZ is a subsidiary of AbeBooks, a leading Internet book retailer, representing more than 13,500 independent booksellers.

Tricia of Read_Rover_Books has used FillZ for several years, ever since the software became available. "They manage my inventory across 12 different sales venues with little additional effort on my part," she noted. "Their service has been extremely reliable, robust, and is constantly upgrading to meet the demands of the marketplace and has been instrumental in helping me to add new venues and grow my sales across multiple venues."

Figure 5-7. FillZ handles inventory management for media sellers.

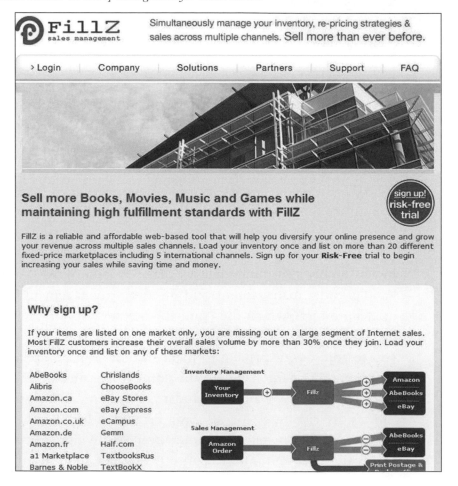

Monsoon (http://www.monsoonworks.com/)

The same people who created the website for Powell's Books are behind Monsoon (see Figure 5-8). Powell's, of course, is one of the world's largest independent booksellers, but it claims it was also Amazon's first Marketplace seller. Monsoon is geared to people who sell books, music, CDs, or DVDs on eBay or Amazon.

Monsoon works just fine with Seller Central. You can use it to list inventory, download and process orders, and price and reprice inventory. Four versions are available, depending on the volume you handle: Express, Edge, Pro, and Pro Warehouse. As with FillZ, Monsoon lets you list items across several channels. The software will also track your total inventory, so if you sell an item on Amazon all of your inventory records will reflect that.

Switching from a Third-Party Program to Seller Central

We don't know how important this will be to you, but we feel compelled to warn you. Amazon states clearly that changing records you've created in a third-party program and importing them into Seller Central is irreversible. If you are converting say, Monsoon files to Seller Central, you need to ensure that the application supports Seller Central before you make the switch.

Other Helpful Tools from Third Parties

Even if you're not quite ready to make the commitment to a software suite that will manage your entire business, you may be ready for some tools that will address specific business needs. Here we've gathered together a variety of such tools, all recommended by successful sellers who are convinced that life is better since they discovered these.

Feedback Forager (http://amazon.wolfire.com/)

One of the challenges Amazon sellers face is that only a relatively small percentage of customers (we've seen estimates of from 10 to 20 percent) leave feedback. Amazon has started doing its part to change this by e-mailing buyers after they've made a purchase, encouraging them to leave feedback. Still, there's something endemic to the Amazon culture that makes leaving feedback unusual.

Figure 5-8. Monsoon is another popular program for media sellers.

Sellers need that feedback, however, to encourage other buyers to feel good about doing business with them. To the rescue is Feedback Forager, a program that sends carefully worded automated e-mails to past customers to seek feedback. The manufacturer claims that users of the software not only receive more feedback, they receive more five-star ratings, too. You can download a demo version of the program, and if you like it buy it for $49.95. Kirk of Cosmic-King is one of Feedback Forager's fans; the only problem with it, he jokes, is that it can also remind customers of a bad transaction! Given Kirk's current feedback rating of 4.8 stars out of a possible five we know that he doesn't often deal with customer complaints.

Gary's Feedback Forager Tips

Our tech editor Gary Richardson is also a big fan of Feedback Forager. Here are his six tips for getting the most out of it:

1. Select only the best transactions to solicit for feedback.
2. Packages shipped priority mail often have a higher satisfaction level than media mail.
3. If you have a product that is highly rated, you would want to select it, while excluding a product that has a poor feedback history.
4. Select transactions that are geographically close for foraging, while avoiding those that are far away, such as international, APO/FPO, freight forwarding addresses, Alaska, Hawaii, and U.S. territories.
5. Non-English speakers or persons with e-mail addresses with negative connotations would also be candidates to avoid if you send a feedback request, for obvious reasons. Never request feedback more than once.

6. You can remove the 1, 2, and 3 feedback options by editing the program's settings, leaving only ratings of 4 or 5. There's no sense in helping someone to give you bad feedback. To be fair, you can replace those ratings and add a sentence that says, "Why no ratings of 1, 2, or 3? Please contact us at (insert e-mail address or phone #) if we have rated less than 4 of 5 on this transaction."

Price Management Software

What if every time a competitor came along and beat your price, you had a software program that could automatically adjust *your* prices accordingly? You can stop dreaming, because such software is a reality, and many Amazon sellers use it, either as a standalone program or as part of a full-featured program such as FillZ or AManPro.

Using this software, though, is a bit more complicated than just setting it to lower your prices every time your competitors lower theirs. If too many sellers do that, the end result can be scads of sellers all offering the same book for a penny! There are all sorts of strategies on how best to use this software, and we recommend you read Amazon's seller boards before using it yourself. For example, as Gary Richardson tells it, some competitors will set their software purposely to "bait the repricer down to a penny." The seller will then snatch the book for a penny and the seller's own price automatically rises back to "normal." So, theoretically, this seller could buy a $50 book for a penny plus shipping. If the penny seller decides not to sell the item, it risks getting bad feedback!

Sometimes you need to wait out the competition. That is, let all those other sellers play the repricing game and sell out their inventory, and when they do, swoop in with your own more realistically priced wares. Gary also suggests that you set your repricer to raise prices when market conditions allow.

Raise Your Fist for Jungle Disk!

OK, we admit it wasn't *necessary* to include Jungle Disk (www .jungledisk.com) in this book, but with a name like that we couldn't resist. Besides, one of our Amazon superstars, Rene Klassen of Musicnmore, recommended it, so here goes. Jungle Disk lets you store your files and back up your data right to Amazon's site. You can use it to back up your whole computer or any part of it. It sits on Amazon's servers and is easily accessed (it appears as a J drive), backing up your data for pennies a month. If you upgrade to another computer, migration is easy. It costs $20 and is available for both Windows and Macs.

There's no rule that says you can use only one program at a time. Why not build a suite of programs that you find meet your own particular needs? For example, Musicnmore's Rene uses Amazon Services Order Notifier (ASON). That's a desktop application (Figure 5 9) from Amazon that runs in the background whenever you turn your computer on. When you receive a new Amazon order, a window pops up to give you the good news. You can set the software to poll Amazon for new orders on your behalf every so often (just how often is something you can set). With ASON you can also view up to 30 days of order history. For more information, see the Seller Central help files. Although the program is free, as we write this it runs only on Windows. So be sure to check the site for the latest details!

Software for Bigger Sellers

In the Internet world, Amazon is an old-timer, but as Xavier Helgesen of Better World Books noted, Amazon's tools are adequate only up to a certain point—in that seller's opinion "the small seller with a spreadsheet." Not every seller would agree with that, but it's a fact that Amazon's tools won't help you sell on eBay, or your own website. That makes sense; after all, Amazon wants you to stick with selling on Amazon. But this limits the software, since selling on more than one marketplace is a reasonable goal for any e-commerce business. You want to feature your inventory wherever buyers happen to be.

Figure 5-9. Amazon Services Order Notifier (ASON) runs in your computer's background and alerts you when a new order has arrived.

Using ASON

The System Tray Icon

When you launch the Amazon Services Order Notifier (ASON), an Amazon.com-style "a" icon is shown in your Microsoft Windows system tray, just like an e-mail notifier or instant messaging icon. The system tray is located in your Windows task bar next to the clock, usually in the lower right-hand corner of your screen.

Right-click the ASON icon to open a pop-up menu with the following options:

- *Check for new orders now* – ASON will immediately retrieve any new orders that are waiting for you.
- *View Order History* – The Order History window opens. (You can also double-click the ASON icon to open the Order History window.)
- *Settings* – The Settings window opens. Here you can change connection settings, notification pop-up style, and how often ASON checks for orders.
- *About* – The About ASON window displays the ASON release number.
- *Exit* – ASON closes.

The Pop-up Notification

When new orders are retrieved, ASON displays the number of new orders in a pop-up notification in the lower right-hand corner of your screen. These pop-ups are partially transparent and include the ASON logo.

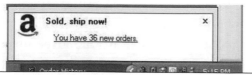

ChannelAdvisor (http://www.channeladvisor.com/)

When you're ready for the services of a company such as ChannelAdvisor (CA) you'll probably know it. Your sales volume will place you among the top tier of sellers, you will have repeatedly heard the company's name mentioned by other sellers, or at trade shows you've attended, and perhaps most important, you will be selling (or at least ready to be selling) on more than one channel. *Channel*, in this case, has nothing to do with your television but refers to the various online marketplaces, such as Amazon and eBay.

As a CA client, you will still set your own prices, describe your products, track inventory, and handle shipping and customer service. CA will handle every other aspect of your business.

Specifically, it will create and manage the inventory pipeline from which your products flow onto the various channels you use to sell your products. So if you're selling on Amazon, eBay, or your own website, for example, CA will manage this process all from your one inventory pool. It will also work to ensure that your products get maximum exposure on comparison-shopping engines, such as Shopping.com and Shopzilla, and also on search engines such as Google. CA has been in this business more than 10 years, and handles about $2.5 billion in merchandise sales for its thousands of clients. You will also have access to its in-house *account strategists*, who can assist you in reviewing your business and ensuring it's as profitable as possible.

ChannelAdvisor knows what it's doing, but, obviously, all this expertise comes at a price. CA charges a monthly software license fee, plus a percentage of each sale. It refers to this as a "commission based model that incents them to help you grow your sales." We recommend that you take your time exploring ChannelAdvisor's site before formally contacting anyone at the company for specific pricing information and advice about your own situation. Yes, read about the company and its services, but also read the various blogs, take a look at the white papers, and certainly check out the case studies. They're free for everyone to learn from.

Channel Velocity (http://www.channelvelocity.com/)

Michael Jansma of GemAffair agrees with Xavier of Better World Books that Amazon's tools are in their infancy. "We need a much more robust tool, so we've gone outside the Amazon platform to find them," Michael explained. "We looked at a lot of products, but Channel Velocity's OnRamp was the most robust." GemAffair is now able to sell on Amazon, Overstock, eBay, and its own WebStore. "I have used them all from Infopia to ChannelAdvisor to Marketworks," said Michael. "But Channel Velocity is three to five years ahead of everyone else. They only deal with very large customers. They built this complex software, and large sellers get that complexity and don't need a lot of attention to use them."

As Michael suggested, Channel Velocity's software was designed with sellers selling on multiple channels in mind (see Figure 5-10). Sellers with a lot of inventory, many customers, and warehouse operations will find it especially suited to their needs. The cost? The company estimates that to be $5,000 to $10,000 to get set up, and then a minimum of $3,000 per month. Company president Wes Shepherd was frank with us in suggesting that not every seller is ready for Channel Velocity, recommending that you consider it once your sales have reached the $1 million to $2 million a year mark. We hope that's you!

Go Your Own Way

Once you get large enough, you can also look into the cost effectiveness of writing your own software. Many sellers do just this. And if the software you create works with a variety of inventory types, you

Figure 5-10. Channel Velocity's OnRamp service is for large Amazon third-party sellers.

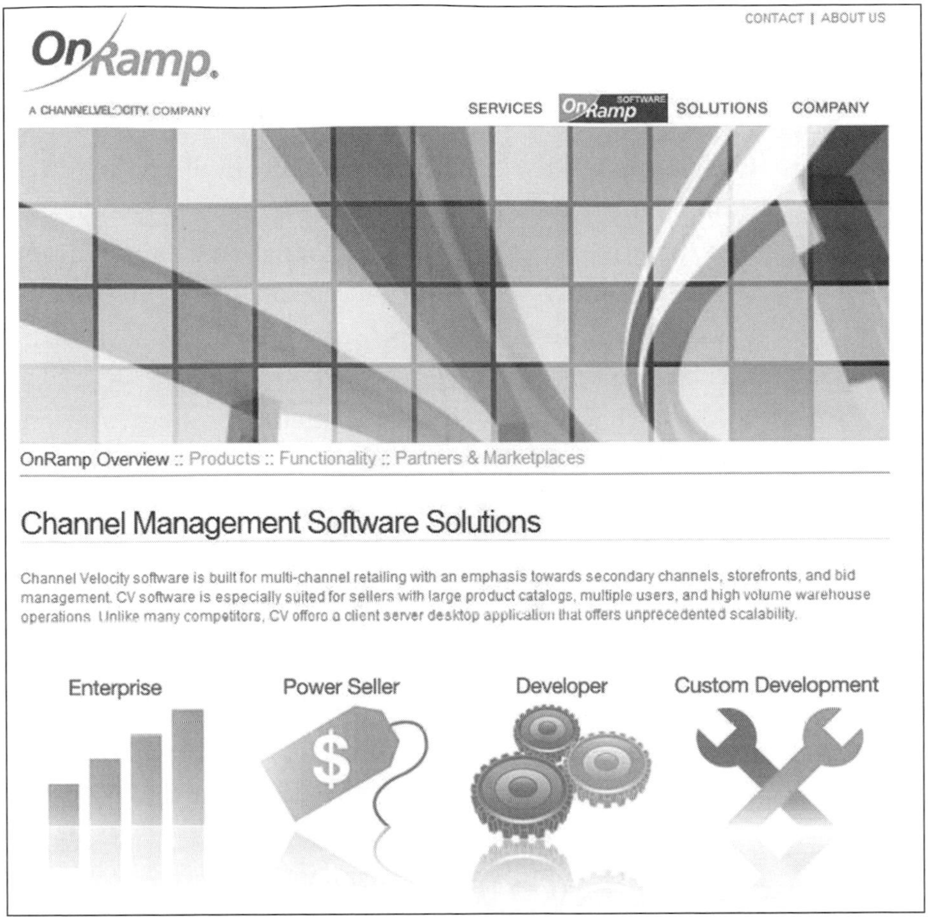

may even be able to license it to others. Better World Books is an example of a company that created its own software, which it dubbed Indaba (sounds like something Fred Flintstone might have used, don't you think?). "Indaba keeps your inventory current across the multiple sites you sell on," says spokesperson Xavier Helgesen. "So you can list the same book on half.com and Amazon and if a half.com buyer buys it, it will no longer be for sale on Amazon." Better World Books licenses its software to larger businesses for now, not individual sellers. For more information click your way to www.goindaba.com.

What I Wish I'd Known Then, but I *Do* Know Now

It's not every day that you get the opportunity to learn at someone else's expense. Even when people are willing to warn us, we often don't want to hear it. Or we don't believe that their experience is all that directly related to our own. Well, here's a golden opportunity that comes along only once or twice in any book. Here's a chance to learn a valuable lesson, and our technical editor, Gary, paid the tab on this one.

"I wish I would have had a picture strategy, and especially a data feed file," he said. "If you start with these two things no matter how big you grow, or to which e-commerce site you move, your life will always be easier. The text data feed file is the common denominator for all service providers, except when it comes to *exporting* your data from them. In that case, they don't want to make that too easy since it would make moving to another site simpler! You can use a data feed file (called an Inventory File on Amazon) for just about everything from Amazon to Google Product Search, and comparison-shopping engines such as Shopzilla. With a data feed file, no provider or venue can ever hold you hostage."

In order to build your own data file you'll need some tools. Here are the ones Gary suggests:

- Picture hosting account
- FTP software
- Spreadsheet software

Gary recommends three specific products:

1. Free office suite software, http://www.openoffice.org/
2. FileZilla, the free FTP solution, http://filezilla-project.org/

3. Godaddy hosting as low as $3.65 a month, http://www.godaddy.com

Think of the feed file as a central database of all your stuff. The minimum requirements for a feed file are title, description, price, location link, and picture link. Google has a great tutorial for creating an open office feed file that you'll find at http://services.google.com/bulkupload/openoffice/.

The FTP software will be used to move your pictures to your hosting account, and your flat file (which Wikipedia defines as a plain text file that usually has one record per line) will contain links to your pictures on your hosting account. With your pictures centrally located, you will not have to upload them separately to every service, venue, or provider you encounter in your e-commerce venture.

Note: Amazon maintains examples of these files in Seller Central, including templates for creating files for uploading your products to Amazon.

Looking Ahead

With your head full of automation thoughts, you're moving along the path from beginner to advanced e-commerce seller. You've got your inventory in place, you've made countless decisions about the processes you'll follow as you list, sell, and manage that inventory, and you're ready to go. Now, it's time to get back to the most basic aspects of operating your business, but also the most important. No matter how many different opinions we've heard from successful sellers, one always rings true. Your customer service policies must be the best you can bring to your business. No business will thrive without good customer service, but building a business on Amazon means making customer satisfaction your top priority. That's simply Amazon's way, and fortunately, the successful sellers we've encountered have lots of great advice to help you join them in this task.

An Amazon Success Story

Andy and Deb Mowery have been among eBay's top sellers for a long time. By now, you've noticed we've mentioned their business, debnroo, many times throughout this book. We've known the Colorado-based couple for years, and we've long marveled at their ingenuity and business acumen. Over the years, we've talked often with them about making the move to expand beyond their wildly successful eBay business, but the couple had never found a solution for multichannel selling that fit their business model. Within the last two years Deb and Andy branched out onto Amazon, and now there's a new story to tell.

Today, debnroo is a Featured Merchant enjoying wonderful success on Amazon, selling home and garden products and pet supplies. Andy has found a world of difference in his new environment. "It's the seller support that's making people run into their arms," he told us. He notes that his first step in solving any problem is to call the Amazon staff. Now, of course, debnroo warrants a personal contact at Amazon, but even before that, Andy said, "the Amazon staff is extremely helpful. They take a no-nonsense approach." Andy also described Amazon as "brilliant," referring to the company's WebStores by Amazon offering. Andy especially likes how Amazon encourages you to open separate niche WebStores to really focus on a market, and it does this all as part of the normal WebStore subscription. What's more, debnroo had just begun taking advantage of Fulfillment by Amazon when we spoke.

Andy and Deb stock their business with products they understand and endorse. Often the couple will add an item to their product line because they bought one for themselves and like it. Andy believes it's important that he and Deb share the thinking that went behind a decision to add an item to their product line. Toward that end, Andy blogs about a lot of the products they sell.

He also adds a good deal of content to their WebStores by Amazon pages, which helps drive traffic to his product pages through searches on Google and other search engines. You can see some examples of this content at pet-water-fountain.com. One article we especially appreciated discusses how veterinarian Mary V. Burns, inspired by her cat Buckwheat (a "constant faucet drinker"), developed the Drinkwell Pet Fountain. Our own cat Max is also a faucet drinker, and would no doubt be overjoyed if he had his own Pet Fountain!

When debnroo branched out to Amazon, one thing the couple didn't have to change was their commitment to customer service. Amazon's A-to-z Guarantee is not a problem for these two, who have devoted themselves to providing the best customer experience possible. On eBay, that was one of the main features distinguishing debnroo from many of its competitors. Without struggling to always offer the lowest price, Deb and Andy were able to build a successful business based on the service they were committed to providing their customers. Everything from a customer service phone number, to a money-back guarantee, to the best professional shipping, combined to make debnroo a crowd standout. With those systems in place, it made the move onto Amazon, known for its world-class customer service, natural.

Overall, life in this corner of the e-commerce world is expanding, challenging, and even, after all these years, surprising. We can't wait to see where Andy and Deb take debnroo next!

CHAPTER

6

Customer Service Without the Smile

The good news is that Amazon attracts customers who trust the marketplace and want to conduct their business in that marketplace with a minimum amount of angst and trouble. Amazon's already created that environment for you. The bad news is that you're going to have to bring the best of customer experience to your own operation in order to stay competitive and thrive on the site. You may think of your business as a little mom-and-pop operation, perhaps a cozy little bed-and-breakfast. But you're going to have to serve your customers with the five-star-quality service you'd expect from the Ritz or the Hilton. Anything less than that will hamstring your business from the very first day.

The day you decided to bring your business onto Amazon, you made a commitment to providing your customers with the very best shopping experience possible. Your Amazon customers come to you expecting nothing less than 100 percent satisfaction guaranteed. So, from the first e-mails that pass between you and your customer to the careful packing and shipping you provide, you'll need to be as close to perfect as possible. Whether or not you consciously and actively took on that level of commitment prior to joining Amazon is irrelevant. Now, as a representative of Amazon, you must align yourself with the customer experience goals Amazon sets for itself, and those are stringent. Happily, you're probably further along toward building good customer service into your operation than you realize.

"We wanted to be on Amazon, because they align themselves with our core beliefs," explains Michael Jansma of GemAffair. "If your customer is happy, they come back for the next purchase." Other successful sellers agree that being on Amazon actually makes their customer service operations simpler. Each seller knows exactly what is expected, so building your operation to create the best possible customer experience will come naturally to you. You're being held to the gold standard of customer service, but there's no reason to feel intimidated. You've been planning to serve your customers all the while you've been planning a successful business.

You chose your product line carefully, with an eye toward quality and value. You've worked automation into your operation through Amazon's own software tools or others you've found on your own (or maybe a combination of both). This helps you keep careful track of your work flow and keep those orders moving! Your product detail pages really sparkle and present your products brilliantly. Now they're irresistible. You've been honing your shipping operations, too. (And when you read Chapter 8, you'll hone those even more.) Each one of these things moves you closer to excellent customer service. As you can imagine, serving your customer doesn't begin when you have a problem to resolve. It starts before the first e-mails are exchanged. It's part of your every decision as an e-commerce merchant.

Online Versus Real-World Merchants

Being a merchant in a virtual world makes customer service a little different from the type of individual attention you can show a customer who has walked through the glass door of your bricks-and-mortar store. You can't, for example, smile at each one who comes through the door. You can't put soothing music on in the background or offer anyone a plate of cookies. But, realistically, that's not what shopping is like for most of us these days, anyway. We're all a lot more likely to be going to that big-box store to buy a present, for example, rather than to that charming little gift store.

As someone selling on Amazon, you can still present a great customer experience. Reach out to your customers and make them feel you're glad they've taken the time to stop by and see what you're offering for sale. By the layout of your store or product pages, the policies you set, and a hundred other things, you can make them see that you're there to make shopping easy and even fun. Do it right, and your online venture, although it may never quite feel like the little neighborhood bakery of our nostalgic memories, will certainly be much more personal and friendly than the mass-market service most consumers get in today's real world. You certainly can make shopping with you easier, and more friendly and cheerful, than that last trip to Wal-Mart!

Set Your Goals

As you create your Amazon business, consider customer service as the central hub of the wheel. This viewpoint will help you choose systems, policies, and processes that will make pleasing your customer the likely outcome of all your interactions. "Amazon's strength in the marketplace is the high trust it has with buyers," notes Asad Bangash of Beachcombers! "All of their programs, like the A-to-z Guarantee, help in boosting exposure and sales." So, providing good customer service is not just part of your Amazon business, it's the central core of it. "Aim for fanatical customer support," agrees Dan Morrill of Alternating Reality. Setting your goals, policies, and procedures from the very beginning will help you build customer confidence while your business grows. Surprisingly, most customer service decisions come down to an ancient and well-taught rule: Do unto others as you would have them do unto you. Put yourself in your customers' shoes, and you'll know exactly how you'd wish to be treated. Helping you to create the systems you'll use to achieve these goals is where we come in.

Learn from the Mistakes of Others

As you go about deciding how you'll serve your customers, research your competition to see what kinds of mistakes they're making. Then build your system around avoiding them. "Customers tell why they're angry in commentary on other sites," notes Dan of Alternating Reality. "You don't have to make the same mistakes. Read every feedback comment on your competition's feedback pages and solve the problems they had. Then keep that as part of your store's operation procedure." Once you've identified the weaknesses in your competition's customer service, you can offer your customers the types of things they are looking for. If you find your competitors are disappointing customers by how they describe their items, you'll see it's better to under-promise and over-deliver on your goods. If there are lots of comments about shipping speed and package quality, you'll know that's a place where you can shine. Would your product line lend itself to gift-wrapping and personal messaging? Well, there are two ways you can stand out.

That's what we mean by world-class service. You'll know what your customers will come to really appreciate as that "something extra," whether it's a guide to caring for their new shoes, or even a great classic bookmark if you sell books. You can bet most of your competitors don't add these little touches, which is exactly why you should.

Learn from Your Own Mistakes

"Amazon's A-to-z Guarantee helps us catch things we missed," notes Eric Lau of Visiondecor. Once you realize a mistake has been made, and all of us make them, consider it a lesson. Find out how the mistake happened and think about what you can do to prevent it, or similar mistakes, from happening again. Eric shared an example with us:

A customer contacted us regarding a sofa she never received after three weeks of waiting. So we investigated, and noticed that we were provided with the phone number the customer entered in with her billing info, but not with the shipping info. As it turns out, the numbers didn't match. We inquired with Amazon and they said that the billing info is what is provided, so when we provided that phone number to our shipping company they were unable to contact the customer for an appointment. This resulted in a few things. We immediately took care of the order for the customer and worked with Amazon to refund her shipping for the inconvenience. Then what really mattered was, we

worked with Amazon to provide more accurate customer information to be provided to our shippers. And
we then requested our shippers immediately notify us
if there were going to be delays with deliveries. Finally,
we now have checks to ensure deliveries are made
when expected to customers, and if otherwise we
check with all points of contact to get customers their
orders with minimized delays. This is a good example
of how we used what everyone deems as a hassle and
turned it to a positive. This way we will not make the
same mistake twice.

Building Your Operation

As you begin to define your own operation, based partly on what
you've learned *not* to do, you'll have decisions to make and procedures to create on several different fronts. You'll have to think about
how you want your customers to contact you. And you'll need to
quickly and competently prepare your packages for shipment, and
more. You'll be automating your operation and, at some point, likely
hiring staff.

   If everything goes well, you'll be in touch with your customers
several times before they ever receive their orders. You'll keep them
informed and up-to-date each step of the way. Creating a system of
automated e-mails will make this communication simple and efficient. If something doesn't go well, you must step in quickly and do
everything you can to assure your customer that she is in professional hands while the trouble is resolved. For the vast majority of your

transactions, the standard communication will be sufficient, and that means e-mail. When you have to fix a problem, however, very often the phone works best. Integrate both e-mail and phone service into your customer communications from the start.

Customer E-Mail

It is standard now for sellers to send an automated e-mail in response to each e-mail they receive. It's a way to make sure whoever is trying to reach you knows you're there to serve. Most of the sellers who spoke with us use this approach. The response should thank the customer for the e-mail and offer a promised timespan in which the sender should receive a personalized response. The next step, of course, is to follow through on that promised response. That means that checking and sending e-mail must be scheduled into your routine workday with fanatical devotion. Quickly responding to your e-mail not only makes it more likely that a customer will buy from you but it also helps to smooth out suspicion if trouble occurs.

"I always keep my correspondence professional yet casual," says Kathy Wojtczak of Element Jewelry & Accessories. "I find issues are better resolved when the customer feels I am addressing them as a peer." When you respond to a question about a product before the purchase, thank the shopper for his interest and then be sure to toot your own horn a bit. Include a signature line featuring your shipping promises and return policies. Make a professional impression right from the start. If you're responding to a question or concern from a customer awaiting a package or dissatisfied with an order, be sure to offer assurance that you are committed to 100 percent satisfaction for your customers. You'll take the steam out of the kettle quickly.

So, what e-mail exchanges should you build into your daily operation? Just model yourself after Amazon, and you'll be fine. You should certainly send an e-mail in response to every order you receive. Thank your customers and let them know when you expect to ship their items. This e-mail should include the shipping address you plan to use so that any mistakes can be caught before you ship. When the package is ready to go, let your customers know through an e-mail that includes all the tracking information necessary. Finally, many sellers follow up their orders with a quick note, once again thanking the customer, extending wishes that the shipment was satisfactory and, of course, gently encouraging positive feedback. (Note: If you're on Seller Central, you can set your setting under *Manage Orders* to control the messages Amazon will send on your behalf, such as a message confirming an order was received.)

Phone Support

To be considered a professional, you have to provide your customers with telephone support. We know that seems so last century, but, and here's the good news for the descendants of Alexander Graham Bell, it's still an essential part of your communication plan. Now, we're not saying you should encourage each and every customer to call you. In fact, once you offer telephone support, do everything you can to avoid having your customers use it! "We're an Internet company," explains Gary Richardson of Goggles and Glasses. "Phone transactions are not efficient time-wise for a small company." Still, not only does Gary offer phone support, he also offers a toll-free customer service number. Then, he gets busy with a series of e-mails to limit the number of customers who feel the need to call. Andy Mowery of debnroo agrees about the inefficiencies of telephone support. Still, for many years Andy has maintained a customer service phone number and published customer service hours for receiving calls. His strategy has worked well in that he rarely, if ever, receives phone calls outside his regular hours, and he still deals directly with customers when necessary. What Andy and Gary don't agree about, however, is whether you should invest in toll-free customer service for your business.

Get a Toll-Free Customer Service Number

Gary is a big proponent of toll-free service. He's found an inexpensive source for his 800 number through www.tollfreenumber.org, shown in Figure 6-1. "We use our number for customer service reasons," explains Gary. "I want to make contacting me easier than it would be to leave bad feedback." Gary doesn't use his 800 service for marketing purposes on small orders. "On the front end, we advertise our regular number for sales under $25.00," he said. Rather, he saves his toll-free service for larger orders or orders that will require the human touch. "A toll-free number helps establish trust, enhances your company image, increases sales, and makes for happier customers. I spend about $10.00 a month for my toll-free number," Gary estimates. "It's definitely worth it."

Don't Bother with Toll-Free Calling

Andy hasn't gone with toll-free customer service. "This is somewhat of a unique position we've had," Andy told us. "Basically, since there is a wide array of flat-rate packages for phone service, and since calling a toll-free number from a cell phone is not necessarily free, we just don't understand the need for the expense," Andy says. "Frankly, it seems that a toll-free number is basically an unnecessary cost in the current environment." Andy recognizes that perception is key in customer service. From time to time, someone does criticize him for not having toll-free service. Then he recommends checking into flat-rate long-distance service or calling for free through Skype, shown in

Figure 6-1. This toll-free number organization can provide your business with an inexpensive 800 number.

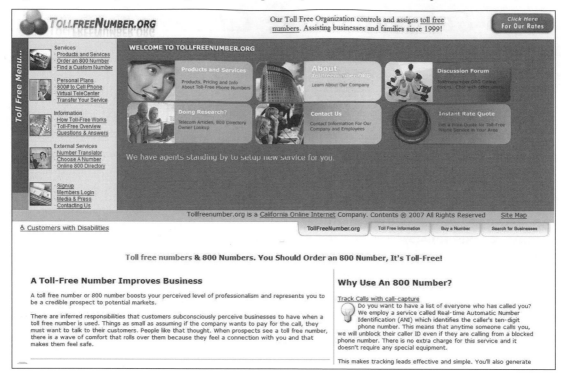

Figure 6-2. Andy admits that toll-free service may get extra sales from customers who would not have called if the call weren't free. "In our case, we don't really want phone sales," explains Andy. "It is not our most efficient channel." Plus, Andy points out, he already provides that quick and free customer service through e-mail and Skype. "Besides the cost, we would be encouraging people to contact us in the most inefficient way possible on our dime, when no dime really needs to be spent," Andy notes.

Packing and Shipping

The impression you'll make when your customer receives your product is so important to your business's success that it's the subject of Chapter 8. But we can't discuss customer service for an e-commerce

Figure 6-2. Using Skype is one option for telephone support. However, your buyer has to have the program installed as well.

business without touching on shipping here. "The key is to go above and beyond the expected level of customer service," notes Kathy of Element Jewelry & Accessories. "If their product is out of stock, I might offer a replacement item at up to 20 percent off. If their package was delayed, I will credit their shipping charge." Even knowing you'll cut your profit on that particular sale, the shipping charge credit will make the delay much more palatable to your customer, and as Kathy notes, you'll be likely to "turn a dissatisfied customer into a happy customer who hopefully returns for future purchases."

Of course, you have to prepare a secure and attractive package that you ship quickly by the most efficient method possible. Chapter 8 is full of practical and tested advice to help you do that. But, what can you do from a customer service perspective to make the most of your packaging preparation? Some pretty basic things might just help.

Consider offering gift-wrapping and personal messaging as a service. At first, you will handle each shipment yourself anyway. The only real commitment required to provide this service is an investment in attractive supplies and extra time for package prep. You may have fewer requests than you expect, but the message you send to all your prospective customers is that your aim is to please. Charge a modest fee, and although you may never earn enough to make it a profit center, you will be showing your customers that you're offering extra services to fulfill their specific needs.

Signature Confirmation

Signature confirmation can boost your customer image, and also protect you from unjustified claims and scam buyers. It's more expensive than its lesser cousin, delivery confirmation, but in some cases, you'll agree it's worth the extra expense. Signature confirmation is the only way to prove that your package arrived. A person must sign for it. Delivery confirmation only proves that the package arrived at your customer's stated post office. It can't account for whatever happens between the post office and your customer. So, if, for example, a package gets stolen from a front porch, you'll still be responsible. You won't be adequately protected from an A-to-z Guarantee claim placed by a criminal instead of a customer, either. If the buyer claims he didn't receive it, nothing you say or do with your delivery confirmation receipt will protect you from a chargeback. You can't prove that your customer got the package.

Delivery confirmation ranges in price from $0.75 per package to $0.18 per package. (We'll show you how to pay $0.18 in Chapter 8.) Signature confirmation, by contrast, ranges from $1.75 to $2.10. For U.S. Postal Service packages, you can buy it for Priority Mail and parcels sent via First-Class Mail, Parcel Post, Bound Printed Matter, or Media Mail rates. For complete details, go to www.usps.com. Most likely, you won't use signature confirmation for most of your packages, but you should keep it in mind as part of your shipping tool chest. One prominent seller of books has set a threshold of $40.00. Above that value, he ships with signature confirmation. He's learned that with signature confirmation, there is a very good chance he won't lose a claim made to Amazon against his shipping. Still, he was quick to encourage us with the fact that of the 5,000 orders he processes each month, he experiences a problem with only one or two of them.

 ## Beware of Orders Getting Old

If you use Seller Central for managing your shipments, you won't by default see orders that are older than seven days. For example, if Amazon holds an order because of a problem with the customer's credit card or bank account, that order will stay visible on the default setting of Seller Central for only seven days. After that, it drops off your orders to be shipped, and you'll lose track of it until you get a negative feedback from the buyer or an A-to-z claim for a product never delivered. In the meantime, Amazon has cleared the problem, but you didn't notice the order was ready to have been shipped.

At the end of each day's shipping effort, select the 90-day view of orders to be shipped on your Seller Central account. You'll quickly see which orders are older than one week but are now ready to be shipped out. It's just a simple and quick check as the last step of shipping, and you'll protect yourself from missing a delivery, guaranteed.

 ## Train Your Staff

Maybe you don't actually have a staff yet. But as long as you're working on your customer service policies, you might as well also think about how you'd expect an employee to treat your customers. Tuck those expectations away for the day you'll be able to pull them off the shelf and start training. In the meantime, thinking like a boss will help you create and enforce your customer service procedures even while you're the only employee who has to obey them. The e-buck stops with you.

Your first employee will likely be there to help with shipping. Make sure you train that person to prepare the packages to your specifications. Keep careful control over who answers the phone for your business, and train your employee carefully before allowing him or her to contact your customers even through e-mail. Until you're certain that your new hire is ready to represent your business well, keep those parts of the job to yourself.

Cross-Train Your Staff

Once you do start adding staff, make sure everyone clearly understands your whole operation. Employees must know exactly how you expect them to interact with customers. You don't want them to give inaccurate information or communicate in any way less than 100 percent professional. "Your workers are your front line," says Xavier Helgesen of Better World Books. "They may well be the ones who deal with most of your customers, whether it's online through e-mails, or through telephone calls." Xavier trains his staff so that everyone is capable of doing every aspect of the work. His employees can handle shipping and inventory and everyone knows what to do for customer service. That way, no matter who happens to answer the phone or check e-mail, he knows his customers are getting reliable service. He's instituted the policies himself and trained everyone to handle things the same way.

Amazon Metrics and Reports

As a third-party seller on the Amazon platform, you'll receive timely updates about just how successfully you are serving your customers.

Yes, Amazon tracks these metrics to ensure customers shopping on Amazon are having the superior shopping experience they expect. But, the information is at least as valuable to you as you build your successful business. Amazon measures seller performance using three primary criteria: feedback, A-to-z Guarantee claim rate, and media refund rate. These ratings go beyond your feedback record to give you insight into areas of your operation you'll need to improve.

View your Performance Summary by logging into your Seller Central account and following the menus. Your Performance Summary gives you details for the last 30 days. You'll be able to view your Ordered Product Sales, your Shipped Product Sales, Refunds, Customer Feedback, and A-to-z Guarantee claims. Now you can compare your numbers to the customer service levels Amazon requires. Here they are:

- **Feedback:** Negative feedbacks should be fewer than 5 percent of your total feedback.
- **A-to-z Guarantee Claim Rate:** The rate should be less than 0.5 percent of orders received.
- **Refund Rate:** The number of media products refunded within a calendar month should be less than 5 percent of the total sold.

Failure to meet these requirements won't automatically get you booted off Amazon, but if you don't improve your scores, your future on the site is in doubt. Amazon expects to see your performance improve within 60 days. Of course, if Amazon detects a serious instance of negligence, it won't wait. The company reserves the right to immediately close the seller account. For your purposes, however, these performance measures are all to the good. Checking your performance statistics carefully can really help you hone your operation. Problem areas become apparent pretty quickly when you can see your results in clear numbers.

Study Your Customer Experience Newsletter

Gary of Goggles and Glasses sells through Seller Central. Periodically, he receives an Amazon Customer Experience newsletter providing insight into how successfully he achieves his customer service goals. Customer experience history is measured against four key criteria:

1. **Order defect rate (ODR)** represents the orders for which you have received a negative feedback, an A-to-z Guarantee claim, or a credit card chargeback.

2. **Pre-fulfillment cancellations** will show you how many times a customer attempted to buy an item that you did not have in stock. You had to cancel the order, because you couldn't fulfill it.

3. **Missed promises** show you how effectively you are meeting your customers' shipping expectations. Amazon expects you to promise to ship the item within two business days. Any orders confirmed to have been shipped three or more days late are counted as having missed the promise.

4. **Percentage of orders refunded** shows, if the number is high, that you are refunding too high a percentage of your products.

Amazon holds specific acceptable standards against these performance measures. Your order defect rate (ODR) is expected to be below 1 percent. Your pre-fulfillment cancellation rate should stay below 2.5 percent, and your missed promise rate must be below 5 percent. Keep in mind that these are just baseline numbers. Many merchants achieve far better performance statistics than these. Use your Customer Experience newsletter to hone your operation. It's a report card showing very clearly just how your customers perceive your performance. Consider it money in the bank to be spent on your Amazon education!

Feedback on Amazon

Amazon, of course, is not alone in online merchant platforms that rely on feedback systems to patrol their marketplaces. But, that doesn't mean Amazon does feedback exactly like eBay, for example. Many of the rules are different, but then so is the philosophy behind the feedback. For one thing, fewer customers leave feedback for merchants on Amazon. "On Amazon, only about 10 percent of customers leave feedback," notes Andy of debnroo. These small numbers make it much more important to receive stellar ratings when you do get feedback. A single negative will bring your total percentage down much more quickly with odds like these. Therefore, the quality of your feedback matters even more than the quantity.

Another surprising fact is that Amazon's feedback isn't cast in stone. If you receive a disappointing rating, you're free to contact the buyer and ask for ways in which you could improve the customer's satisfaction with the purchase. You can work to please the customer, and then your customer is free to remove the stain against your reputation. "Amazon does a good job in allowing sellers to resolve issues with customers in a manner that is beneficial to both buyer and seller without getting involved intimately," notes Asad Bangash of Beachcombers!

Because so few customers leave feedback routinely, you'll have to develop some methods for encouraging that feedback. Successful sellers have devised some clever approaches. You'll also have to help your customers understand what the feedback ratings actually mean and how important their ratings are to your business's health. When you make your case, be sure to emphasize that your only aim is to please the customer. That aim is real, and that will make all the other details fall right into place.

But, you might as well face it, it will be impossible to keep your business completely unscathed by negative feedback, whether deserved or undeserved. "It is inevitable that every merchant will run into a difficult customer situation at some time," says Kathy of Element Jewelry. "We do have to face difficult customers sometimes," agrees Bing Yang of Augustina Jewelry. "Sometimes, no matter what we do or how well we do, a particular buyer is not happy. In the end, that's the nature of business. The good part is, most customers are reasonable." Your goal will be to do your best to please every customer, encourage those you please to reward you with positive feedback, soften the blow of the ones who can't be pleased, and keep on selling and building your reputation.

Encourage Customers to Leave Feedback

As you may recall, many of your Amazon customers won't even realize they're not buying their item directly from Amazon itself. It's no wonder buyers don't use Amazon's feedback system routinely. Still, you can take steps to encourage your customers to stop by and add positive feedback to your score. Of course, that would also mean another chance to make a great impression. You'll have the chance to remind customers to leave feedback on several occasions, so be prepared.

Include a Note in the Package

You are free to include a friendly reminder on the packing slip you include with each package. Customize that slip with a friendly reminder and put it into each package you send. Or, create a colorful and attractive business card that sends the message along. Find a clever phrase or use a striking design that complements your product. If you make the customers smile, you're more likely to motivate them to reward you with a quick feedback. You can clearly show your customers that you are an individual—the more human interaction you can incorporate into this online transaction, the more likely it is that a human will respond individually to your effort.

Use E-Mail Reminders

In Chapter 5, we told you about Feedback Forager to automate your efforts in encouraging customers to submit positive feedback. Actually, any system you use to automate your e-mail can be programmed to send an e-mail reminder for feedback. "We send customer follow-up emails about 20 days after the transactions take place," notes Steve Jay of wholesalelaptopbattery. Steve uses SpaceWare to automate his e-mail and a friendly reminder for feedback is part of that automation.

When you send your reminder, make it clear that your first concern is the customer's complete satisfaction. Encourage your customers to contact you directly with any questions or concerns they might have with the order or the product. Then go ahead and bring up the subject of feedback. Your note might look something like this:

Thank you very much for your recent order of the mahogany jewelry box. By now you should have received your package, and we hope you are 100 percent thrilled with the quality of the box and the quick service we've provided for you.

If you have any questions or concerns, or if by chance your order has not yet arrived, please contact us via e-mail at [email address] or by telephone at [phone number and customer service hours] so that we can provide you with the personal service you can expect each time you purchase an item from us.

If you have received your item, and you are pleased with your purchase, may we please ask you to take a moment to leave a positive feedback comment for us? Our feedback score is a vital part of our online business, and we depend on good customers like you to spread the word about our work. Leaving feedback on Amazon is quite simple.

We thank you for your kind support and look forward to serving you again in the future.

Best wishes,

[your name]

· ·

By making this note friendly and personal, you've connected with your customer and shown yourself as a partner in the transaction, rather than just a nameless source of commodities on the big, impersonal Internet. With automation, you haven't expended too much energy, but your customer will surely feel personally addressed. Not everyone who receives your e-mail, of course, will bother to comply, but you'll be surprised at the number of people who do feel connected. If they're pleased, some of them will be happy to step up and help you out with a quick positive feedback.

Educate Your Customers About Feedback

Because most customers don't leave feedback, it's easy for the customers who do to misunderstand feedback terms. The results can be disappointing. You're hoping for a five-star rating, of course. "Any feedback less than a five will bring down your overall score," explains Tricia Records of Read_Rover_Books. "Fours can hurt as much as ones or twos if you get enough of them." When you reach out to your customer to request feedback, you'll include the link to make it easy to find the feedback form but also include a little advice about what each score means. Here's how the ratings break down:

- 5 (Excellent)
- 4 (Good)
- 3 (Fair)
- 2 (Poor)
- 1 (Awful)

It is very possible for a casual shopper to consider a rating of 3 to be a fine review. He ordered, you shipped it, he's happy, but he may not be thinking of the interaction as anything more than routine. He didn't have any problems to warrant a lesser score, but perhaps you sold him a commodity he needed (say, a laptop battery charger), not something that it necessarily thrilled him to buy. You may have done everything right, but his reaction to the whole event is fairly neutral. He took care of a problem. Without knowing that a feedback score of 3 represents only a fair rating for your service, he'll consider his transaction complete. But, a 3 score will drop your overall rating. "A single 3 rating dropped our feedback score from 100 percent to 98 percent," reported Gary of Goggles and Glasses. Remember, you're talking about a small percentage of your customers who will ever leave you feedback, so each single rating has a greater effect on your overall score. So, again, when you reach out to solicit feedback from your customers, include a brief description of what each rating means. Not only will you be making the whole process easier for your customer, you'll be increasing the chances that the feedback you receive will be strong and positive.

Dealing with Negative Feedback

When you do get less than stellar feedback, and you will, reach out to that customer to address whatever issue may have led to the disappointing score. A polite e-mail asking which part of the transaction was less than satisfactory can open a dialogue with your customer and even help you to improve your operations. Kirk Holbert of Cosmic-King reports that he will plead with an Amazon buyer who is dissatisfied, even offering a 100 percent money-back guarantee. His feedback score is more important to him than the revenue he'll lose by refunding the customer's money.

Asking to have a negative feedback score removed can be a delicate procedure. Your first step is to assure your customer that you are disappointed that the transaction was not a good experience. Then you'll offer to make things right. *Finally*, you'll explain the impact this comment has had on your Amazon reputation. Your first concern should be to correct any issues with the customer. It's not in your best interest to emphasize how damaging this score is to your reputation. If your customer is truly dissatisfied with his purchase, why would the person care about what that means to you?

If your first attempt doesn't bring the results you were hoping for, try again. Gary of Goggles and Glasses will send three e-mails and then call the customer if necessary. Sometimes through the course of this correspondence, you'll find that you actually have made a mistake, and rather than addressing you about it directly, this customer went straight to feedback. Gary told us a story of a customer who bought a pair of sunglasses and then left a feedback rating of 3. She agreed that the quality of the glasses was excellent and the service was good, but the glasses were way bigger than she thought they'd be. Since they proved to be different from what she expected, she left a disappointing feedback. Through a series of e-mail exchanges, Gary learned that he'd actually sent her the wrong pair. He sent the correct pair through expedited delivery and offered her a free glasses case for her trouble. Of course, she removed the disappointing feedback score. Not only did Gary salvage his Amazon reputation, he turned an unhappy customer into a happy one. He also showed her the person behind the faceless online business. Since this customer told Gary that she buys a lot of sunglasses online, who do you think she'll come to next time she wants a new pair? If you've done your best to correct the problem that led to your disappointing score, and your customer still won't remove it, what can you do next? Sadly, there's little more to do. If your customer leaves something obscene or reveals your personal contact information, you can turn to Amazon to have it removed (http://www.amazon.com/ gp/help/customer/display.html?nodeId=1161284&#remove). But other than that, you're stuck. You can't enter into this venture with the expectation of never disappointing a single customer. If the negative feedback comes and you can't get it removed, pick yourself up, brush yourself off, and keep on going. In time, that negative comment will scroll off the first page of your feedback record and fade from memory. It's more important for you to address whatever issue may have caused the negative response, and then get back to the business of pleasing more customers.

True or False? You Can't Leave Feedback for Buyers

Even some long-time Amazon users assume that feedback is a one-way street on this site. Your customers rate you, but you can't rate them. That's simply not true. Through your My Account page, you can click on any completed order and rate your customer with feedback. However, Amazon will not block a poorly rated customer. Most buyers never check their feedback ratings, so your difficult customer may never even see your remark. Why bother, then?

If you've had a horrible encounter with a highly unpleasant customer, don't you think your fellow Amazon third-party sellers deserve fair warning? If sellers took a minute to rate an impossible buyer, you'd be able to check out a buyer's reputation at the very beginning of a dispute. As soon as the trouble arises, you could check out the buyer's feedback to see if this is a reasonable buyer who may have a legitimate claim, or a chronic malcontent who will never be happy with anything you do to improve things. It can help you plot your course in response to the problem. If you see you've gotten into a tangle with someone who can't be pleased, you can quickly refund the money and get back to work building your business.

Turning Good Feedback into Reviews

Okay, enough about negative feedback and negative customers. Once you start getting positive feedback, turn those comments into product reviews. In Chapter 7, you'll learn what an important marketing tool product reviews on Amazon can be. The more reviews your products receive, the more visible and competitive they become on the site. Once you start to accumulate positive feedback, you can approach those customers and request that they write a review. You've already pleased them, so requesting a review can be a natural next step. Of course, since you're asking your customer to do you a favor, you'll want to offer something in return.

Approach your customer with an e-mail expressing your gratitude for the positive boost the comment is to your reputation. Offer that happy customer the opportunity to write a product review, and be sure you include the link to the reviews page to make it simple. Your incentive, in return for the time and trouble your customer will take to write the review, can be a free gift or a deep discount on the next purchase. The cost of your incentive will be money well invested as you build your reputation on Amazon. Those reviews are so important to your reputation that you should consider these incentives part of your start-up costs.

Turn Negative Feedback into a Review

It may be easy to understand why a satisfied customer would leave a product review, but how can you expect a dissatisfied one to do the same? It all begins with that e-mail you send when you receive a negative feedback. If you find that the reason your customer left a negative comment was because she was disappointed with the product, consider this a chance to help the buyer learn how to more effectively shop on Amazon. Explain the difference between critiquing a product and rating a seller. Show the buyer a more effective way of sharing opinions about the product itself without damaging your reputation as a seller. Gary of Goggles and Glasses shared the following e-mail with us so you can see exactly how he handled just such a case.

....

Thanks for removing that feedback. I appreciate it. Our feedback is important to us and prospective customers. That's how they determine if we are "safe" to buy from. Amazon.com also uses it to evaluate sellers' performance. It's our report card, per se.

If you would like to rate a product on Amazon, you can do so on the product page. Truthful reviews, even if negative, are helpful to other consumers and welcome. If you were to write a review saying your purchase was "cheesy," I can guarantee there is some buyer out there looking for "cheesy." On the other hand, someone who wants to avoid "cheesy" finds that review helpful, too. That helps the merchant.

We just got some new sunglasses, and I'd be happy to send you a free pair. Just e-mail your shipping address.

....

When Things Go Bad

It would be nice to plot a happy, smooth road to a successful business humming along on Amazon, but as comforting a thought as that might be, it's not going to be the path you take. Your road to success is bound to be paved with more than a few rocks. You're bound to face disputes with customers, your competitors, and even Amazon itself. Knowing how to set things right when they've gone wrong is part of your education. By now, you've seen lots of techniques for dealing with unhappy customers. We hope you see the big take-away on the subject is this: Do everything you can at every possible encounter with a customer to provide extraordinary customer service to go along with your great products. Dealing with disputes with your competitors and Amazon.com itself can be a different story.

Dealing with Competitors

Don't escalate conflicts with your competitors. Competitors can easily cause all types of trouble for you in an online market. "There are too many ways to sabotage someone on any online venue," says Tricia of Read_Rover_Books. When you get contentious with a competitor, you're likely to end up battered and bruised and far-afield from your goal of building a thriving business. An angry competitor can damage your feedback score by leaving negative comments, for example. Tricia calls that *feedback bombing* and notes that even when it's fraudulent feedback, it can be very difficult to prove its impropriety and have it removed. So, stay polite, keep your distance, and do your best to get along with your competitors.

If you suspect a competitor is working to sabotage you despite your honorable intentions, you'll have to stay vigilant and be ready to work to protect yourself. One thing a competitor might do is post a poor review of your product. If that's the case, read it carefully for loopholes that might get Amazon to remove the review. We once had a disgruntled "reader" write a scathing review of a very successful book we'd written. The reviewer was clearly grinding a personal axe. We were able to submit an appeal to Amazon, based on our findings that the review was inflammatory, and Amazon agreed. It removed the review. If you think something is funny about a review you receive, don't hesitate to appeal to Amazon through e-mail at community-help@amazon.com. The response can be very quick and quite satisfying.

Working with Amazon's Customer Service Department

You've already seen that Amazon.com is quite a powerful and reliable business partner. For the most part, you can expect fair treatment, rewarding sales, and a good relationship together. But, Amazon.com is also big, and it can be anonymous. It's possible to get caught up in a conflict with the company that threatens your standing on the site. You know Amazon holds all sellers to strict performance levels, especially customer service performance. You're working hard to meet the Merchant Performance Standards you know Amazon requires of you as a merchant. One important measure of that performance, of course, is your feedback.

You also know that few of your customers will bother to leave you feedback of any sort. Of those who do leave feedback, many of them will be unclear about what the feedback score means, leaving ample opportunity for a feedback rating that doesn't accurately reflect your performance. You'll be especially vulnerable to this problem as you just start out. All new sellers with little feedback behind them risk falling below Amazon's standards. Here's an example.

Suppose you sell 20 items and complete those sales without incident. Of those 20 customers, 18 are perfectly happy, but don't bother to leave feedback. Only 2 customers leave feedback. (This ratio is realistically what you can expect in terms of feedback rates.) If both of those ratings are negative, you'll have a 100 percent negative feedback score, well below the Merchant Performance Standards Amazon enforces. You'll likely be swept up in a numerical analysis that pops up to warn Amazon's Alliance Program of sellers who are failing to meet their standards, and you'll be blocked. Your account will be suspended, you'll receive complete information about how you can refund or ship your last transactions, and Amazon will hold money to cover any possible outstanding A-to-z Guarantee claims or chargebacks.

Be prepared to document your case and get in touch with the Alliance Program at alliance@amazon.com right away. Request a review of your case. Be prepared with all the facts of the transactions and any e-mails you sent attempting to satisfy your customers. If you can show that you are doing well, despite the statistics, you're likely to have your account reinstated. The e-mail you get informing you of your reinstatement will also outline specific steps you can take to improve your operation and increase your performance rating. Don't underestimate the power of appealing directly to Amazon.com when trouble crops up. The company is big and you can get lost, but the customer experience Amazon provides for shoppers is reflected in the company's interactions with you as a third-party seller. "Amazon has done a good job of protecting both the buyer and seller," notes Asad of Beachcombers! Amazon "lets individuals find solutions to benefit both parties."

Looking Ahead

We've talked a lot about building and keeping a sterling reputation as an Amazon merchant. Absolutely, your sustained efforts to please your customers with great products and service will be a cornerstone of your thriving business. But, every business has to establish a brand and build a name for itself. Building lasting customer relationships and making your business stand out among the other million-plus third-party sellers can be challenging. Chapter 7 will give you lots of great ideas for marketing the thriving business you're building.

An Amazon Success Story

When Asad Bangash and Jody Rogers brought their online business Beachcombers! to Amazon, they'd already established a successful operation both on eBay and the Web. The partners specialize in ethnic Indo/Pakistani women's fashion shoes and accessories. They already had established reliable suppliers and built an attractive and varied product line. You can see for yourself at www.shopbeachcombers.com. "We have always taken an active interest in expanding our sales venues whenever possible," said Asad. "We had just expanded onto Overstock and a few other venues." Asad and Jody had been considering Amazon for some time, and started selling on the regular marketplace. They soon saw this venue would be too limited and lacking in automation for them to build the kind of business they wanted to have on the site. "As luck would have it, just as we started the formal invitation process with Amazon, we received an offer from our American Express merchant account with a formal invitation to sell on Amazon as a Pro Merchant," he noted. As we write, Asad and Jody have been selling on Amazon for nearly two years.

Asad finds Amazon's high-trust marketplace to be a perfect match with the customer service philosophies he and Jody have always brought to their business. They also consider Amazon to be a good business partner in providing an online platform to expand their business. Asad is able to provide his customers with the service they deserve, and at the same time he feels well-supported by Amazon.com. When they first came to Amazon, he and Jody spent hours researching all the tips and tricks that Amazon has available on the FAQ and help pages. "We followed 99 percent of their recommendations and built our listings based on their best practices," he said. For the most part, Asad uses e-mail technical support when he encounters a problem. "We typically e-mail questions through this channel, and it has served us well, so far," he said. "We tend to get a different rep each time to help us, but this does not pose any issues with good follow-up to our questions."

Asad and Jody face some special customer service issues that cause them to think carefully about every aspect of their business. For example, not only do they have to do the same work every other online merchant has to do to keep their product line fresh and their inventory updated, but they also have to present their wares carefully, educating their customers as they showcase their products. "Our items are ethnic," explains Asad. "Many customers do not understand some of the finer points of our products, and we do not want them to be disappointed when the issue could have been resolved prior to ordering. To address this issue, the couple includes very careful sizing and ordering details. They have also created guides to educate shoppers in such matters as how best to break in their new shoes to make them perfectly comfortable and how to put glass bangles on without breaking the bracelets or cutting your arm.

Yet another customer service challenge can be the number of international sales the partners process. The biggest challenges to international sales are "expense of shipping to the customer, education of importing by the customer, and speed of shipment," explained Asad. "We try to find a cost and acceptable speed of delivery that the customer will find fair and that we can still keep profitable." As for educating international customers about the details of cross-border purchases, that is another task in itself. "Many international customers do not know that many times there are customs, taxes, and fees due when the shipment arrives to them. We make our best effort to explain this prior to purchase in all our policies, shipping text, and communications with our international buyers."

Whether through Amazon sales, eBay sales, or their own website, Asad and Jody have created a dynamic and growing business selling beautiful things to both domestic and international customers. They've identified a niche in a thriving market, and created a means of presenting fine-quality, attractive items to that market. Of all the venues the couple shares, their own website accounts for the largest portion of their sales. "We look at Amazon and eBay as marketing and customer generation," noted Asad. If we get a new customer from these venues and then have them shop from our website or offline, then those venues have served their purpose." It sounds like a pretty good plan, and another Amazon success story to us.

CHAPTER

7

Marketing Your Amazon Business

Talk to a few Amazon sellers and you may hear the same thing over and over: "Amazon is a great place to operate a business, but it's very difficult to build your brand there." We agree, and will go so far as to say that Amazon purposely makes it so most third-party sellers seem almost indistinguishable from Amazon itself. That's not because Amazon isn't a good business partner, but it's in keeping with Amazon's goal of providing the best possible customer experience. If you want to operate on Amazon, you must be prepared to operate your business with the same standards of customer service that Amazon itself provides. The customer shouldn't be able to tell who is actually fulfilling the order, because that order will be fulfilled so professionally and smoothly that it might as well be coming from Amazon itself.

This philosophy, at first glance a strike against your own personal business goals, is actually quite a potential boost to your bottom line. Amazon attracts the customers with its name recognition and reputation for reliable, dependable service, and then you get to be the one who actually makes the sale. "The Amazon brand adds value to our own brand," notes Michael Jansma of GemAffair, who has found Amazon to be very supportive of his efforts to create his own brand and image on the site.

Although it is true that having a presence on Amazon is bound to be a boost to your traffic, many of the traditional tools for marketing your e-commerce business, such as amassing a customer list, collecting e-mail addresses for e-mail marketing campaigns, or offering customers an opt in to a newsletter, may simply not work on Amazon. As a matter of fact, trying to use them on Amazon can actually get you thrown off the site.

Before you wonder, then, why we even devoted a chapter to marketing an Amazon business, let us reassure you that there are a lot of innovative and interesting ways to build a brand, even on Amazon. Forcing you to think of some new ones will open entirely new opportunities for you. If the perception is correct—that you can't build your brand on Amazon—why have our in-depth interviews revealed so many great and creative marketing strategies? Where there's a will there can be many ways, and additional opportunities coming along all the time. Think creatively, and you'll find lots of ways to attract and retain your customers. Fail to market to those customers, and your business is likely to stagnate and eventually die as your competitors pass you like a sprinter passing a spectator.

Start with Best Practices

By now, many of the things you've considered have already started you down the path of marketing your business. When you create great product detail pages with keyword-rich titles, you are marketing your business. When you take clear and professional images of your products, you're creating good marketing tools. When you ship your products quickly, neatly, and professionally, you are literally reaching out to your customer to make a marketing presentation. So, from the very first day of operation, you are wise to be following Amazon's own "best practices" advice for operating your business. After all, Amazon has learned over many years what works to build a great customer experience, both for the company and its third-party sellers. So let's look at some of those best practices with a marketing point of view.

- **First on the list of best practices is providing world-class customer service.** That means answering e-mails promptly, professionally, and in a friendly tone. Any time you are interacting with a customer or prospective customer, you must expect to be offering that customer your very best possible service.

- **Only list items for sale that you actually own.** Amazon's rules expressly forbid you from selling things that you don't currently have in stock. Unless your items are nestled and waiting in your own little corner of a Fulfillment by Amazon warehouse, you need to make sure they're right there where you can see them, pull them, and ship them within the two-day limit stipulated by your agreement with Amazon. The one exception would be if you were to use Amazon's own Drop Ship by Amazon program, discussed in Chapter 8.

- **Ship your items within that two-day limit.** Maybe it's no fun to send orders out every day, but that's the promise you made when you signed up with Amazon. Aside from Sunday or a holiday, you should be expecting to process your orders on a daily basis.

- **Handle all refunds and returns promptly and professionally.** You may very well not want to refund the money; we understand, but you still have to do it. So do it with a little grace and finesse to prove that you are exactly what you're expected to be—a professional e-commerce business owner. Following through with a disappointed customer can actually result in good feedback for you. It's easy to forget a seller who did what was expected by quickly shipping the product purchased. It's quite a bit more memorable to find a seller who took a disappointing interaction and made it right. You may find some of your best and most important feedback comes from a disappointed customer you then went on to please.

Understanding the intricacies of Amazon's feedback system will also provide you with marketing opportunities. Feedback, always hard to ensure, is difficult to amass on Amazon, since most buyers never bother to add it. That means when you do get feedback, you need to be prepared to make the most of it. We'll show you how in the following pages, but for now, tuck the feedback opportunities into your travel kit, and let's be sure you clearly understand that which is simply not possible on Amazon.

Amazon Rules for Third-Party Sellers

We've firmly established that you must be very careful about how you reach out to your customers on Amazon. The company is fairly unforgiving about violating the rules, and you don't want to do anything that will permanently remove you from the Amazon site. That will surely stop your business in its tracks. So, let's gain a clear understanding of what you can't do before we look more closely at all the things you can do. "On Amazon you have painfully little visibility to your customers," notes e-commerce consultant David Yaskulka. "By and large, to them it will appear as though they bought the item from Amazon, not you. Amazon's rules for communicating with customers give you no opportunity to reach out to customers." Tricia Records of Read_Rover_Books agrees. "Amazon does a really good job of keeping their customers defined as their own, and they take strong measures against those who cross the line and market directly to them," she warns. Here's a look at exactly what the Amazon Services Business Solutions Agreement states:

••

Use of Amazon Transaction Information

You will not...use any Amazon Transaction Information for any marketing or promotional purposes whatsoever (except as permitted below), or otherwise in any way inconsistent with our or your privacy policies or applicable Law; (c) contact a Person that has ordered Your Product that has not yet been delivered with the intent to collect any amounts in connection therewith or to influence such Person to make an alternative purchase; (d) disparage us, our affiliates, or any of their or our respective products or services; or (e) target communications of any kind on the basis of the intended recipient being an Amazon.com user.

••

Okay, so let's translate that into some very specific no-can-dos. You will not be permitted to do any of the following:

- Amass a list of your customers and their contact information.
- E-mail or send postal letters to your customers for marketing purposes.
- Use URLs to other merchant sites within your product detail pages.

- Create a logo that contains or displays a URL to another site.
- Cross-sell for another merchant or any third-party product.

All of these prohibitions are not meant to discourage you. There will still be plenty of opportunities for you to reach out to your customers. You just need to be clear about what is permitted and what is not before you can proceed with what is. Let's take a look at the many things you can do to build your brand.

Your Brand on Amazon

Just as you brought your own personality, interests, and skills to deciding which products you'd source and sell on Amazon, you'll bring those same things to the manner in which you list and sell those items. You couldn't help but project your personality into these aspects of your business, even if you weren't trying. You might as well think carefully about them as you build your business to make them work in your favor. Consider every aspect of what you bring to the market and how you can best distinguish your business from your competitors. Specifically, we want you to think about everything from your logo to your descriptions and photos to your packing slips and the boxes you ship your products in. Each of these elements combined will help you create a distinguished brand. We can't promise your business will someday become a verb like Google or Xerox, but everyone has to start someplace, so you might as well consider starting from a strong position.

Promote Your Name and Logo

In Chapter 2, we looked at some practical considerations for selecting your nickname on Amazon. We hope by now you've found something that pleases you, because this name will easily become the cornerstone of your every marketing effort. "We developed our brand by getting our own logo," Dan Morrill of Alternating Reality books told us. Figure 7-1 shows you just how intriguing and memorable that logo is. By making sure that the logo met the standards set forth in Amazon's rules, Dan is able to include it in all of his product detail pages. (Note that one of those rules states the logo must be no more than a 120 x 30 pixel image.) That means that every time a customer opens one of his pages, it's instantly clear that a specific third-party seller is in the house. Dan was also wise enough to tie his image into his genre of science-fiction books. That makes it all that much more enticing and memorable for his customers. You may have to invest some money with a graphic designer to come up with a great logo, but that will be money well spent when it appears all over Amazon, the Web, your e-mails, your boxes, your packing slips, and … well, you get the point. Sites such as guru.com can provide you ready access to many capable designers, who will gladly bid for your services.

Figure 7-1. Alternating Reality's logo paints a memorable mind image.

 ## *Brand Your Correspondence*

With your logo and business name defined, put them both to work. Include them in the signature of all your e-mails. Print them on your packing slips. Invest in business cards that you'll drop into every package you send, and consider printing your own logoed boxes for shipping all your items. "I also ship out all of my orders in Element Jewelry–branded gift boxes, which helps build a return customer base," notes Kathy Wojtczak of Element Jewelry & Accessories. Tricia of Read_Rover_Books agrees, and includes business cards and coupons in her shipments. By offering coupons for repeat shopping, Tricia is working toward building brand loyalty and repeat business while still staying within the boundaries Amazon has defined. Even if you don't get the repeat customer, you can never tell when the delivery person who handles your package will see that label or logoed box and get curious enough to check out your offerings and become a new customer.

Brand Your Product Detail Pages

You can create your own particular style with your product detail pages. Perhaps you'll define specific expressions, terms, or details that make your pages stand out from all others. "The way we write our descriptions is also a form of branding that separates us from other sellers on Amazon," notes Xavier Helgeson of Better World Books. Writing descriptions with lots of content will not only make your pages stand out on Amazon, but the content will make it more likely that your product detail pages will be picked up in results of searches through Google or Yahoo! when people go looking for information that relates to your products. Remember our profile in Chapter 5 of Andy and Deb Mowery of debnroo, who made that a priority on the WebStores by Amazon pages. As long as you know folks will be looking for information relevant to the products you sell, why not include some of it on the pages you use to sell those products?

Your images are another place where you can make your brand stand out. "We brand our images in the way they are taken so that

visually there is a difference from our pictures to the competitors',"
said Xavier of Better World Books. If your images stand out, those
visuals are bound to stick in your customers' memories. Find a way
to distinguish yours from your competitors' that ties in with the
theme of your products and you'll strike yet another chord with the
shoppers who are already curious about what you sell.

Cast a Wide Net

As soon as your systems are in place and you're ready to process
orders and ship quickly, start listing as many items as you can manage, and keep at it. "We list every product we can on Amazon," said
Michael Jansma of GemAffair. "That gives us a wide net." Just based
on sheer percentages, the more you list, the more likely your products are to appear on search results pages. Of course, that will back-
fire if you list more than you can reasonably process, but your goal
should be to have your product, along with your nickname and logo,
all over the Amazon site.

Building a Brand Before You've Built Your Brand

Until you build name recognition and can reach a higher level of effi-
ciency, how are you going to proceed? When you first begin selling
on Amazon you won't have any feedback. It will be very difficult for
you to stand out from the crowd on your reputation alone. Amazon
helps you to get started. In the place your feedback statistics would
normally appear on a product page, Amazon places a cheery icon
with the words "Just Launched" under it. That actually gets you off

to a good start, makes you stand out, and may make some people willing to give you, the newcomer, a chance.

As such, you must be especially careful to follow all of Amazon's rules and best practices. This is not only to build up that feedback rating but also to ensure that you get paid. Amazon will hold funds until the company is certain your first few transactions went well. That is, Amazon may have collected your customers' payments, but they will not actually transfer the funds until it's satisfied that your customers are satisfied.

 # Buy Your Own Products

Unlike an auction format, where bidding on your own products is strictly prohibited, there is no rule against buying from yourself. "Buy some items from yourself if you really believe in your product," recommends e-commerce consultant David Yaskulka. "This will increase its visibility as you go from no sales to one. When you do that, in effect, you are paying Amazon for better placement."

 # Offer a Discount in Return for Experience

David further recommends that you enlist friends and colleagues in your buying campaign. "If you are a member of a group, say the Internet Merchants Association (IMA) or the Professional eBay Sellers Alliance (PeSA), encourage other members to buy your products, perhaps offering them a 50 percent discount. Then have them give you frank and honest feedback. If the feedback is positive, they can post it." If the feedback is negative, have them discuss it with you personally so that you can address the flaws in your operation and improve your business. Consider the cost of the discount as part of your start-up expenses. It will help you overcome the early days with no feedback, and gain some good experience in completing sales, processing orders, and serving your customers.

Maximize Amazon's Tools for Building Your Brand

Our discussion so far has focused on what you can do to maximize your opportunities for branding your business, and our efforts until now have been in building your branding into the basic operations and best practices of your business. That certainly is the place to start. However, Amazon offers you quite a variety of tools you can use to drive traffic toward your products, and now it's time to get specific about using every one of those as potential brand builders. Before we're done with you, your business and products will be popping up all over the site. Then we'll move on to spreading your word across the Internet at large. Amazon, in keeping with its standing as a good business partner, will help you every step of the way.

Your Own Amazon Pages

Let's put first things first. Begin building your presence on Amazon by completing every page available to you. It may seem intuitive, but in the rush to build your business it can be easy to overlook the details. "I've completed every available seller-page," noted Chris Schlieter of timezone. In time, your seller profile will be filled with feedback from your customers, but while you're waiting for that to happen make sure you make the most of the pages you have. Figure 7-2 shows a seller's feedback page. Notice the tabs along the top that take shoppers to policy descriptions from shipping to returns to more detailed feedback. The *At a Glance* page is the first thing your customers will see. Use it to personalize your business. Andy Mowery of debnroo added a photo to that page with a bit of company history to go along. When you click on the *Seller Help* tab, as you can see in Figure 7-3, you hop right to an expanded history of Andy and Deb's company, complete with pictures. It's as close to making personal contact as you can get on Amazon. By the time you've finished reading about the couple and their business, you can certainly feel that you've found a trusted merchant worthy of your business.

Figure 7-2 A seller's feedback page is vitally important.

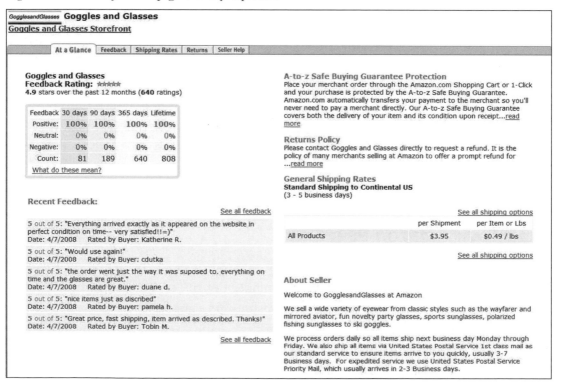

Figure 7-3. Notice how seller debnroo has personalized the Seller Help page.

Don't Forget a Link to Your Store

Your *At a Glance* page also offers a link to your WebStore by Amazon. As soon as you've got your store up and running, update the page with a link. "Customers can link directly to my WebStore from the *At a Glance* page," noted Kathy of Element Jewelry & Accessories. "They can choose *See Other Products by Element Jewelry & Accessories.*" Once customers click that link, they are no longer operating on Amazon at large, they're visitors to your very own store. You've got them one step closer to being customers of your own, rather than just Amazon customers.

Make Your Feedback Work for You

Once you start to amass feedback, you can put those comments to work. "Satisfied customers can leave telling and complimentary feedback comments, which can, in themselves, serve as a kind of promotion," commented Barry Mark of Treebeard Books. Although you can't leave feedback for your customers, you can add a reply to the feedback they leave for you. Certainly in the case of a negative or neutral feedback rating, you'll want to add a note explaining what happened. Even if your note says, "We're so sorry for this disappointment. A full refund has been issued," that will go a long way toward softening the negative statement and retaining your image as a professional seller. But, even if the comment is a good one, you may decide to follow up. A "Thank you for your good words. We're delighted you're so pleased with the jewelry box," will give you one more opportunity to shine a spotlight on your product.

Gather Amazon's Reviews

One of the strengths of the Amazon market is that it allows "word-of-mouth" advertising. One of the easiest ways to spread the good word about your products is through the site's Reviews features. Anyone who is registered with Amazon.com is eligible to write product reviews. It doesn't even matter whether the person bought the item on Amazon. If you see something for sale on the site, and you have an opinion about it, you're free to add your opinion in the form of a review. It doesn't take shoppers very long to determine that they are better off buying what others have already tested and approved. Good reviews for a product lead directly to increased sales. We can speak to that personally, as we've watched sales of our books increase along with the number of positive reviews we've received.

There are a variety of ways you can go about legitimately adding positive reviews to your product detail pages. We say legitimately, because you can't just review your own products using a pseudonym. Not only is that dishonest and unethical, but if you're discovered, the folks at Amazon would consider this a serious breach of trust.

Ask Your Customers

As we've already mentioned, every package you ship to a customer gives you a chance to reach out to your customers in a very concrete way. In addition to the personal thank-you you'll include, here's a chance to ask those customers to speak up on your product's behalf. You may include a little coupon offering a discount on a future purchase in return for a positive review. Or, you may offer a small free gift in return. Simply decide on the incentive that feels right to you and start soliciting those positive reviews. Gary Richardson of Goggles and Glasses uses both his shipment notification e-mail and his packaging to invite customers to add a product review.

Ask a Reviewer

You can find a list of popular reviewers on Amazon at http://www.amazon.com/gp/customer-reviews/top-reviewers.html (see also Figure 7-4). These are folks who enjoy reviewing books, music, videos, or any number of other items and writing about them on the site. Some of them had more than 15,000 reviews listed when we checked! You can browse this list for people who are interested in products similar to those you sell. You'll find all the necessary contact information, right along with the reviewer's profile. Send an e-mail

Figure 7-4. Amazon lists its Top Reviewers right on its site.

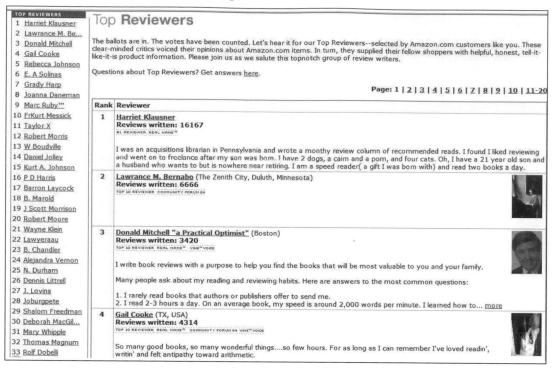

to see if the reviewer who appeals to you is willing to give your product a try. The most you have to risk is a sample that you'll donate to the effort, but if the result is a good solid review, you'll earn back your investment many times over.

Love That Listmania!

Another word-of-mouth option for Amazon users is the Listmania feature open to anyone registered with Amazon.com. This handy and simple tool lets you create lists of your favorite things. Simply create a title for your list, and then you can add up to 40 items relevant to that title. When someone searches for an item you've included on your list, your entire list will appear on the product detail page for that item. So, suppose you sell items for babies. You may create a Listmania list titled: *Essentials for New Parents*. Now go ahead and populate your list. Your first entry should be one of your best-selling products, because that item will appear complete with an image whenever your Listmania list does. Be sure to include items on your list that are truly of value to new parents. You want your list to be viewed as more than just shameless self-promotion. You want to reward whoever opens your Listmania list with information that truly will be valuable. Of course, creating these lists won't be hard for you, since you're selling and dealing with items you know and love. You'll be able to create a number of valuable recommendations to your customers and promote some of your best products at the same time.

Include Popular Items You Don't Even Sell on Your Listmania Lists

"Create lists for all kinds of products and include popular products whether you sell them or not," recommends e-commerce consultant David Yaskulka. "Be sure to include highly rated or reviewed items, too," he advises. These lists will appear whenever someone searches for any of the items you've included (see Figure 7-5 for an example). By including popular and well-reviewed products, you increase the opportunities for your own products to pop up in search results.

David further recommends that you link current popular books or videos to your Listmania lists, even if you don't sell them. As long as they are relevant to the subject of your list, you'll be taking advantage of the fact that many people will be searching for them. So, for example, if you're selling pearl earrings, including the book *Girl with the Pearl Earring* by Tracy Chevalier will increase the chance that someone will find your earrings when searching for this popular book. Add the movie, and you'll get results when someone searches

Figure 7-5. Creating Listmania lists is another way to advertise your products.

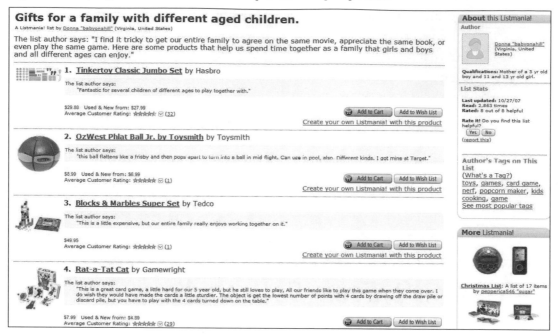

for Colin Firth or Scarlet Johansson. Add a book about Vermeer's painting, and you'll get your earrings into yet another corner of the market. By now, you probably have the idea, right?

David also recommends that you create specific *granular lists*. Our example of a Listmania for new parents is just one example. You could take it a step further and create a similar list for *Great Gifts for New Parents Under $50*, or *Absolute Must-haves Before Baby Comes Home*. Not only are you gaining the opportunity to spread the word about some of your own products, but you'll also be providing a shopping service to prospective customers. When you've completed these lists, you'll gain direct exposure from them when they appear in the following places:

- Your relevant search results
- Your product detail pages
- Your *competitor's* product detail pages

Every product detail page on which they appear will provide you with a cross-marketing opportunity.

Great Granular Listmania Ideas

Here are some ideas for granular Listmania lists that could support your line of jewelry:

1. Great cameo pendants under $100 (add others under $150, $200, etc.)
2. Great sterling silver cameos
3. Great gifts for Mother's Day (including lots of cameos)
4. Great wedding jewelry (including blue cameos)
5. Reproduction cameos just like Grandma had
6. Her first cameo
7. Classic and timeless jewelry every woman should own

TIP

Play Tag!

We talked about tags on Amazon in Chapter 4 as we looked at defining and selecting effective keywords for your product detail pages. Now you can use tags to increase the chances that customers will use them to click through to your own listings. Once you've got your products up and running, think about what other items your customers might be shopping for. For example, if you sell automotive supplies, you may want to spend some time trolling around in the home and garden section or the sports and outdoors area.

You can place your tags on any page, so think about the products your customers are likely to be using in addition to your own, and see where you might find them outside of your immediate category. Catching a customer who didn't even stop by to search for what you sell is gravy for the meat and potatoes you need to run your business. Tags are free and simple. The more you place, the more likely one of them will catch a customer.

Become a Featured Merchant

We've advised that you become a Featured Merchant, and who among you doesn't want to reach this goal? Featured Merchants, in addition to all the other benefits they receive, gain marketing advantages. "As a Featured Merchant, my logo appears in search results," noted Kirk Holbert of Cosmic-King. Plus, in a search results list of third-party sellers, the Featured Merchants appear first, complete with the logo that makes them stand out. So, as you can see, as your business grows, opportunities for increased visibility also grow. You are at least thinking about that logo by now, aren't you?

Your Amazon Business on the Web

It may seem obvious, but simply by virtue of the fact that you're building your business on Amazon, you are also taking a place on the Web at large. Amazon exists within the context of the greater Web, and so does your business. You'll have plenty of opportunities to use the Web as a vast ocean of customers just waiting to float your way. To make them more likely to drift your way, we'll show you some bait that has been tested and confirmed by successful sellers. We'll also try to steer you clear from the offers you'll find that don't necessarily provide the return on investment you were hoping for.

Now, we can't get too boastful here. The field of Internet marketing is broad, complex, and changing all the time. We'd have to write another whole book in order to begin to do the subject justice, and somehow, we suspect our current editor would frown on our doing that when we've made the promise to finish this one. So, with that in mind, we'll give you a look at some of the things successful Amazon sellers are currently using. We'll offer you some resources for learning more, and we'll help you distinguish between which efforts are interesting and intriguing and which ones are actually likely to generate some revenue. Then you can decide how you want to divide your resources of time, money, and effort to pursue the options that seem right to you.

Write for the Web

You already know a good deal about the items you sell. You also know more about operating an e-commerce business than most people do, and you're learning more about that every day. You most likely have other hobbies, interests, life experiences, and points of view that others would be curious about. One of the best ways to get yourself out on the Web is to simply start writing articles. Just as you turned to reviews on Amazon to generate interest in your products, articles on the Web can attract people to your business. Make sure you comply with the rules for each site that accepts articles for publication in terms of including links and promoting your business, but at the very least you can include your business in the biographical information that appears at the bottom of almost all articles published. Here is a list of some of the best sites for publishing articles provided for us by Dale King of GuruKnowledge.org with some free advice thrown in too!

The 10 Best Article Directories

From GuruKnowledge.org

Writing articles is quickly becoming the most popular way to drive targeted traffic to your website. The reason I like article marketing so much is because it's free, and also because articles are viral. In other words, if you write articles and allow them to be freely published, your articles become viral, meaning your articles can actually spread like a virus and have the potential to be viewed by thousands of Internet users.

Also, search engines love articles. And if you write lots of good, quality articles, you can expect to get linked to by many high-profile websites, thereby increasing your PR (Page Rank) and traffic as well. There's also another important byproduct of article marketing: Credibility. Other than receiving testimonials from well-known experts, writing articles is the quickest way to establish credibility online. And if you write good-quality content, not only will your articles get published regularly, they will also brand you as an expert in your field, which will instantly enhance your reputation and bottom line tremendously.

Don't know how to write? No problem. Hire an affordable ghostwriter over at http://elance.com. Just make sure you check their credentials carefully. After all, all writers are not created equal.

Now there are literally thousands of article directories on the Internet. Here are the 10 best, according to search engine results for Google PR and Alexa traffic rankings.

1. EzineArticles.com is a matching service between tens of thousands of expert authors and millions of readers & publishers looking for expert solutions to millions of problems. EzineArticles is owned by highly respected entrepreneur Chris Knight, and is arguably the king of article directories. EzineArticles has been around since 1999. (http://EzineArticles.com)

2. GoArticles.com is owned by Canadian publishing giant, Jayde Online, Inc., and has been around since 2000. (http://GoArticles.com)

3. WebProNews.com is an articles and newsletter database covering a variety of e-business topics, including SEO, SEM, Affiliate marketing, and e-business site design/development. WebProNews has been around since 2000. (http://WebProNews.com)

4. ArticleDashboard.com bills itself as "the premier source of free content for newsletters, ezines, and websites." The site also offers free syndication services for authors and publishers. ArticleDashboard has been around since 2005. (http://ArticleDashboard.com)

5. SearchWarp.com is one of my favorite article directories, because it feels more like a friendly community than an article directory. It's very colorful and vibrant. Another reason I like it so much is because it publishes the author's picture along with the articles. In fact, I liked the concept so much, I borrowed it when I started my own article directory. SearchWarp has been around since 2002. (http://SearchWarp.com)

6. Isnare.com is an outstanding article directory owned by Glenn Prialde of the Philippines. Isnare has been around since 2004. (http://Isnare.com)

7. Buzzle.com features its own directory, free e-mail, message boards, news, articles, and short stories online. Buzzle provides information on health, travel, science, technology, and lifestyles. Technically, Buzzle is an online news magazine. But you can submit articles to Buzzle once you pass its approval process. Buzzle has been around since 1999. (http://www.buzzle.com/authors/become-author.asp)

8. AmericanChronicle.com is another one of my favorite article directories. Actually, it's a family of 21 different article directories. Like Buzzle, it's technically an online news magazine. And also like Buzzle, you can still submit your articles, once you pass its approval process. AmericanChronicle has been around since 2004. (http://www.americanchronicle.com/notices/submit_info)

9. IdeaMarketers.com is a great article directory that will not only let you submit articles, [but also let you] build your own ezine as well. IdeaMarketers is owned by highly respected entrepreneur Marnie Pehrson. IdeaMarketers has been around since 1998. (http://Ideamarketers.com)

10. ArticleCity.com bills itself as "your one-stop source for free articles." Not only can you submit articles, but you can submit press releases as well. ArticleCity has been around since 1999. (http://ArticleCity.com)

One last thing: I get a lot of e-mails from people asking me if they should use software to autosubmit their articles to hundreds of directories at a time. In my opinion, you shouldn't. Here's why. New article directories come online every day, and many disappear as quickly as they arrive on the scene. As a result, you have to update your software on a regular basis. In addition, while quicker than manual submissions, it still takes time to set up the software and fill out all the forms for your articles. Also, many article directories do not accept or approve articles that are autosubmitted, and they have sophisticated detection methods in place to catch violators. For best results, manually submit your articles to the 10 best directories listed here, and you'll be just fine.

Reprinted with permission of Dale King, owner of GuruKnowledge.org.

Websites and Blogs

Having a website or blog was once thought highly advanced, but it really is no longer a big deal. Lots of people have them. Just try to find a new parent who doesn't have a place to share photos or, increasingly, videos of the bundle of joy. In time, you'll have a website that is e-commerce compatible so that you can actually sell products there, and we'll look at these more closely in Chapter 9. Maybe that will be through WebStores by Amazon, and maybe not, but before you reach that milestone, you can easily carve a corner of the Web to call you own. There you'll be able to market your business and generate interest among potential customers. As a marketing opportunity, you can't afford to delay taking this step for too long.

Once you have your own blog or website, you gain lots of marketing opportunities. "We talk about the books we are selling, with links back to that particular entry," said Dan of Alternating Reality. "We use our own blog, which has been effective at driving customers to our site. We discuss the cool things that you can find within our store and on Amazon in general."

You can install links directly to your product detail pages, you can buy Google AdWords to direct customers to your products (we'll look at this closely in Chapter 9), and you can use your site to increase the likelihood that you and your products will pop up in the search results anytime someone searches for a subject relevant to what you sell.

Suppose you sell camping equipment. You do that because you love camping, know lots about it, and have been at it for years. That's how you knew which products you'd like to include in your product line. Now, create a blog or a website devoted to camping. You're not going to strictly use this as a list of products you sell, because that turns people off. Instead add content about your favorite camping trips. Write reviews of the best National Parks you've visited. Provide lists of must-have emergency equipment. How about some recipes you've enjoyed? The 10 most annoying camping companions you've met along the way? Include funny photos of camping trips, and even disasters. You know what other campers would like to read about, because you're marketing here to your own kind. Reward the camping enthusiasts who stop by, and you'll get them dropping back in from time to time to see what you're up to. Now that you've got their attention, you can include links back to your Amazon products.

Use Amazon's Widgets

Amazon offers a variety of simple and dynamic tools that allow you to link Amazon products to your website or blog. The first step is to join the Amazon Associates program, if you haven't already done so. At the bottom of each Amazon page is a link to get you signed up. Then you can add all types of Amazon content to your site, from product detail pages, to the widgets we're currently addressing. Plus, these handy little tools are free, and when someone clicks from your website to Amazon to buy the product you feature, you'll get a little kickback from Amazon for the referral. You can go to widgets.amazon.com for a complete list of what's currently available. When we last checked, you had 19 offerings from which to choose, ranging from slideshows to unbox stores, to Kindle Chiclet. We've used a slideshow to feature our books for years. You'll find our working example at bradanddeb.com. Widgets are free, easy, and fun to create. Why not give a few a try to see which works best for you and your audience?

Search Engine Optimization (SEO)

It won't do you very much good to create lots of great and interesting content for your website or blog if no one can find it. The Web is so vast—and growing larger every day—that, left to its own, your little corner is likely to be overlooked in the crowd. Once you have your content up on your blog or website, you'll want to be sure you're doing everything you can to encourage potential shoppers to come by and see what you have to offer. By now you've surely noticed that throughout the book we have discussed how important it is to have your products show up when people search for those items through search engines like Google and Yahoo! Unfortunately, you have a lot of competition on the search results pages that appear.

To make sure your products are near the top you need to do some *search engine optimization,* or SEO.

Wikipedia defines SEO as "the process of improving the volume and quality of traffic to a website from search engines via 'natural' ('organic' or 'algorithmic') search results for targeted keywords." It goes on to say that "usually, the earlier a site is presented in the search results or the higher it 'ranks,' the more searchers will visit that site. SEO can also target different kinds of search, including image search, local search, and industry-specific vertical search engines."

From there, the definition quickly devolves into a discussion of search algorithms and the like. While SEO is beyond this book's scope, there are lots of genuine experts out there. Many of them write blogs. We asked the folks at OrangeSoda.com, a prominent SEO company, which blogs they read. Their list follows. The comments following some of the blog listings are also from OrangeSoda.com:

OrangeSoda.com's Favorite Blogs

These are some of the best blogs to follow.

General SEO/Search News

- Searchengineland.com—Only a few years old, but possibly the strongest search news source
- Seobook.com
- Seomoz.org—Trendy, but worthwhile.
- Searchenginejournal.com—Oldie, but goodie
- Searchengineguide.com—Oldie, but goodie
- Bruceclay.com/blog—Very up-to-date. Real-time blogging during major search conferences

Famous Googlers

- Mattcutts.com/blog—Lead spam engineer
- Vanessafoxnude.com (no longer with Google)—No nude pictures, just good insight into search

Local SEO/Small Business SEO

- Localseoguide.com
- Blog.kelseygroup.com
- Gesterling.wordpress.com
- Blumenthals.com/blog

List of top search-related blogs

http://www.toprankblog.com/search-marketing-blogs/

Web 2.0: Destiny or Distraction?

Web 2.0 is one of those terms that lots of people use, but many of us aren't too sure exactly what it means. Web 2.0 makes you feel like you've got to adapt to some new version of the Web. That can be intimidating, and besides, technological advances are hardly news. Web 2.0 goes beyond mere technological advance—as a matter of fact, the technology that allows Web 2.0 behavior has been around a long time. You're using it to have your website or blog.

The phenomenon behind Web 2.0 has more to do with generational advances than technological. The people who have now lived for many years on the Web are finding lots of ways to make that Web their own. They're bringing creativity, self-expression, and self-determination to the Internet, and of course that changes everything. You just saw how simple it is to bring your own blog to the Web, about any subject that you happen to find interesting. Welcome to the next generation of the Web!

Here people have created communities populated by other people who share common interests or goals. Web 2.0 generally refers to websites that promote sharing and connecting with other members of the Internet community at large, or subsets of that community. Through blogs, wikis, social networks, and video sharing, people are sharing their life experiences like never before. Your customers, from now into the future, are likely to be the people who use this new generation of the Web in the same way you've always turned on your car radio in the morning.

If you can reach them through Web 2.0 activities—really learn to operate in the new world that is Web 2.0—you're likely to have customers for a long time to come. We'll get specific about how you can venture into Web 2.0 to boost your sales and expand your market. There are plenty of opportunities for you to explore. But, we're going one step further with this. We're going to guide you toward the most cost-effective and direct ways to get started. You can spend an incredible amount of time learning about, understanding, developing strategies, and creating content for this new venture. We're here to tap you on the shoulder and remind you to get back to selling your products. Web 2.0 is evolving, and you're surely going to be operating there into the future, but let's get our feet wet realistically with projects that can help you start building sales right now. That way, we can keep Web 2.0 your destiny rather than letting it turn into a distraction.

Social Networking Sites

As the name suggests, websites that bring people together for social sharing of interests, events, videos, and friends are called *social networking sites*. By now, we all know of MySpace and Facebook, to name just two. It was once the domain of the high school and college kids, but that was then. As of the fall 2006, ComScore Networks, a global leader in measuring the digital age, reported that 68 percent of MySpace users were over 35. Many of these are your potential customers.

Let's consider some guidelines as we begin. First of all, it's important for you to understand the demographics of each social network you plan to occupy. MySpace has grown older. Facebook, although maturing all the time, is still heavily populated with college kids. Other sites such as Friendster have yet other demographic expectations. Understand these before you try to create a marketing campaign that will appeal to the site. Also, avoid crass commercialization. Sure, you want to sell your products, but enter these communities planning to share information and experience, too. Social networking sites have brought about "social shopping," defined as buying things based on recommendations from trusted sources. You'll want to become one of those right away. Once you do, social networking can take you far through its strongest advantage—word-of-mouth marketing. The good word spreads through social networking sites almost as fast as the bad ones do!

We're going to give you a head start with MySpace and Facebook. By the time we're through with those, you'll have a lot of ideas about what you might want to try, and a much clearer understanding of how to go about fitting these tools into your business toolbox.

MySpace (http://www.myspace.com)

Of the many social networking sites, MySpace may be the best known. It's certainly quite popular (55 million people visited it in January 2008, according to Nielsen Online). MySpace users can create their own personalized MySpace profile, add videos, blogs, pictures, art—you name it—all with the purpose of communicating to their MySpace friends. (Friends are people who are part of your

MySpace community, who share information, and so on, with one another.) To find out if there was a way to create a MySpace profile, and then use it to lead people to your Amazon store or listings, we spoke with Charise Richards. Known on various sites as one_chic_lady or mrpayne2, Charise is one of MySpace's biggest boosters. Not only does she have several MySpace sites of her own, but she's also creating them for other people. She loves MySpace so much that she creates sites for fun, not money, although at least one grateful customer PayPals her some funds once in a while.

At first, most MySpace profiles may seem like a jumble of art, pictures, words, and even sounds. That's because many are just that. But there are ways to include links and other things to turn visitors to your profile into customers. (Plus, don't forget the people who get to your profile as it shows up in a Google search, for example.) Figure 7-6 shows part of Charise's MySpace profile at http://www .myspace.com/one_chic_boutique. The Amazon logo on her page is as clear as a bell. Click on it, and you're whisked away to Charise's Amazon store.

Although many of the products Charise sells through her Amazon store are listed on her site, they are not hyperlinked. What good are they, then? They help make it so Charise's MySpace site appears when people search Google, and other search engines, for the products she carries. Once they get to her MySpace profile, the hope is that they will go to her Amazon store, too. To make her site more interesting to people who buy the unusual products she carries, she'll blog about some of them on her profile page. Oilily Voyage Diaper Tote Saddle Bags is one example.

MySpace doesn't seem to mind the Amazon link, as Charise hasn't exactly turned her MySpace page into an e-commerce site. There's still plenty there of interest for the average browser. Plus, MySpace can add its own advertisements from Google AdWords to her page, which generates money for them.

If we take a look at a page that Charise has created for someone

Figure 7-6. Charise Richards's MySpace site is one way she advertises her Amazon business.

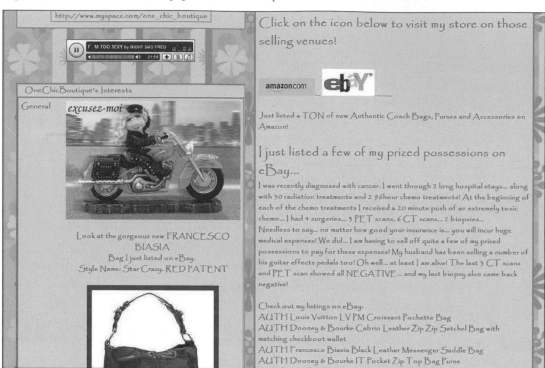

else, we get a better feel for some other ways to "monetize" your MySpace site. Figure 7-7 shows a site she designed for Robert Keeley, who sells products for guitarists. Charise is the behind-the-scenes person for this site, providing updates and sometimes even communicating with Robert's many MySpace friends (4,183 at last count). Robert's site includes video clips you can download (of interest to guitar students and experts alike) and pictures of his exhibits at various trade shows. These items help paint a picture of him as a true professional. There are many links on the site that will take you to Robert's WebStore, where you can buy some of the items pictured. His profile is at http://www.myspace.com/keeleyelectronics.

Figure 7-7. Robert Keeley's MySpace page helps him sell guitars.

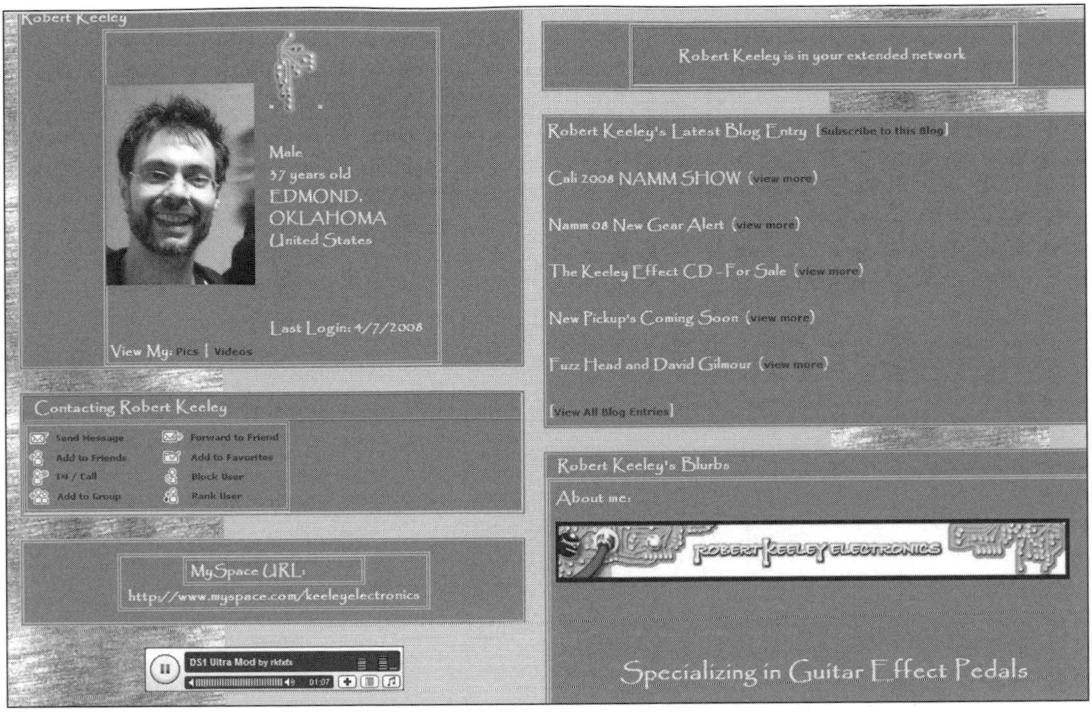

Robert Keeley

Male
37 years old
EDMOND,
OKLAHOMA
United States

Last Login: 4/7/2008

View My: Pics | Videos

Contacting Robert Keeley

Send Message   Forward to Friend
Add to Friends   Add to Favorites
IM / Call   Block User
Add to Group   Rank User

MySpace URL:
http://www.myspace.com/keeleyelectronics

DS1 Ultra Mod by rktefx   01:07

Robert Keeley is in your extended network

Robert Keeley's Latest Blog Entry [Subscribe to this Blog]

Cali 2008 NAMM SHOW (view more)

Namm 08 New Gear Alert (view more)

The Keeley Effect CD - For Sale (view more)

New Pickup's Coming Soon (view more)

Fuzz Head and David Gilmour (view more)

[View All Blog Entries]

Robert Keeley's Blurbs

About me:

ROBERT KEELEY ELECTRONICS

Specializing in Guitar Effect Pedals

How Charise Got Started on MySpace

It wasn't that long ago that Charise didn't know any more about MySpace than my mother does. To learn, she began by looking around the site, of course. But to start designing her own site she went to a MySpace layout site. There are thousands of these, and you can get to them by Googling those search terms. Charise learned how other people created MySpace sites and then did her own coding to create a unique background and font that's just her own. How she created the background is an interesting story in its own. She found the wallpaper at a site owned by a wallpaper company (real world wallpaper, not computer wallpaper). She saved an image she liked, and the rest was easy.

Although it's difficult to track just how many dollars a MySpace site will generate for you, eBay and Amazon's WebStores data can show you where your visitors come from. People using that data say that having a MySpace definitely generates traffic. So should you have a MySpace page? Of course: They're free, and if your competitors don't already have one, they're probably thinking about it.

Facebook (http//www.facebook.com)

Mark Zukerberg, founder and CEO of Facebook, began the site in February 2004 as a private place for fellow Harvard students to connect online. By the end of that short month, more than half of Harvard's student body was registered. By the end of that academic year, Zukerberg and his business partner Dustin Moskovitz had moved to Palo Alto, California, and the rest of the story is now part of Internet folklore. Today, Facebook claims more than 67 million active users, more than half of whom are not in college. That user base expanded naturally from Harvard students to college students in general, to high school students, and finally, to anyone over the age of 13 with a registered e-mail address.

According to the company, Facebook includes over 55,000 regional, work-related, collegiate, and high school networks. The fastest-growing demographic reported is among those users over the age of 25. So, a Facebook presence is definitely a good idea if your products are likely to appeal to a younger audience. At the time of this writing, the sellers we spoke with were more likely to have a presence on MySpace than Facebook. Of course, with the rate of change in the world of Web 2.0, by the time you read this, that may have changed.

Video on the Web

The arrival of high-speed Internet access has turned the computer into a video viewing device, and it seems that's just what we've all been waiting for. Today, you can hardly log on to to a website without being offered the opportunity to view a video moment. Whether you're catching a snippet of Oprah's latest celebrity interview or watching a hilarious moment captured by an amateur, you've literally got millions of videos available to you through simple searches. Plus, these videos travel across the Web fast through word-of-mouth marketing. Who among us doesn't have at least one relative who insists on sending clever little clips to everyone in the address book several times a week?

But video, well placed and planned, can be a powerful tool for spotlighting your products. Some items lend themselves more naturally to benefiting from a video presentation—say, products that move or unfold. But nearly anything can have a video application. Think about your product line to determine which items would be compelling. Do you sell something that requires some assembly? Do you feature a product you could show being used and enjoyed? Since you know your products better than anyone, you're bound to come up with a clever way to feature them in video.

As of this writing, there are many videos online. As a matter of fact, search engines like Google and Yahoo! will let you confine your search terms to nothing but video. But, when you think Web video, we must admit only one word comes quickly to mind. That word is YouTube.

YouTube

It's easy to think of YouTube as an entertainment site rather than a place where real business can happen. But if you were to think that way, you'd be wrong. While few sellers right now are using YouTube as their primary marketing vehicle, more and more are posting videos to the site and giving it a try. When you consider these statistics from ComScore, one of the leading Internet market research companies, the argument for YouTube gets even easier to make:

- In January 2008, YouTube received more than 9.8 *billion* video views.

- In the United States, 139 million or so Internet users spent more than 3 hours watching video online that month.

- Again in the United States, more than 75 percent of all Internet users have viewed video.

The question remains, though: Is video a tool you as an online merchant should look into? After speaking with online sellers, and professionals who make their livings creating videos for sellers, we believe the answer is a qualified yes. Video should be part of your marketing tool chest—if it is done right. Once you have your video up on YouTube, not only will you have access to a vast audience, but also you'll gather reviews and comments from that video that are free market research about your customer base. Plus, done right, you're video is likely to show up all over the place as all those relatives of ours make it a part of their routine e-mail correspondence!

What Works in Video

A representative from The TalkMarket (www.talkmarket.com), a company that helps online merchants create polished videos (their slogan is "Show, Tell, Sell"), recently spoke at an Internet Merchants Association (IMA) meeting we attended. The company will work with you to create a polished video, with its payment being 5 percent of any sales attributable to the video. Right now, the completed video must be posted to its site, but the company, which actually used the IMA show to launch, was evaluating letting customers post their finished videos elsewhere.

Here are some of the guidelines the company gave for what constitutes a "good" video:

- You won't have a TV production crew at your disposal. Most likely, you'll shoot your video with a single camera, while professionals use three cameras. You can simulate a multicamera effect by shooting the speaker sitting in one position, then having the speaker move and shooting him again in the new position.

- Music is important—a video that doesn't have it sounds empty. Music can add an emotional lift, and it frees the speaker from talking during the entire video. You should realize, however, that you can only legally use music that's been designated as being in the public domain.

- Go for those "across the fence" sales, which are another way of saying to pretend you're speaking directly to your customer, as one neighbor might speak to another. This means your video does not have to be scripted. Share your passion for the product but remember that people don't like to sit through commercials.

Speaking of commercials, we don't want this section of the book to be one for The TalkMarket, so be sure to check out others like TurnHere (www.turnhere.com/).

Of course, YouTube isn't your only alternative. Once you have a completed video, you can post (embed) it on your website. And while Amazon currently prohibits sellers from posting videos of their own products, reviewers can submit videos for any products they'd like. The company advises that posting videos makes the most sense for products that are "innovative," or with complex features. For more information, send an e-mail to mediatech-submit@amazon.com.

Your Marketing To-Do List

Now that we've explored many different ways for you to spread the word about your business and your products, let's put some perspective on where you should begin. Without a roadmap, you are likely to scatter your marketing efforts and spread yourself and your marketing budget thin without gaining the benefits you were hoping to achieve. Because of the learning curve and expense, both of which are lessening all the time, video isn't the first or even second marketing tool you should invest in.

Your first marketing efforts should focus on Amazon's offerings. Creating Listmania lists, soliciting product reviews, and creating great product descriptions all come before creating a video for your business. "Since Amazon buys search engine ads for my products on Amazon, customers are brought to both my Amazon listings and my WebStore through Amazon's own marketing," notes Kathy of Element Jewelry & Accessories. "In fact, if you search for 'Element Jewelry' on Google, you'll not only see links to my WebStores, you'll also see ads for my products in the Google-sponsored Results section that will direct customers to my listings on Amazon." It should be clear that building your listings on Amazon is more cost-effective as you begin than spending a few days creating a video.

Once you've explored all your options for promoting your products through Amazon, your next step would be to build your own website or create your own blog. Then you'll want to make sure you apply the rules of SEO to increase your traffic. Building a MySpace or Facebook presence is simple enough, so that's a reasonable next step. Only after you have all those things in place should you consider rewarding yourself by creating video. It's quite easy to get so caught up in promotion that you forget your main job. According to Steve Grossberg, president of the IMA, eBay PowerSeller, and Amazon success story, "I see my job as buying and selling product." Steve sells video games, and his philosophy must be working. The day we spoke, he was planning to ship 500 to 600 orders that evening. All told, he shipped 150,000 orders last year!

Looking Ahead

It may be some time into the future before you're ready to match Steve's shipping operations, but everyone has to start someplace. As you think about your next marketing moves, we'll turn our attention to shipping your items. Successful shipping policies and practices are vital to the survival of your business, not to mention its success. Chapter 8 will help you establish some best practices, and someday you may just stand toe-to-toe with Steve.

An Amazon Success Story

We started this chapter with an image of the logo Dan Morrill created when he started his online bookstore, Alternating Reality. We've mentioned him more than a few times throughout this book, because he's worked hard, done his research, and set his course for success. Although he hadn't been selling on Amazon for very long, when we spoke, he'd been working in Internet marketing for years and immersing himself in all things science fiction for far longer—more than 35 years, as a matter of fact. When he decided to open his online bookstore he chose Amazon as the platform he'd use.

He also researched other online options for booksellers, and considered each carefully. He was finding out how difficult it would be to sell on each venue. He explored Alibris, Biblio, eBay, and Amazon. "Amazon had the lowest cost of entry," Dan told us. After researching for about three months, he bought his first inventory and opened his doors. "I have not been sorry," he said.

Dan said that when he first started selling, he found help and support easily on Amazon. "The Amazon success and sellers boards have been great," he noted. He used the Amazon boards to establish his best practices and eliminate trouble right from the start. He also made sure to study his competition. "When we were doing our customer research, the comments the customers left on our competition were the most valuable," Dan said. "We spent days reading what ticked customers off, and came up with a top five list of things never to do with our store."

You'll find Dan's blog and website at www.alternatingreality.com. It's a fully functional, beautifully designed site full of book reviews, news, and even free downloadable books. Dan also has a forum feature so visitors can exchange thoughts about their interests, making the whole experience interactive. Of course, widgets take you right to the Amazon page for every book listed or discussed. There's plenty of great content to keep science fiction and fantasy enthusiasts checking back in, and it couldn't be easier to make a purchase when you do.

Of course, it wasn't enough just to create and maintain a great website. Dan also used his SEO experience from years of working in Internet marketing to spread the word about the site across the Web. "I have done a lot of SEO to make sure that it gets customers," he said of the site. "We still have a long way to go but have made excellent first steps."

What advice would Dan offer other sellers who are just starting out? "Don't expect to sell out day one," he noted. Realistic expectations are important, of course, and those combined with hard work have brought Dan a professional, highly functional, and rapidly growing business selling the things he loves best. It sounds like a success story to us!

CHAPTER 8

Shipping: The Workhorse of Your Operation

Sold, ship now. Your Amazon sale is official! This is the message sellers get when they've made an Amazon sale. Receiving it often, of course, is your goal. Although we've sold many things online, we still get a tickle when this e-mail message pops up. Even the big sellers admit it's a thrill. Yet, in many respects, the part of the transaction that happens *after* you get this message is likely to be far from your favorite part of the job.

Your shipping operation will make your business possible. But it's also mundane and relentless. It's easy to view it as much more like a chore than the other parts of your operation. Admit it. You chose your product line based on your interests and tastes. That makes the research you do for sourcing your products interesting and exciting, even if it can be laborious and frustrating. Your marketing efforts give you the chance to show off your creative side. Your customer service tasks connect you with the people you've come to the market to serve. But, your shipping just plugs along day after day without let-up or relief. (At least that's what you're hoping for!) So, in many ways the shipping part of your business is like the horse you'd have used to plow your fields if you'd been a farmer a hundred years ago. The horse needs to be reliable and sturdy, able to manage heavy loads, but not necessarily beautiful. It's your job to keep it healthy and strong so you can keep working.

Shipping is the one concrete and tangible way you can touch your customer. Getting this part of the transaction right is imperative. Customers make purchasing decisions based on a good-faith estimate of what they expect to receive. If an item is delivered quickly, at a fair price, and in a package that's been carefully and professionally wrapped, isn't the customer likely to feel pleased before the box is even opened?

The workhorse is the most valuable unsung piece of farm equipment. Likewise, unsung as it may be, a successful shipping operation is at the core of your business's infrastructure. Not only is it your most direct link to your customers, but how efficient and cost-effective this department is will directly impact the amount of money you can earn and the rate at which your business will grow. Speaking of which, your shipping operation will probably be the first place you'll add employees, expanding you from business owner to employer. Let's take a look at some ways to tend, train, and feed the workhorse your shipping department is bound to become.

Tend That Workhorse

Your shipping department will require care and maintenance to ensure that it's reliable. You'll have to house it, supply it, and keep it neat and orderly. Already, this is sounding like the care of a living thing, isn't it? Plus, like a living thing, it will need to grow. You have to design your shipping operation with an eye on how you will expand, because you will, if all goes well. Let's look at some of the issues you'll need to address as you build your operation.

Where Will You Work?

Just as a farmer will always need a barn to keep his horse, you'll need a place to do your shipping. It's not good enough to gather some shipping supplies, stick them in the corner of the dining room, and call it the shipping department. You might start out just fine that way, but trust us, it's not a long-term solution. Plus, if your family operates anything at all like ours, every time you go to complete your orders, you'll need to search for the scissors someone needed for homework or the tape someone filched for wrapping a present. You'll spend time organizing your operation that you should spend shipping your orders. So, whether you select a spare room, a corner of the basement, or part of your office, make your shipping area segregated from your living space, and enforce some rules to make sure your supplies are always at hand.

Your shipping operation should include a sturdy table and storage areas for all your supplies. You can start out by prepping your orders on the floor, but your back won't agree for long. Make sure you organize everything within your reach, and, of course, consider your dominant hand. If you can set up this operation within the reach of your inventory storage area, that's all the better. We've actually listened to conversations among large sellers who discussed the increased efficiencies that came from moving their work table three feet away from their shelves rather than five feet away. They were measuring their shipping efficiencies in terms of steps and turns of their bodies.

To complicate the process, you'll factor in expansion. Can you look at your plan and see where you'll add work space and storage space as needed? If not, keep thinking. The day may come when you actually have to move the whole operation to gain more space, but before then, you want to be able to expand without disrupting your process too much. The least amount of disruption possible is your goal. Every hour you spend shipping is an hour you can't spend sourcing and listing, so build efficiencies into your operation from the very start. (Fair warning: You're very likely to hear this theme repeated at least a few times before you get to Chapter 9!)

Use High-Quality Shipping Supplies

In the early days of online shopping, individual sellers could get away with all kinds of innovative and creative shipping supplies. Recycling and reusing supplies is still the order of the day on other online shopping venues, and we've recommended it ourselves. But, that's not going to work for selling on Amazon. Your Amazon customer is accustomed to receiving a professionally packed, clean, and secure package. You will be held to the same standard. "Amazon has caused us to step up the game in the shipping department," says Gary Richardson of Goggles and Glasses. "There is zero room for mistakes. Mistakes are fatal and show up as red marks labeled 1/5, 2/5, or 3/5 on your feedback rating." Gary goes so far as to suggest that you "vacuum and dust your shipping area often. Be careful with tape, as it attracts hair and dust, which usually ends up in a very visible spot on the exterior of your package. That does not impress customers!"

"Shipping materials for Amazon customers, in my opinion, should be clean and new," agrees Tricia Records of Read_Rover_Books. Your customers wouldn't have made the purchase if they didn't really want your products, and yet, customers take a leap of faith to make the purchase with you. Make sure you impress them from the instant they receive your package. You want them to take one look and breathe a sigh of relief. "Make the receipt of your products an enjoyable event, realizing that the buyer has anticipated its arrival (sometimes with trepidation if they've had a negative buying experience before with someone else)," notes Tricia.

So, how are you going to budget and plan for these new supplies?

A trip to your local office supply store will show you just how quickly some of the money you'd hope to put toward product sourcing will have go for shipping supplies. Not to worry. We have plenty of good cost-saving advice for you. Start by weighing the economics of going with the free Priority Mail supplies from the USPS. "Well over 95 percent of my stuff goes into Priority boxes," says Chris Schlieter of timezone. "They're sturdier, and they get recognized as Priority. They get better than first-class treatment at the Post Office," Chris says, "85 percent of your domestic continental shipments get to their destination within three days," using Priority Mail.

Set Watches to the Customers' Time Zone

This was a tip Chris used for his eBay business, and he's found that it's carried over well to Amazon. As he prepares his watches for shipping, he sets them to the buyers' time zone. He feels this helps minimize his return rate, "since the buyer can enjoy his/her new watch immediately upon receipt." Now that's smart marketing.

You'd Better Shop Around

"Purchase your supplies from Uline.com (Figure 8-1), a company that bills itself as the shipping supply specialists," recommends Gary of Goggles and Glasses. "They sell everything you might need, from cushioned envelopes to bubble wrap to scales." Other sellers find their own sources of inexpensive supplies, "I buy from Costco," says Dan Morrill of Alternating Reality. "Everything you need is at

Costco, and the prices per unit are much better. I can get bubble envelopes and paper bags for about $0.40 each on the envelope and less than $0.01 on the paper bag. If I go anywhere else, bubble envelopes can come in as much as $3.00 each!" Other alternatives might include shopping around for local cardboard manufacturers. If you can buy locally, you may be able to negotiate, and you can also avoid shipping charges for your shipping supplies. Finally, consider buying only several times a year, but in bulk. Bulk shopping can really save money, as long as you have a clean and dry place to store your supplies.

Hold the Plastic

Many online merchants use a credit card to order supplies. It simplifies record keeping and adds a bit of buyer protection. In this case, however, it may be wise to deviate from that practice and establish a commercial line of credit (LOC). Gary Richardson notes that Uline is one of the easiest places to establish commercial credit lines. He advises readers to make their first purchases with a credit card, and then open a *house account*. Next, bill your second order to that house account. Uline will send a bill that you have 30 days to pay. "Pay this ASAP," Gary says, and they will then report your account as paid on time to Dun & Bradstreet (D&B), which will establish a LOC in your D&B credit file."

Don't Forget That Digital Scale

It's easy enough to recognize that you'll need boxes, padded envelopes, tape, labels, and such, but don't forget to include a digital postal scale on your list of shipping supplies. Your shipping costs will be based on weight, and even a few ounces in either direction will make a difference in what you'll spend to send your packages. (We

Figure 8-1. Uline is one of the largest suppliers of packing materials to small- and medium-size businesses.

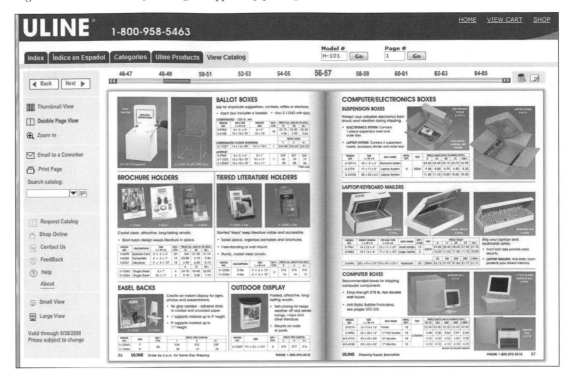

contacted Mark Taylor, chief logistics officer of RedRoller.com, a company that supports online sellers in their quest for answers on all things shipping. He has much more to say on this soon.) Don't guess. Get a digital scale, so that you are precisely measuring the weight of your total package. Then you'll know exactly how to calculate your sale price to keep you from using some of your profits to cover your shipping.

Hitch That Horse to a Plow

Now it's time to make all your planning and tending pay off as you get your shipping workhorse hitched to the plow and ready to work. "The same things you want from a company when you order something are the things every customer wants," says Asad Bangash of Beachcombers! "Speed, shipping notification, accuracy, and safe packaging of the products." You've got your work cut out for you. To achieve your goals, you'll need to consider your shipping charges, your choice of carriers, and your communication with your customers. Let's start with that last one. It may not be as concrete or obvious as the first two, but it's at least as important.

Keep in Touch

When it comes to shipping, "it's the basics that apply," says Asad. As an Amazon merchant keeping your customer well informed, this is one of the most important of the basics. As a matter of fact, it is so basic that Amazon built this kind of messaging into its Seller Central program to help sellers automatically keep in touch. Whether you use Seller Central or not you're still expected to keep your customers informed throughout the shipping process. You learned in Chapter 6 that quick e-mail response is vital to good customer service, and that includes the service you provide when shipping your products.

Chris Schlieter of timezone notifies his customers not only when he receives their orders, but also when he expects to ship the order. Then, when the item is actually shipped, he sends along the tracking number. If you follow suit, you'll actually reduce your e-mail load. As long as you're letting your customers know every step of the way, you lessen the number of questions you get about the order. So, keeping in touch with the ones who buy from you actually increases your efficiencies.

Communicate Your Policies

By now, you've had many opportunities to clearly state your shipping policies, but as long as you're sending e-mail along anyway, here's another chance for you to make everything clear. Don't forget to include your return policies. When you're sending e-mail along to inform customers of their purchase's arrival, you've got their attention. Include the information in the form e-mail you create, and you'll at least have something to refer to if your policies are tested or questioned. It's also a good idea to include return policy information within the package itself, just as Amazon does. Your customer will appreciate it.

Determine Shipping Charges

For those of you who will sell strictly on the Amazon Marketplace, there's little to consider in establishing your shipping charges. As you saw in Chapter 2, Amazon itself does that for you, and your challenge is to make the shipping credit Amazon gives you work. You'll do that largely by purchasing your shipping supplies carefully, and setting your selling price to give yourself a little buffer on shipping. If you end up having to spend more to ship your item than Amazon has credited to you, the difference comes directly from your profits. There is no way for you to increase the cost to your customer. When you ship internationally, you will be responsible for complying with all domestic and foreign tax laws and you will be subject to all foreign tax obligations that apply to sellers.

Use Seller Central to Set Default Shipping Methods

You can set your shipping settings by clicking on the *Settings* tab through Seller Central. Customers see the settings you've set when they go to your *My Info and Policies* pages (Figure 8-2). Seller Central sets your default settings, which are based on the areas you ship to, the delivery options you offer, and price (Figure 8-3). That's probably good enough. But if you choose to change any settings go through the *Settings* tab. There may be times when you want to override your settings, according to Amazon, and choose not to ship that television to Canada without exploring all of your options.

Figure 8-2. The My Info and Policies *page is where your settings appear.*

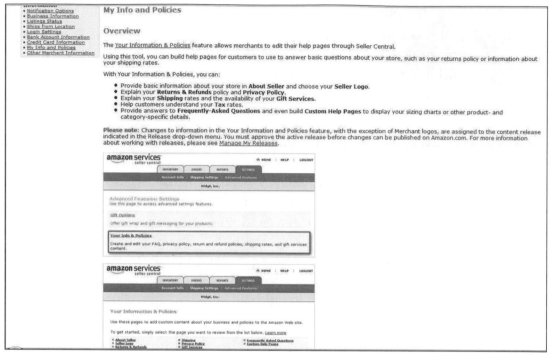

Offer Expedited Shipping

One way to help offset your shipping expenses is to offer expedited shipping. "It's amazing how many people will pay extra to get their items right away," says Gary of Goggles and Glasses. He shared with us the story of a buyer who ordered a pair of designer sunglasses for $19.95, and then paid $23.00 for expedited shipping! Obviously it didn't cost Gary $23.00 to overnight the glasses, so he made a bit of extra money on the deal. "I'm thinking if we could teleport items we could charge more," Gary laughed. "We live in an age of instant gratification," agreed Kathy of Element Jewelry & Accessories. "The sooner you can deliver a product to a customer, the better." To be fair, expedited orders may not earn as much extra money as you first thought, because they have to take precedence over everything else.

Figure 8-3. These are the default Seller Central settings.

Standard Shipping Rates	Rate Components	Service Levels			
		Standard	Expedited	Two-Day	One-Day
Continental US Street	ETA	3 - 5 business days	1 - 3 business days	2 business days	24 hours
	per Weight (lbs)	$0.50	---	---	---
	per Shipment	$4.49	---	---	---
Continental US PO Box	ETA	3 - 7 business days	1 - 3 business days	---	---
	per Weight (lbs)	$0.50	---	---	---
	per Shipment	$4.49	---	---	---
APO/FPO Street	ETA	3 - 7 business days	1 - 3 business days	---	---
	per Weight (lbs)	$0.50	---	---	---
	per Shipment	$4.49	---	---	---
Alaska and Hawaii Street	ETA	3 - 7 business days	1 - 3 business days	---	---
	per Weight (lbs)	$0.50	---	---	---
	per Shipment	$4.49	---	---	---
Alaska and Hawaii PO Box	ETA	3 - 7 business days	1 - 3 business days	---	---
	per Weight (lbs)	$0.50	---	---	---
	per Shipment	$4.49	---	---	---
US Protectorates Street	ETA	4 - 8 business days	2 - 4 business days	---	---
	per Weight (lbs)	$0.50	---	---	---
	per Shipment	$4.49	---	---	---

TIP *Read This Blog!*

The Amazon discussion boards are full of questions about shipping practices. You're likely to find people there who are working to solve many of the same problems you're facing too. But, beyond Amazon, you'll find a wealth of information at http://shippingcoach.wordpress .com/, shown in Figure 8-4. Mark A. Taylor runs a company that consults on such matters with the likes of Ford Motor Company and Michelin Tire. He uses this blog to help small businesses and online sellers negotiate the ins and outs of shipping efficiently and cost effectively.

Figure 8-4. Mark A. Taylor's shipping blog can really help you save on your shipping expenses.

Choose Your Carrier Wisely

It may seem that the choices are clear here, and in a way they are. You go to the USPS or use UPS for shipping. Yet, as Eric Lau of Visiondecor points out: "all shipping vendors are not equal." Eric, as you may remember, sells furniture and home accessories. His shipping needs are likely to be more extreme than those of the average seller. "Depending on the product you ship," he explained, "each shipping vendor has different rates/discounts/processing methods that benefit specific metrics per industry. For example, we need carriers that can effectively ship large bulky items, and some of them just cost too much or aren't good at doing it." So, as you can see, what you ship will help you decide which carrier to use and may push you away from the most common choices.

Other things to consider may simply relate to geography. If you have a UPS drop-off site in your closest shopping center, it may pay to ship there, rather than the post office across town. Other sellers might find the economics work in favor of FedEx or DHL, depending on the size, shape, and weight of their items, the delivery services each company offers, and the geography of their particular locations.

Compare USPS to UPS

For the most part, it's safe to assume that the bulk of your shipping will go through either USPS or UPS. Let's look at the advantages and disadvantages of each. On the one hand, USPS is simple and reliable, and you can also get free shipping supplies if you use Priority or Express Mail. For the most part, your charges through USPS will be less than through UPS. On the other hand, UPS gives you a higher weight limit than the USPS; 150 pounds rather than 75 pounds. Also, factored into the higher cost is free delivery confirmation and insurance coverage of up to $100. As you can see, it's very difficult to make a blanket statement that one or the other service is always best for all purposes. You will, ultimately, be in the best position to assess each service and decide for yourself which one is best for you.

Five Shipping Tips for Amazon Sellers

Mark A. Taylor, DLP, is the chief logistics officer of RedRoller and is president of TAY-LOR Systems Engineering Corporation. With three decades of experience, he has met with thousands of parcel shippers. He has been featured as an industry expert on ABC News and in the *New York Times* and is the author of *Computerized Shipping Systems: Increasing Profit & Productivity Through Technology*. His blog at http://shippingcoach.wordpress.com provides tips and advice for shippers.

Taylor has been named a Distinguished Logistics Professional (DLP) by the American Society of Transportation & Logistics in recognition of the contributions he has made to the field of logistics during his 30-year career and can be contacted at (734) 420-7447 or Mark@RedRoller.com.

He offers these shipping tips:

> Most Amazon sellers make mistakes when shipping packages. When you sell an item on Amazon's Marketplace, you receive a fixed amount as a shipping credit to help cover shipping costs, so it is important to know your shipping costs or you could lose money. If you ship smart, you can make a profit. The following tips can help you save on shipping and fulfill your customer's expectations.

Taylor's Tip #1: "Compare rates and services among multiple carriers."

> Most Amazon sellers assume that Media Mail, available from the United States Postal Service (USPS), is the least costly method of shipping and don't even bother to compare rates. This is a mistake. If you have a package that weighs less than 8 ounces, then you should consider First-Class Mail. The USPS has a special rate for packages weighing less than 13 ounces, and for lighter-weight packages it is cheaper than Media Mail! First-Class mail is delivered in three days or less, so your

customers should be delighted. You can also add delivery confirmation.

If you choose to offer expedited shipping for your buyers, Amazon tells your buyers that they should expect to receive their order within two to six business days after shipment. For one-pound packages, Priority Mail is generally the least expensive, but not always. The retail cost (2008) is $4.80. If you are shipping to a commercial location that is in a nearby destination (zone 2), the cost with another carrier, such as UPS, FedEx, or DHL could be less—$4.46 the day I'm writing this. If your package is two pounds, the disparity can be even greater—75 percent more!

The cost to ship a package depends on over 30 factors, including the distance, content, weight, and whether or not you're shipping to a residential or commercial destination. No carrier or service is the best for every variable. The only way to ensure you are getting the lowest cost is to compare rates and services among different carriers.

Amazon expects the seller to ship the product within two days of receiving the order and sets an expectation for the buyer to receive the order within 4 to 14 business days for "Standard" delivery.

According to the USPS, the delivery standard for Media Mail is 2 to 9 days, so shippers who process their order within the two days of receipt should have no problems with their buyers. Media Mail is an inexpensive way to ship, but there are some caveats.

Here are two things shippers should know about Media Mail:

1. Media Mail is only for books, film, manuscripts, sound recordings, videotapes, and computer media (such as CDs, DVDs, and diskettes).
2. Media Mail cannot contain advertising except for incidental announcements of books.

As of May 2008, the basic cost for a one-pound package shipped anywhere within the United States for Media Mail is $2.23, or a little more than half of the $3.99 fee that Amazon provides for shipping. The problem comes if you have a book over six pounds. In those cases, sellers should be aware that they will not cover their costs for shipping, and should make sure that they have enough profit in the book sale to justify the sale.

Taylor's Tip #2: "Don't pay retail."

A little known secret is that the parcel carriers have two set rates; one for retail customers and a different one for commercial customers. The rates for commercial customers are less. You can qualify for a commercial rate with most carriers by signing up for an account or shipping online. Even the USPS offers two sets of rates. Commercial rates average 3.5 percent less for Priority Mail and 3 percent less for Express Mail than the retail customer will pay. You qualify for the lower rates by shipping online! (Shipping online simply means paying for the shipping and printing out the shipping label through the U.S. Postal Service's website. You would then drop off the package at your local post office.)

Taylor's Tip #3: "Don't wait in line; ship online and save more than a dime."

The carriers want you to ship online because it saves them time and money. You can qualify for lower rates with the USPS by signing up to ship with Click-N-Ship by going to www.usps.com and selecting "print a shipping label."

This is how much you will save by shipping online:

- Priority Mail: 3.5 percent average
- Delivery Confirmation: Free with Priority Mail

- Express Mail: 3 percent
- International Priority Mail: 5 percent

When you ship online, you can actually print out the address label with the postage. Although you can get some of these savings using the USPS Click-N-Ship, you cannot ship Media Mail.

There are a number of third-party vendors that offer PC Postage, which provides for online discounts and discounted rates for Delivery Confirmation:

- http://www.endicia.com/
- http://www.pitneyworks.com/
- http://www.stamps.com/
- http://www.redroller.com

The cost for this software runs about $15.00 a month, and the good news is that all of these vendors offer free trials. And, some of these software applications provide the capability to compare rates and services, some with multiple carriers. The savings from rate shopping alone can justify the investment for the monthly fee.

Taylor's Tip #4: "When shipping with the USPS, use delivery confirmation."

Sometimes, customers ask, "Where's my book?" Negative ratings can hurt your sales. My suggestion is that it is worth the money to purchase an extra service, delivery confirmation. Experienced Amazon sellers have reported to me that when they reply with the delivery confirmation number, nine times out of ten they never hear from the customer again.

Delivery confirmation provides the date, ZIP code, and time your package was delivered. If delivery was attempted, you will get the date and time of attempted delivery. You can access the information at http://www.usps.com/shipping/trackandconfirm.htm.

The cost for delivery confirmation is $0.75 retail and $0.18 if you purchase it online.

Taylor's Tip #5: "Use an accurate shipping scale with a digital display."

The rates for shipping are determined by the weight of the package. As we discussed earlier, even one ounce can make a difference. If you are using USPS Priority Mail, one ounce will cost you big time. The difference between 1.0 pound and 1.1 pounds is $4.80 compared to $8.25 (USPS Zone 8). One ounce is 70 percent more!

You can check the accuracy of your scale with five U.S. quarters. The display should be one ounce.

Make Your Carriers Compete

Mark A. Taylor touched on this, but let's go into this a bit further. Just because the major carriers post prices doesn't mean there's no wiggle room in those fees. Surprisingly, you can negotiate prices even with the likes of UPS. Prepare a sample package and go to the local UPS store, for example. Ask how much it would cost to ship that package in whatever quantity you anticipate processing each week. Don't be surprised if the price quoted is significantly less than the individual price of each package. We even know of one seller who scheduled pickups at his site at the same time for both UPS and FedEx. When both drivers arrived, he asked them which one would give him the best price!

Buy Your Postage Online

As long as you have that digital scale, you can weigh your packages and purchase your postage online. It doesn't matter which carrier you use—they all have this feature available through their websites. You can also turn to companies such as Stamps.com or Endicia.com. One of the best things about Endicia, according to one Amazon apparel seller, is being able to create USPS return labels that you can mail, fax, or e-mail to your Amazon.com customers for returns. "Return labels are standard with Amazon, and customers have come to expect that level of service," she said. With your postage complete, you can schedule your carrier to pick up your shipments, or simplify your trip to the postal center by having everything ready to go. The less time you stand in line waiting to post each item, the faster you can get back to listing and selling your products.

Determine Whether to Get Insurance

No matter which carrier you select, the subject of insurance creates a good deal of discussion among experienced online merchants. Some wouldn't ship without it, while others feel the expense of insuring every shipment is greater than the cost of replacing the occasional order that doesn't arrive at its destination. Still other sellers buy global insurance for their merchandise that covers damage to their inventory both during shipment and while the items are stored in their warehouses. Whether or not you will insure your items depends on many factors, including the value of each order you ship and the nature of the products you sell.

Decide Whether to Use Delivery Confirmation

You can find a great deal of discussion among sellers about the merits of delivery confirmation. Most of the Amazon sellers we spoke with use it, as Mark A. Taylor suggests. "I ALWAYS use delivery confirmation," notes Kathy of Element Jewelry & Accessories. Many sellers have found that delivery confirmation is a good way to scare away scammers who make purchases and then claim never to have received the items you ship. However, delivery confirmation only proves that the package was delivered, not that the buyer actually received it. It won't completely protect you from A-to-z Guarantee claims where the package has been stolen, for example, from a buyer's front porch. But, it will likely chase that scammer on to the next, less savvy seller, who can be bilked by the sad story of the package that never arrived.

Teach That Workhorse a Few Tricks!

Now that we've made our way through the practical considerations of your shipping operation, let's take a look at how you might use your workhorse to enhance your business and maybe turn it into a bit of a show pony after all. Tricia Records of Read_Rover_Books notes that if you do shipping well, "you will be rewarded with a higher percentage of positive feedback." Not only will your reputation on Amazon grow, but you will reduce your customer service encounters, and if you're creative, you can turn your shipping into a good marketing opportunity, too.

Use Branding

You saw in Chapter 7 just how challenging it can be to make your business stand out on Amazon. Shipping is one opportunity you have to do that. Sellers have found many creative ways to reward their customers when their orders arrive. For example, Asad of Beachcombers! sells ethnic Indo/Pakistan clothing, shoes, and accessories for women. With each shipment, he includes a free tube of henna as a gift. Of course, the tube includes his logo and website address, where the happy buyer can go to get directions for using the henna.

Other sellers go for a visual impression. "Use color or something else pleasant that the customer may not have otherwise expected," recommends Tricia of Read_Rover_Books. "A packing slip is a must," she adds. "It gives you the chance to communicate your return policies." We agree, and as long as you're including one, you should strive to brand it your own and make it attractive. Not only will this make an impression with your customer, but it could also save the delivery in the event that the package gets damaged in transit. Just make sure both your recipient's address and your own appear on the packing slip, and you'll add a level of protection to everything you send. Finally, don't forget to include your logo within your e-mail signature and have it printed on the labels for the exterior of outgoing shipments, recommends Tricia.

Consider Special Offers

You may not yet be prepared to offer a free gift with every shipment, but that doesn't mean you can't include a special offer from time to time. Many sellers told us they use coupons offering a discount for repeat customers. Or, you can use your packing slip to offer your customers a reward for opting in to your electronic newsletter. Just make sure that you can actually deliver on what you promise, and you may find that your customers are so delighted with your work that you've begun to build a loyal and repeat customer base.

Offer Free Shipping

You won't be able to sustain a policy of charging nothing for shipping. It's expensive for you and all online shoppers expect to pay something to receive their goods. Still, free shipping is a real and proven motivator for online shoppers, so consider how you might be able to use it. Bing Yang of Augustina Jewelry says it definitely helps with sales. "I do offer free shipping promotions regularly when you buy two or more items," notes Charise Richards of OneChicBoutique. If nothing else, consider offering your customers reduced shipping rates for multiple items. It doesn't cost you twice as much to ship two items, as long as you put the order in one box, so pass the savings on to your customer as a sign of goodwill.

Protect Yourself from Fraud

Now, we're not saying you can turn your workhorse into a guard dog, but there are steps you can take to incorporate protection into your shipping operations. As we've already mentioned, there are scammers out there who will attempt to defraud you by saying your package never arrived. There are still others who will claim the merchandise was damaged in transit or the order was incomplete. And that's just a sampling of the tricks some pull. Although you can't possibly protect yourself against every type of thief, the packaging step gives you the opportunity to protect yourself a bit. Here are some tips Gary of Goggles and Glasses has shared to help mitigate the damage:

- We weigh the cost of signature confirmation against the cost of insurance on a shipment if it is going to a suspicious location. Usually insurance is cheaper than signature confirmation.

- We use ultraviolet pens to mark items in a hidden place that are prone to "switched returns."

- I'm now looking at installing a camera over the scales and at the packing table. We seem to have some customers who claim wrong amounts shipped or accessories that are not received.

- Inspect everything!

Shipping Internationally

Selling online gives you the chance to sell to a customer base that spans the globe. Only you can decide how you feel about operating your business internationally, but many of the sellers we've worked with over the years insist that international sales are important enough to warrant the extra challenge that comes from fulfilling your orders across borders. Whether or not you choose to list on Amazon's international sites, your products will be available for international purchase unless you specifically prohibit international sales when you create your product detail pages. You may start out too timid about inviting the world into your e-business, but in time, the growth potential available through the billions of people who don't happen to live in the United States may just prove too tempting to ignore. Most of the sellers we've spoken with agree that although international sales *can* be a bit more challenging, they're certainly worth the extra trouble involved. Let's look at some of the ways you can mitigate the fear and risk of selling internationally.

The first concern you'll have is to deal with the language differences among international buyers. "We've sold to customers in Norway and France," reports Dan Morrill of Alternating Reality. "We use the Babel Fish site (Figure 8-5) to help us translate to each language, and we include an English version of the same message." Remember when you're dealing with international customers to keep your language simple and avoid slang and idioms. Many of those cultural nuances are easily lost on nonnative English speakers.

Of course, shipping internationally means extra paperwork. You'll be required to complete the customs forms that accompany any package shipped outside the United States. These can be tedious, but they're not complicated. Just be sure to be completely honest and transparent about the value and nature of your shipment. Remember that the duties and taxes incurred in international shipping will fall on your buyer, not on you.

Figure 8-5. The Babel Fish Translation tool makes translating brief passages a snap.

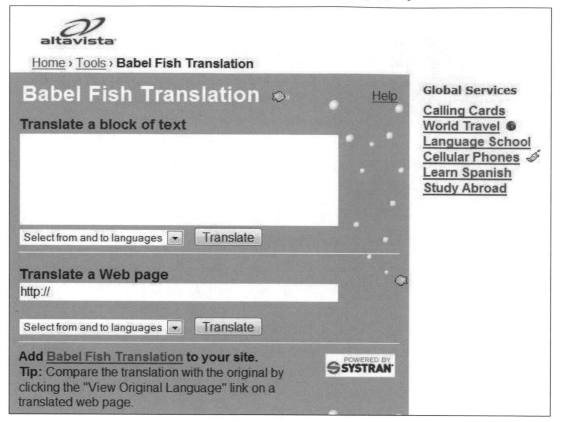

That's not to say you won't have additional expenses when shipping internationally. Of course, shipping is going to cost more. "Finding a balance between cost to the customer and speed of delivery is a tough challenge," noted Asad of Beachcombers! "We try to find a cost and acceptable speed of delivery that the customer will find fair and that we can still keep profitable." Keep in mind, however, that the added expense can be offset by the increases in sales. "For international customers, buying for Christmas may start as early as September or October to account for the longer shipping time," said an experienced Amazon bookseller in the southeast.

Being clear about those shipping expectations is vitally important to serving your international customers. "The biggest challenge is to set realistic delivery expectations," notes Kathy of Element Jewelry & Accessories. "I offer all of my products internationally and have shipped countless orders overseas. In 99 percent of all cases, my products were delivered without incident." Opinions vary between using the USPS or UPS for international deliveries. The USPS doesn't allow package tracking internationally, but UPS is quite a bit more expensive, and often customers overseas don't want to spend the extra money.

Make It Fit Before It Ships

Once you've decided which carrier you'll use for international shipments, make it simple to know whether or not a particular item in your inventory is a good candidate to cross the borders. "For media items, keep a USPS flat rate international mailer on your desk while you're listing," advises Tricia of Read_Rover_Books. "Only enable international sales for those items that will fit into the mailer." That's a brilliant idea, and so simple, too!

Many sellers are concerned about fraud through international sales, but still others insist that the rate of fraud is actually higher domestically. "I haven't had any problems," reports Charise of OneChicBoutique. At the same time, Charise makes her policies very clear. "My terms state that all international sales are final," she said. It's important to find your level of risk versus reward as you decide whether or not you'll sell internationally. If you decide to go ahead, be sure you clearly define the rules that will let you sleep at night and state them clearly to all international customers.

Safeguard Your International Operations

Processing your orders internationally may require you to deviate from the automatic and quick manner in which you process your orders. "We've instituted rules to protect ourselves," noted Michael Jansma of GemAffair. "We manage the method of payment (credit card), the requested shipping method, and the country and address that it's going to. A human looks at every international order before it's shipped. Sometimes we prep the package and just sit on it for a couple of days." Michael noted that credit card companies have gotten good at modeling credit histories, and most cases of fraud are detected within 48 hours. If that amount of time safely passes, he feels more secure shipping his order internationally.

Fulfillment by Amazon

In 2007, Amazon began to offer its sellers a service called Fulfillment by Amazon (FBA). While nearly all the sellers we spoke with were curious and interested in the program, not all of them had yet to take advantage of it. It was still pretty new at the time. Simply put, the program allows you to ship your inventory to an Amazon warehouse, where it is stored until you sell it. Amazon employees then pick your orders, pack them, and ship them on to your customers. (See Figure 8-6).

One of FBA's biggest proponents also happens to be one of our favorite sellers, Andy Mowery of debnroo. When we spoke, Andy had recently sent FBA his first three boxes. He is intrigued and excited by the possibilities. Because of costs, Amazon's economies of scale are unbeatable. "Who has a bigger UPS account? Or FedEx?" he asked.

Figure 8-6. Through Fulfillment by Amazon, you can have Amazon handle your product storage, picking, packing, and shipping.

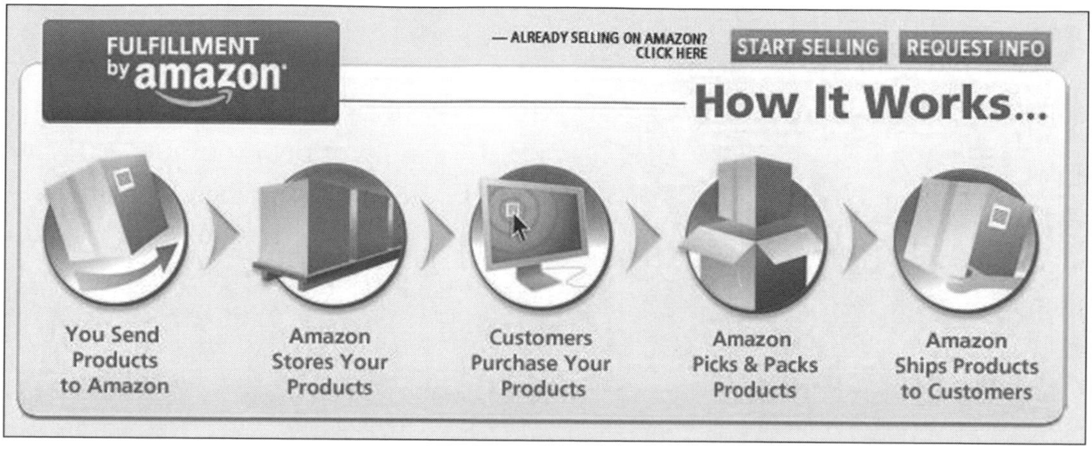

He's sold on FBA. Even though he is based in Fort Collins, Colorado, where land and labor are cheaper than in many other parts of the country, Andy notes that energy and transportation costs are going up. "Running a warehouse is so frustrating. It's the thing that holds me back," he said, referring to his plans for expansion. When you look at a sample of Amazon's warehousing capabilities in Figure 8-7, it's hard to imagine doing it better or more cheaply yourself!

As you can imagine, over the last 12 years or so Amazon has built a network of warehouses and procedures for packing and shipping orders that's arguably unrivaled. The company has invested significant resources in fulfillment as part of its commitment to providing the best customer service possible.

FBA Has Its Advantages

If we haven't convinced you yet that FBA might be a good idea for your business, we've saved the best for last. When you use FBA, your customers can take advantage of Amazon's extremely popular shipping programs, Amazon Super Saver shipping (free "standard" shipping on all orders over $25.00), and Amazon Prime, which gives

Figure 8-7. A glimpse of just part of one of Amazon's warehouses reveals how enormous its storage potential is.

customers unlimited two-day shipping for a flat fee of $79.00 per year. The company says these programs are so popular that they're the best reason to give FBA a try. As Andy of debnroo puts it: "With FBA, Amazon Prime and Free Shipping (orders over $25), are now part of your business, too."

FBA Wins the Buy Box

If getting a spot in the buy box is your goal, and as you know, we've already advised you to do that, signing up for FBA can help. Andy says you can get that buy box a higher percentage of the time if you use FBA. That's because free shipping makes your offer less expensive than your competitor's. They can't touch that, and your customer sees only the total price—product and shipping price combined.

When you use FBA, the fact that Amazon will be fulfilling your order is clearly stated on the search results pages that your customers see. This is another way to make your listings stand out from the crowd. When your customers see that you participate in this program, you'll be able to ease any concerns they may have about how safely and quickly their orders will arrive.

Surprisingly, FBA isn't all that well known among sellers. Yet we agree that it's worth giving the service a try to see if it makes good business sense for you and the products you sell. Others, however, disagree. "I don't trust even Amazon to service my customers," said one wary jewelry seller. Other sellers equate FBA with a drop-shipping service (and boy, do those have a bad name among some e-merchants). Some fear the loss of control over that part of the overall process. For Tricia of Read_Rover_Books, for example, the service doesn't make sense for her right now. "As the majority of my inventory would not be appropriate for FBA due to its nature (out-of-print books can take years to find the right buyer), sending all of it to FBA would be cost prohibitive." Still others see their warehouse as a profit center and don't want to give that up.

FBA Tips

Chris Schlieter of timezone recently signed up for FBA and was testing it when we spoke. He had some advice for those considering FBA.

1. Standard consumer products with UPC codes can be intermingled in Amazon's inventory with the same item from other sellers. So don't use it for products where the exterior of the package would make a big difference. For example, 4GB iPods will all be in one bin, so you can't control the appearance of what your customer actually receives. This is a problem only for standardized items.

2. Read all the instructions Amazon offers so your order isn't held up by mistakes. For example, he can't use packing peanuts or shredded paper.

3. FBA fully leverages Amazon shipping rates so it looks more attractive to customers with lower shipping costs.

FBA's Fees

Now, Amazon isn't going to take care of these chores for you out of the goodness of its corporate heart (as large as that heart may be). In fact, here's a breakdown of all the costs.

- **Inventory Storage:** You will pay Amazon a monthly fee of from $0.45 up to $0.60 per cubic foot of storage that you need. (Note these data are from the 2007 fourth quarter.)

- **Order Type:** If orders came through Amazon.com, your total fees are based on order handling + pick and pack + weight handling. Go to this page to see just what fees apply: http://www.amazonservices.com/fulfillment/pricing.html. If the order is for fulfillment of non-Amazon products, a different rate scale applies. "You should consider these fees as you're evaluating whether to fulfill an item through FBA," advises Barry Mark of Treebeard Books. (You don't have to send Amazon your entire inventory. You can pick and choose.) The cost of using FBA is about $3.00 per item, given all the fees. Then you have to figure in what it costs to acquire the item. You can't afford to give them cheap stuff. One Amazon seller we know feels that he can't sell anything for less than $5.00 through FBA.

By the way, you can use the FBA program to handle orders from your Amazon.com customers, of course, but also from customers who buy things from your website or even your eBay store and auction listings. They will even fulfill orders that came through bricks-and-mortar stores! Andy of Debnroo is such a big fan of the program that he has asked his Amazon contact to look into FBA for all of his shipping (eBay and his own website, too). "Once you get in bed with Amazon, why have anything in your warehouse?" he asks.

An add-on service called Amazon Fulfillment Web Services (Amazon FWS) further automates the process of sending merchandise to Amazon fulfillment centers by using Web tools to create labels and packing slips. The outbound portion of Amazon FWS allows sellers to direct when and to where orders are to be shipped in real time through a Web interface. The upshot is that Amazon FWS, which is free, automates this part of your business even more.

For now, Amazon will ship your orders in its own boxes, not yours. However, the company is looking into the idea of using plain cardboard boxes for FBA. Also, Amazon will use your packing slip, which is a way to get your company's name before your customers (and not just Amazon's). Further, if you wish to bundle your items with a promotional gift or coupon, you can send those along, too. The important thing to consider is that you can't expect Amazon employees to build your order for you. So, for example, if you'd like to include a free gift, each item you send must be complete with the gift so that the Amazon employee will simply pick it and pack it as a single unit.

Amazon Drop Shipping

We've long hesitated to recommend drop shippers. For the few of you who aren't familiar with the term, *drop shippers* warehouse inventory, which they ship to your customer when you receive an order. They spare you the expense of sourcing and then warehousing inventory.

We've spoken with many online sellers who use drop shippers to expand their product mix. But many others won't touch them—they prefer to have their inventory on-hand, where they can see it and have complete control over it. They worry that a drop shipper will run out of stock and cast them, the seller, in a bad light when an order has to be back-ordered. Drop shipping is actually contrary to the rules of Amazon, which insists that you have in your possession the items you are listing for sale on the site.

But what if Amazon were the drop shipper? That is, you, as a seller, could count Amazon's entire inventory as your inventory, which Amazon would then ship to your customers as orders are received. That's a horse of another color, which is why we think you should at least consider the program. Gary Richardson posed an interesting question as we pondered this section: "Would you choose Amazon as your drop shipper?" We had to say we would. What's Gary's opinion? "This is one drop shipper I would trust," he said.

As a seller, you may not offer items to Amazon customers that outside drop shippers fulfill. You can, however, use Amazon as your drop shipper. For example, you could sell an item through your own eBay store, or your own website, and have Amazon ship the products to your customers. Here are the four steps involved in setting this up:

1. Establish a corporate account with Amazon.
2. Add Amazon's products to your own website's inventory.
3. Gather orders. Your customers pay you directly.
4. You electronically submit the orders to Amazon for fulfillment.

The drop shipping service is free. For more information click to http://www.amazonservices.com/dropship/.

Looking Ahead

Now you've explored the challenges of shipping and the opportunities you'll face selling on international markets. In the next chapter, we will turn our attention to the rest of the online world. The Internet is broad and varied. Selling online, of course, did not originate with Amazon, and Amazon may become just one part of your e-commerce business. We'll look at the obvious alternative, eBay, but we'll also introduce you to some corners of the Internet market you may have yet to discover.

An Amazon Success Story

When we met Kirk Holbert, he'd been selling on Amazon for only about six months. Still he was already a Featured Merchant and enjoying great success on the site selling toys, action figures, and collectibles under the name Cosmic-King. Kirk already operated a successful eBay business before he came to Amazon. "I owned my category," he said. He'd been operating his online business for nine years on eBay. His decision to try Amazon came after he met an Amazon representative at an Internet Merchants Association (IMA) meeting. Within six months, Kirk reported that his earnings on Amazon were approximately four times those of his eBay business. His success actually led him to purchase his own warehouse!

Kirk actually applied for Featured Merchant status. He saw that as a Featured Merchant, it's possible to "own the buy box." Once you've got that piece of premium real estate on an Amazon page, the sales really stream in. To become a Featured Merchant, Kirk sent a portfolio of some of his eBay successes to Amazon for review. He received his invitation about six to eight weeks later, and he's been successfully making Amazon his own ever since.

Kirk spends much of his time researching new products and creating his listings. He keeps up to the minute with the e-commerce world by reading *AuctionBytes* and through his participation with the IMA. He's a big fan of that particular organization, noting that it's a "group with personal integrity." He uses the group to keep up with news, information about future products, and also trends. He turns to IMA for advice on best practices, too. Kirk also notes that it's important to be part of a group like this, because being an Internet merchant can be so isolating, and connecting with others is very important.

Selling internationally has worked well for Kirk, although he admits that shipping is an extra challenge. It's far more expensive to ship via UPS when going international, so he tends to stick with USPS. With the USPS first-class

international, you can't get delivery tracking, which is available through UPS, but he finds his international customers don't want to pay the extra fee and brokerage fees for this service. Still, the boost in his sales on Amazon that he enjoyed once he started offering his products internationally was worth the extra trouble.

Kirk makes customer service his number-one concern and so Amazon's A-to-z Guarantee has never been a problem for him. Even before he came to Amazon, he operated his business with a 100 percent satisfaction guarantee. Reading through his stellar feedback on both Amazon and eBay proves that his business practices have built for him a very loyal customer base.

CHAPTER 9

Life Beyond Amazon: Selling Through Other Venues

Few things in life come guaranteed, but one of those few is change. It's bound to take us places we can't foresee, and it's bound to be a constant as long as we live. In 2004, it seemed everyone we met was interested in building an eBay business. Folks couldn't seem to get enough information, guidance, and advice about how they, too, could become successful e-commerce merchants on the site. By the end of 2006, we'd detected plenty of discord among the eBay seller community, and it soon became clear that lots of folks had begun to look around for ways to diversify their business models. By mid-2007, it seemed that a good many of eBay's top PowerSellers had started selling on Amazon, and not only selling, but devoting a lot of the energy once reserved for their eBay businesses to their new market. Amazon's recruiting of these sellers had something to do with that, but sellers wouldn't have gone to the trouble of learning the ways of a new site if they weren't already thinking of ways to branch out.

Many of the new Amazon sellers we spoke with were only sorry they had not started selling on Amazon sooner. Most of these sellers continued to have inventory on eBay but were ready to shift more inventory to Amazon if it made sense to do so. (If you took our advice in Chapter 5 and created a data feed for your inventory, this process is simple.) These smart sellers knew that it was best to become familiar with several channels, and to use a *multichannel strategy* for running their overall businesses. That way, if one channel should peter out for some reason, they could shift to another without too much of an interruption in their business. They've safeguarded their futures that way, and gained more control of their own businesses, in an ever-changing environment.

When we started interviewing what we thought were Amazon sellers for this book, we were surprised to learn that these sellers were truly e-merchants, selling on many different channels, and not just Amazon. When we asked Michael Jansma of GemAffair about building his business on Amazon, he told us he thinks of building his *business*, not building it strictly on Amazon. It struck us at the time as very wise advice. "The way the brand has grown and its well-known customer service philosophy," are the reasons he came to Amazon. Tricia Records of Read_Rover_Books agrees. She sells on 12 different venues, including AbeBooks, Alibris, Choosebooks, Half.com, Biblio, Barnes & Noble, her own website (www.readrover.com), Valore Books, and eBay, among others (see Figure 9-1, for example). The idea is to be where your customers are, which is everywhere.

Figure 9-1. ValoreBooks is one of many online book retailers. It specializes in textbooks, which generally have high price points.

Strategies for Evaluating Other Channels

Starting from the premise that you want to be where your customers are, what other factors come into play when you're evaluating a prospective new channel? For now, let's disregard the fact that people who sell books have many book-centric channels from which to choose, although we'll discuss some top options there, too. But how do you choose among your many other channel options? For some guidance we spoke with David Yaskulka, vice president for auctions-for-charity pioneer Kompolt, and marketing chair of the Professional eBay Sellers Alliance (PeSA). David has also run successful businesses on both eBay and Amazon.

Here are three criteria sellers should use when evaluating other channels, according to David:

1. **Profit participation.** What does the channel contribute to your bottom line? Although his gross revenues were the same on both eBay and Amazon, his profits were better on Amazon.

2. **Velocity**. How quickly can you move merchandise? This is something you have to test. On Amazon his company lowered its prices to match its eBay prices, and its traffic was the same.

3. **"Lifetime customer value."** What's that customer worth to you? When you develop a customer through your own website, that customer is really yours. With 100 percent certainty the buyer knows you are the seller. If you can do cause marketing (as you can through eBay or your own site), this is one way to build a bond with a customer. *Cause marketing* refers primarily to companies that raise money for charities through online auctions.

Other Channels for Booksellers

When we began researching this chapter, we were not sure at all why a bookseller would want to sell anywhere but on Amazon, considering its 76 million customers and sterling reputation for top-notch customer service. But industry insiders made some good arguments for also selling elsewhere, including the fact that you can describe your inventory using your own words, set your own shipping rates, and reach a more select demographic (for example, buyers of antiquarian books would be more likely to turn to AbeBooks than Amazon). There are scores of channels for booksellers, including those specializing in certain types of books, from antiquarian books to textbooks. Here we describe the top three.

Alibris (http://www.alibris.com/)

Alibris (pronounced "uh-LEE-briss") is a huge book marketplace, with 75 million used, new, and out-of-print books available for sale (see Figure 9-2). Like Amazon, Alibris is adding categories of other things you can buy or sell, and movies and music in all their various

Figure 9-2. Alibris specializes in "as good as new" used books.

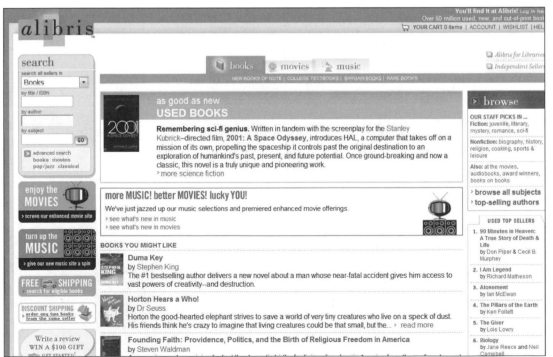

forms are also for sale. We admit we're new fans of Alibris, having bought from a seller there and received coupons from Alibris ever since. On its website, it says it has "millions" of customers from 45 countries. One of our favorite Amazon sellers, Dan Morrill of Alternating Reality, says he also sells through Alibris. If you have many out-of-print books, you might consider this channel since that type of inventory is one of its specialties. To get started as an Alibris seller, you must pay a $19.99 application processing fee; beyond that, sellers pay a commission of about 15 percent of each sale for items under $500, less for more expensive items. Finally, sellers pay a flat monthly fee of from $9.95 to $150, depending on the size of their inventory.

Alibris Versus Amazon

Alibris is one of the leading marketplaces for media sellers. We asked President and CEO Brian Elliott why a seller would want to sell on Alibris, given Amazon's command of the market. His response follows:

- **Alibris helps sellers get access to millions of book, music, and movie buyers.** We bring in buyers from our own websites (Alibris.com and Alibris.co.uk), thousands of libraries through our direct library sales force, and through business partnerships that drive sales to the customers of other retailers.

- **For many sellers, Alibris brings as much volume as Amazon.** For all of our sellers, Alibris helps bring in incremental volume and avoid the risk of putting all of their eggs in one basket.

Alibris also differs in some specific ways:

- **Alibris provides access to more customers.** Alibris invests not only in growing its online marketplace, but in finding library customers, business partners, and new outlets for sellers to help sell their items. Business partners include Barnes & Noble,

Blackwell UK, Blackwell Book Services, Books-A-Million, Borders, Chapters/Indigo, Gardners UK, Half.com, Ingram Book Group, YBP, and others.

- **It allows sellers to manage accounts on other online exchanges.** Alibris helps sellers manage their Amazon.com accounts—for a low per-item-sold fee, Alibris keeps seller inventories on Amazon updated and pulls order information in to the Alibris Seller Hub so that sellers have one place to process orders, print packing slips, generate customer e-mails, etc.

- **It offers cataloging and pricing tools.** Alibris has online cataloging tools that give sellers access to over 10 million book bibliographic entries (including over 3 million pre-ISBN titles) and over 4 million music and movie entries. Alibris makes cataloging pre-ISBN books simple. Alibris also provides market data to sellers so they can price competitively when listing their items, and provides tools to enable sellers to more easily reprice listings as the market changes over time.

- **Alibris handles global logistics.** Sellers ship direct to buyers for most orders in their home countries, but Alibris handles international shipping through its warehouse in Nevada. We also provide consolidation services in our warehouses for customers like libraries that want their orders consolidated and with standard purchase order invoices and shipment manifests.

The average Alibris book buyer isn't average—because we provide access to such a wide variety of channels, our customers include:

- Heavy readers, looking to feed their voracious appetites for more books
- Collectors and others looking for rare and hard-to-find items, pre-ISBN titles, signed copies, etc.
- Bargain hunters, people looking for a good deal on a used book, DVD, or CD
- Library staff looking for out-of-print titles, collection development projects, and books that publishers are out of stock on

AbeBooks (http://www.abebooks.com/)

AbeBooks brings together a network of 13,500 independent booksellers (see Figure 9-3). All told, it provides access to 110 million books of all varieties, including new, used, out-of-print, and antiquarian. It has its own bookstore management software, HomeBase 2.1, available for downloading right from the site. To upload your inventory you can also use FillZ software, described in Chapter 5. As we mentioned there, AbeBooks owns FillZ.

The company says it receives more than 1.5 million unique visitors a week and more than 5 million searches are conducted on its site each day. Fees for listing books on its site start at $25 per month

Figure 9-3. AbeBooks, whose name reminds us of a favorite uncle, represents more than 13,500 booksellers selling over 110 million books. Amazon recently bought the company.

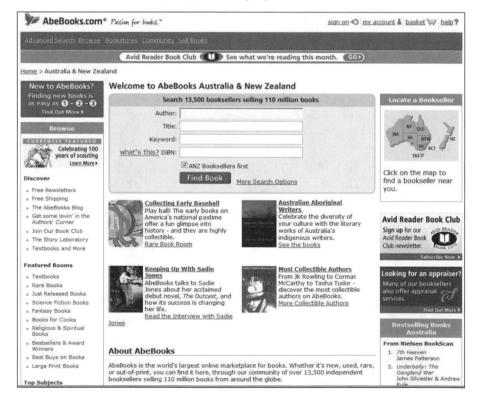

for 500 books, plus a commission of from 8 to 13.5 percent, depending on the payment method used. Booksellers can set their own shipping rates and describe books themselves, rather than relying on someone else's copy. Note that in late 2008, Amazon acquired AbeBooks; however, the company was to operate as a "stand-alone business."

Barnes & Noble (http://www.bn.com)

None of the Amazon sellers we spoke with for this book said that they also sold on Barnes & Noble's website, barnesandnoble.com (also accessible at www.bn.com). However, we'd be remiss if we didn't mention it. The site is undergoing some major changes and may once again become a real force (see Figure 9-4).

According to its website, Barnes & Noble "stocks more than 1 million books," which it claims is more than any other online bookseller. The company has a program for third-party sellers; however, getting information about it is a bit more involved than getting the scoop on Amazon's program. There is little said about the program on its site, so our feeling is that the guidelines for becoming an "Authorized Seller" are more stringent than they are for the Amazon Marketplace, for example. Here are a few details, all culled from the site:

....

Our sellers are independent booksellers and small businesses that have been approved by Barnes & Noble.com. They provide our customers with used and out-of-print books. They become Authorized Sellers by going through an application and approval process. To remain an Authorized Seller, each seller must conform to a set of performance guidelines established by Barnes & Noble.com. The books offered by these sellers are sold by, and shipped by, the sellers themselves. Barnes & Noble.com does not take possession of sellers' books; we facilitate the transaction between the sellers and our customers.

Figure 9-4. Barnes & Noble was supposed to blow Amazon out of the water when it launched its site. That didn't happen, of course, but the site does have a cleaner and more engaging design than it used to.

Before we leave this section, please note that there are also specialized retailers for other types of media products. Music sellers, for example, can sell through GEMM at http://gemm.com/ (GEMM stands for Global E-commerce Mega Marketplace). We've limited our coverage to book retailers, though, since we thought that category would interest a higher percentage of our readers.

eBay

Most of the sellers we interviewed for this book got started on eBay. It was there they learned how to sell products through the Internet as e-merchants. They learned about customer service that is never face to face, and they cut their teeth on shipping and sourcing issues. Steve Grossberg, president of the Internet Merchants Association, remains a big eBay fan. His business does $3 million to $4 million a year. Here's a breakdown of where his sales came from in 2007:

eBay: 65 percent
Amazon: 30 percent
His own website: 5 percent

Yet, as we write this, the tide has turned a bit away from eBay and is flowing toward Amazon. At a recent meeting of the Internet Merchants Association, the body language we saw and the crowd reaction we observed spoke quite loudly about eBay and Amazon's relative standing among Internet retailers. While the eBay executive was waiting to be introduced, he stood unsmiling with his arms crossed over his chest. He looked like he was waiting to see the principal. When his name was announced, he slowly approached the podium. The crowd was still. Compare this to the experience for the Amazon executive. When he was announced, the crowd started applauding before he had even said a word! As you can imagine, he went on to speak with confidence and verve. Admission: eBay will always have a place in our hearts. We've sold stuff there, such as golden-age comic books, old magazines and cut-out doll books, and other "ephemera." Throughout our house are the clocks, posters, photographs, and other treasures we bought through the site. We've even written four books about eBay (all for sale on Amazon, by the way). In the process of writing those books, we spoke with a lot of eBay's most successful sellers, the high-level PowerSellers.

So trust us when we say that for some sellers, eBay is where they should start and where they should stay for a while until they learn their trade. While the company has gone through some changes over the last few years, selling on eBay can still make a lot of sense for certain online merchants:

- Merchants just starting out online
- Those who see themselves more as weekend sellers than as online merchants supporting themselves and maybe others with their businesses
- Those who want to auction their item off rather than just set a fixed price for it
- Merchants selling collectibles, antiques, and other noncommodity items

Besides, you can't just dismiss a marketplace of 280 million registered users worldwide, operating in more than 39 worldwide markets. At any time, there are more than 110 million things for sale on eBay!

In some ways, being an eBay seller is easier than being a merchant on Amazon, because the bar is set lower. For example, eBay doesn't restrict certain categories to preapproved sellers. You can easily get your feet wet in e-commerce by selling off things your kids have outgrown or gifts you've received that you don't want to own. The channel is still a prime market for people who want to turn their online shopping hobby into a business. It's not that you can get away with being careless or dishonest on eBay, because that's not true. It's just that eBay still, to some degree, retains that casual hobbylike attitude. You can use eBay to gradually test the waters of e-commerce selling without investing too much money or effort to get started. If you discover that you like it, you'll work hard to build a business there, but you don't have to take a blind leap into water way over your head.

The venue has historically taken pride in providing a "level playing field." One of the ways this happens is that eBay does not usually step into disputes between buyers and sellers. Although eBay is certainly working hard to make the site safe and reliable, its hands-off attitude gives users a lot more freedom, and sometimes that includes freedom to defraud each other and behave badly. Amazon, by contrast, makes it clear that if you're planning to set up shop, you're going to be held to the exact standards the company holds for itself. Knowing that you are accountable to the A-to-z Guarantee all Amazon customers bring to their purchasing decisions, you have to be on your A-game from the very first day you begin. The result is that on Amazon, the citizens (customers and retailers alike) are almost always law-abiding and the cops (Amazon itself) are tough but fair.

For eBay sellers, this hands-off policy has worked well, because they didn't have to concern themselves with a lot of rules. And neither did buyers. Unfortunately, this has led to a lot of fraud on the site, although it's not as rampant as some in the media would have you believe. Over the years, eBay has worked to hold down the incidents of fraud, but in a community as large and diverse as eBay's, it's difficult to eliminate dishonesty completely. Surprisingly, you'll find fraud running in all directions. You'll find criminals victimizing sellers at least as often as they victimize buyers, so no one group can be held largely responsible for the mayhem. We don't want you to think that *anything goes* on eBay. For example, sellers who wildly overcharge for shipping, or otherwise cheat their customers, are now thrown off the site with great regularity. It's just that the community is vast, and as your business grows from small to large, you won't always find that the folks at eBay can adapt quickly to your growing needs. Many sellers we've spoken with don't feel they get the support or treatment they deserve as eBay "customers" responsible for bringing large sums of money to the eBay corporate bottom line.

Of course, eBay carns these revenues through the generally modest charges you pay to list things for sale on its site, and, more important, through the Final Value Fees it collects when a listing ends in a sale. These Final Value Fees can be as high as 15 percent of the price the seller realizes.

As we've mentioned, it's simple to get started selling on eBay and it's getting easier all the time. First, if you don't know the site, take a look around. Even if you think you know it, you should still look around, because eBay is shaking things up a lot by adding new features all the time. Search for things that interest you, as it makes browsing the site a lot more fun.

Now you can just register yourself as a seller on the site (there's a *Register* button near the top of the eBay home page—see Figure 9-5). Be sure you also register for PayPal, eBay's online payment service, while you're at it. Once you're signed up you can fill out the eBay screens that handhold you through the whole listing process.

We count a lot of eBay PowerSellers among our friends, since we've written so many books about how to successfully sell there. Many of these PowerSellers make great livings from their businesses. They've been generous enough to share with us their best tips for selling on eBay. Because we like you (you're reading our book, right?) we want to share some of those tips with you.

Figure 9-5. Consider listing on eBay if you have collectibles or other used items that would fetch more than a few dollars.

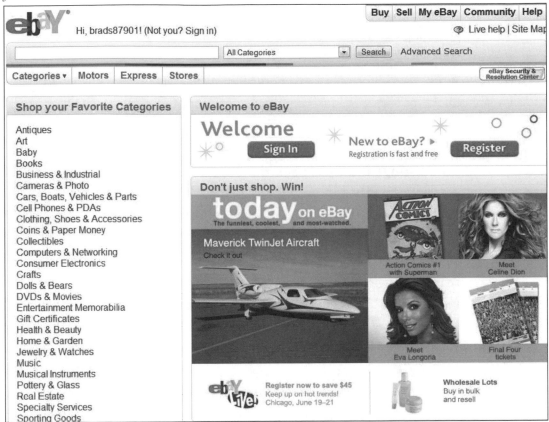

10 Secrets to Success on eBay

1. **Know how eBay works.** Make sure you've bought a few items off the site before you try to sell anything there. That way, you learn more about the whole process and how the site works. Stay updated by subscribing to online publications and joining professional associations like the Internet Merchants Association (IMA) and the Professional eBay Sellers Alliance (PeSA).

2. **Plan to work hard.** Sourcing the right products, pricing them correct-

ly, shipping items, offering customer service—all of these things eat up a lot of time. Frankly, except for a few PowerSellers we know who have been selling a long time, most work very long workweeks. Most people in retail do, as a matter of fact, and online retailers are no different.

3. **Source your products very carefully!** As in any business, sourcing your products for resale will take up the bulk of your efforts as you begin and for a long time into the future. Research, research, and more research is the only way we know to successfully source for eBay or Amazon selling.

4. **Create listings that really sell the product.** Successful eBay sellers know their markets and how to best appeal to them. Check completed listings and pay special attention to the ones that resulted in a sale.

5. **Automate your business.** You have to hand it to eBay on this score. For years, eBay has offered free software on the site for sellers to use to automate their businesses. This software lets them list more products, do it more quickly, and better run their businesses on a day-to-day basis. They can easily list as many items as they want. We know PowerSellers who list thousands of items per month.

6. **Be smart about customer service.** Bad feedback is bad feedback, whether you sell on eBay or Amazon. More and more on eBay, bad feedback will "disadvantage you," meaning that when a buyer does a search, your items may not appear on the first page of results. So not doing the right things on eBay can directly affect your business's health. That's why PowerSellers are careful to provide good customer service (e.g., offering a money-back guarantee) and to ship items quickly and carefully so that they will continue to be allowed to sell on the site.

7. **Keep careful track of the money.** More than one sad story can be told about the PowerSellers who lose track of the actual profits. When things take off quickly, and on eBay they can, and the money starts pouring in, it may seem like a fortune. But the more you sell, the more you list, and the more you list, the more you pay in eBay and PayPal fees, shipping expenses, employees,

and countless other things required to run your business. Stay very clearly focused on your spending, as well as your earnings. It's a double-edged sword. Lose track of the expenses, and you'll lose your business. Just make sure you know what's going out as clearly as you know what's coming in.

8. **Cultivate customer lists.** On eBay, you can still snare important information about your customers, and then reach out to them with other offers, send them coupons, and suggest they visit your website. Take advantage of every opportunity you have to build a list of customers. Those customers you make on eBay become your own in a way your Amazon customers will not.

9. **Get those PowerSellers discounts.** The vaunted level playing field model started to break down around 2007, and by the beginning of 2008, eBay knew it had to start treating its PowerSellers differently—even offering discounts of from 5 to 15 percent off their bills (Final Value Fees). These discounts are tied to very stringent Detailed Seller Ratings (DSRs) and are challenging to achieve, but do set your sights on achicving them.

10. **Sell on other channels.** That's right; eBay is just part of most PowerSellers' venue mix. They've seen the site change too much, and they know not to rely on it for as their sole income for too long. So they're selling on other sites (like Amazon, for instance), and also selling through their own websites.

Other Sites

You already knew about eBay of course, and you may even have been aware of the many book-related e-tailers. But aside from those sites, there are so many other places on the Web to set up shop. How in the world do you choose among them? We decided to feature only those sites that our Amazon superstars recommended. This is just to get you started; you will certainly know or hear of others as you expand your business.

Neweggmall.com

This site was just being built when we looked in on it, but Gary Richardson of Goggles and Glasses has high hopes for it, and after checking it out, we can see why. Neweggmall.com was positioned to be the general merchandise offspring of newegg.com, the Web's largest online-only supplier of electronics ($5 billion in sales in 2006). With that kind of pedigree behind it, it's no wonder Gary has high hopes for Neweggmall.com.

As we write this, Neweggmall.com plans to open by featuring merchandise in categories that it sees as the highest-grossing, including:

● Accessories (jewelry, watches, purses, belts, hats, etc.)
● Apparel
● Auto and hardware
● Beauty
● Health and wellness
● Home living
● Luggage and bags
● Outdoor and garden
● Sports and toys

The company will charge merchants on a "cost-per-order" basis, and they are free to list as many items as they want to. Apparently, there will also be a membership fee (currently projected at $29.99 per month), as the site mentions that new merchants can receive six months of membership at no charge. To get started, all you need is a flat file, as we described in Chapter 5. (You have been working on that, right?) Once your listings are up, if you don't sell anything Newegg doesn't earn any commissions, so the company promises aggressive merchandising and advertising campaigns to help drive business your way. Already, Neweggmall.com has a base of 8 million customers, with credit cards on file from its electronics business to build on. Clearly, not all the details were available at the time of this writing, but based on Gary's enthusiasm and the success of its parent company, we definitely feel you should explore it for yourself. For the latest details, go to http://www.neweggmall.com/.

UBid (http://www.uBid.com)

Despite all the griping about escalating fees, management trip-ups, seller unfriendly policies, and much more, eBay still has no real competition. It sits alone on the top of the online auction site mountain. One competitor that Bing Yang of Augustina Jewelry uses is UBid, where you can buy a variety of new and refurbished items. UBid prides itself on offering a buying and selling environment that is fraud-free, because all of its merchants are "certified." Much smaller than eBay, it claims to have helped "7,000 business liquidate more than $2 billion in excess inventory," over the last 10 years. This is a fraction of the business eBay does in a quarter.

craigslist (http://craigslist.com)

If you would like proof of the impact that craigslist has had, take a look at your newspaper's classifieds section, and then try to remember how it compares to just a few years ago (see Figure 9-6). Chances are, that section is much thinner than it was, and craigslist has as much to do with that change as anything.

Started by Craig Newmark in 1995, craigslist began as an e-mailed list of events in the San Francisco area. Today, it provides local classifieds and forums for 450 cities and is used by 25 million people in the United States alone. Many people like craigslist because it still has a homey, we're all-in-this-together feel to it. Postings are free, and the traffic is good (all told, it gets more than 9 billion page views per month!). Although Craig is no longer company president, he still works full-time in the customer service department!

Figure 9-6. craigslist is a good place to buy and sell large items, because you can see the item in person. There's bound to be a craigslist that covers your area.

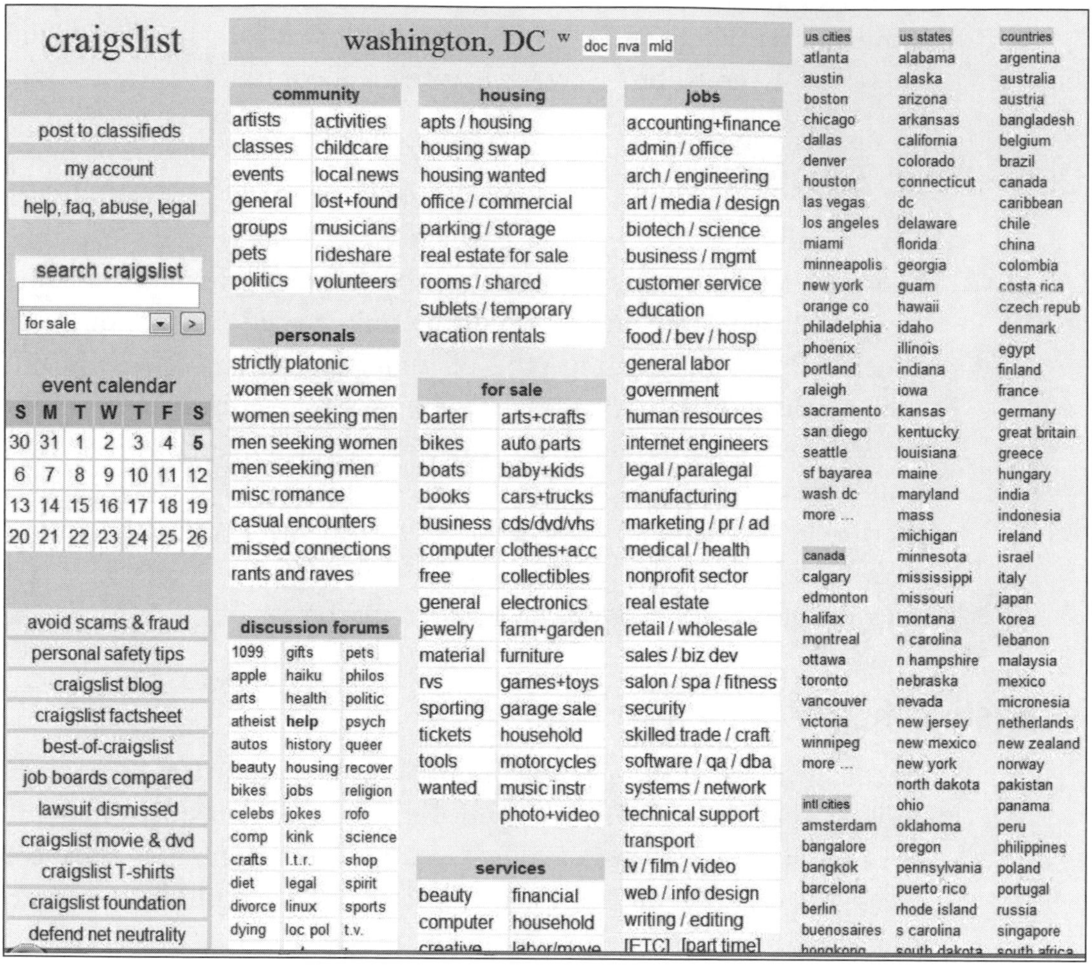

Comparison-Shopping Engines (CSEs)

One of the great things about computers and the Internet is the ability they give you to scan across unimaginable amounts of data, and then sort that data in many different ways. Take comparison-shopping engines (CSEs), such as Shopping.com and Shopzilla. We bet you've used these or others like them many times. Plug in a product you're thinking of buying, and you can immediately see who's selling the item, at what cost, and how the sellers stack up against their competitors. It's incredibly easy to see who's offering the best deal.

Because we're good consumers, we'll test one out now and show you the results, as a refresher, of course. Let's go to Shopping.com and see what Video iPods are going for these days. We found nearly 60 different iPods for sale, ranging from about $100 to nearly $500. With a single click, we could line up our favorite choices and see where they were being sold, and the details of the sale, such as shipping and availability. Not surprisingly, more than a few were listed for sale on Amazon and eBay! We could quickly redefine our search based on storage capacity, battery power, and color, just to name a few qualifiers. It wouldn't take us very long to see where the best deal was, and our choices included both Internet and physical store locations. Too bad, Brad's still not getting one—we need a new kitchen!

We've just looked at CSEs from a buyer's viewpoint. As a seller, all of these engines represent another place for you to sell your products. Of course, these CSEs won't make that happen from the goodness of their hearts. You're going to have to pay for it. CSEs will cost you, mostly in the time it takes to get set up there. Then there's that other cost: money. Most CSEs charge you for customers they deliver to your site. For this reason, ChannelAdvisor president and CSE expert Scot Wingo says they are relatively expensive, so you should use them to drive customers to your own WebStore, rather than to eBay or Amazon, to get the best return on your investment (ROI).

There are many comparison-shopping sites now (50 to 100 or more), and posting your products to them may differ a bit from site to site. One option, of course, is to work with a company such as ChannelAdvisor, which will take the entire task of posting to these sites off your shoulders for a fee. They can also make sure you're posting to the best ones for your product lines, in other words, those delivering the greatest ROI, also known as *bang for your buck*.

You may think you know about comparison-shopping engines, but like the Internet itself, new ones doing new things pop up all the time. We've already mentioned Shopping.com and Shopzilla, which have been around for a while. Here are some others worth exploring.

Ciao! (http://www.ciao.co.uk/)

Ciao! is a European-based shopping engine that was just opening a U.S. site as we wrote this. The beta site we saw had a lot of product reviews (more than 4 million) and a Web 2.0 feel to it. You must contact the company directly to learn about the fees involved in becoming a Ciao! merchant.

NexTag (http://www.nextag.com)

NexTag features a spartan, Google-like interface. Charges are based on a cost-per-click model that vary with the product category.

Pronto (http://www.pronto.com)

Pronto is fast and easy, colorful, and fun. When you search for a product, you not only receive a list of stores selling that product, but you can also read reviews left by other Pronto users (see Figure 9-7). Pronto bills itself as "shopping gone social." To list, you pay a cost-per-click charge that varies with the category.

Smarter.com (http://www.smarter.com/)

Smarter.com includes the usual price information and reviews but also features video reviews and news about coupons and rebates. Listing on the site starts at $0.15 per click.

CSEs are an area you need to stay on top of, as innovation is endemic to this field, with new, feature-rich engines appearing all the time. A good blog to bookmark is Comparison Shopping Engine Strategies at http://www.csestrategies.com/.

Figure 9-7. Pronto is one of a new breed of comparison-shopping engines that you should check out.

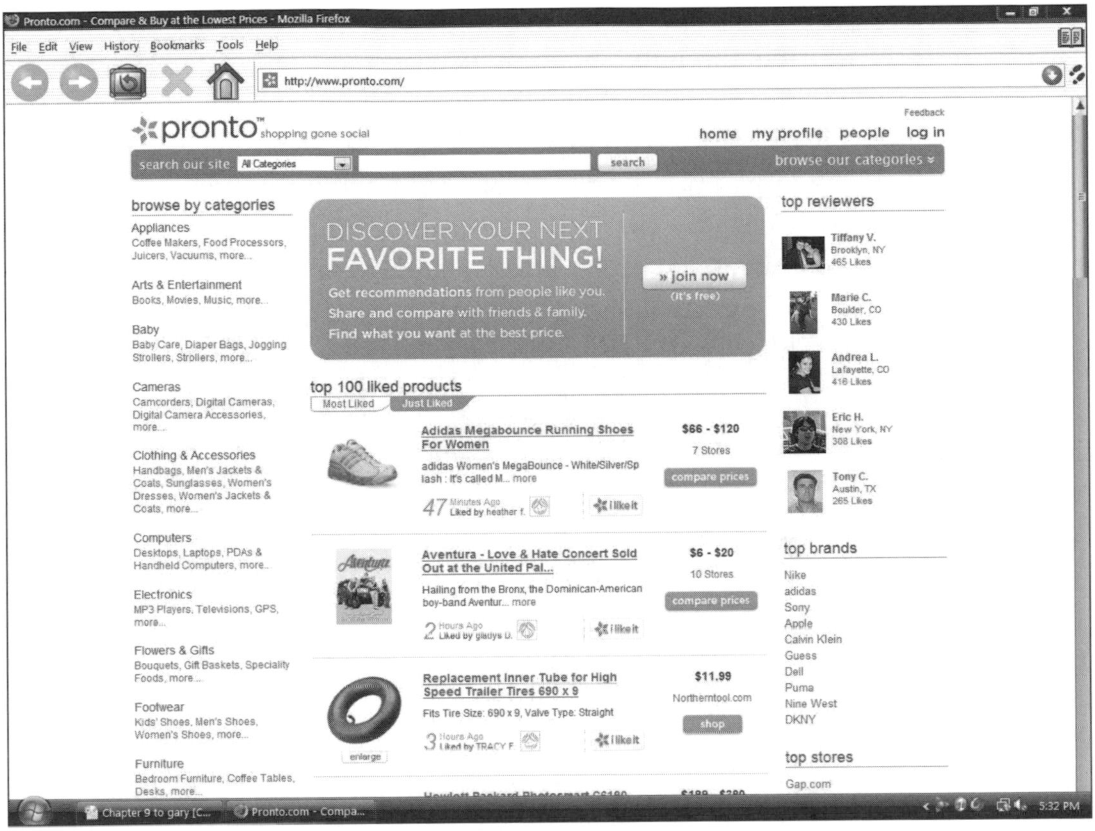

Start with Google

The first comparison-shopping engine you should list your products on is Google Product Search (http://www.google.com/products). You may have used this when it was called Froogle, and since Google Product Search is technically in beta, it may be called something else by the time you read this (see Figure 9-8). No matter, you need to list there!

You can post your products to this site for free. That's right, no cost-per-clicks to worry about. Lots of people get to it through the link available through Google, which, as you can imagine, really adds to the traffic it gets. In fact, Gary Richardson says he gets more traffic from the products he has listed on Google Product Search than from anything else. "The ROI on that freebie is incredible," he said. Those merchants who also sign up for Google Checkout (Google's online payment system, which is a competitor to the better-known PayPal) get pushed to the front of the line when someone does a search. Their products appear at the top, with a nifty Google Checkout shopping cart icon.

Your Own WebStore

Almost all of the most successful e-commerce merchants we know have their own WebStores. We're not talking strictly about participat-

Figure 9-8. Google Product Search provides more bang for your buck (it's free) than any of the CSEs.

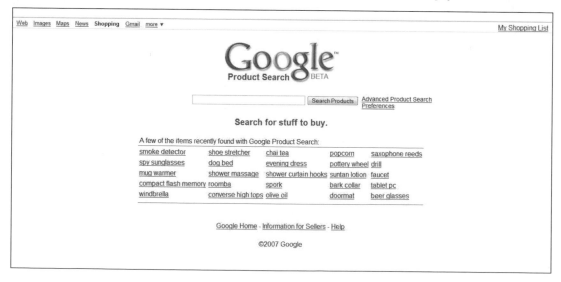

ing in WebStores by Amazon, although many of them do. We mean their own independent e-commerce sites, where they control everything. Of course, this means they have to work that much harder to drive customers to their stores because they won't have the marketing muscle of Amazon to help them out. However, many of the marketing techniques we discussed in Chapter 7 will work for your own website, too.

In creating your own store, you have two options: If you already work with an auction management company such as ChannelAdvisor, you can let it do all the heavy lifting, as creating WebStores for its customers is part of what it does. If you go this route, you can be assured that everything works seamlessly from channel to channel—that is, that your inventory is updated in real time and order management is built-in, as well. The services of companies such as these aren't cheap, however, but you may feel the results are worth it. Fortunately, there are more economical ways to build your own little store on the Web.

Companies such as ShopPal and Miva Merchant can have you up and running in a very short time. They offer templates and other Web tools (Miva even offers shopping cart software that's time-tested) to make building a WebStore relatively simple. You'll pay a start-up cost and then a monthly fee that will vary, depending on how much inventory you carry.

You can also get help from professional website designers through sites such as Guru (guru.com), shown in Figure 9-9, and Elance. There you will put your project up for bid (providing a rough budget) and sit back and wait for the proposals from professionals to come in. You can evaluate their work through the samples they provide and the feedback other customers have left. So as you can see, there's no need to go it alone when you decide it's time to create your own WebStore. See Figure 9-10 for an example.

Figure 9-9. Guru matches freelancers with employers and can be a great source of inexpensive talent.

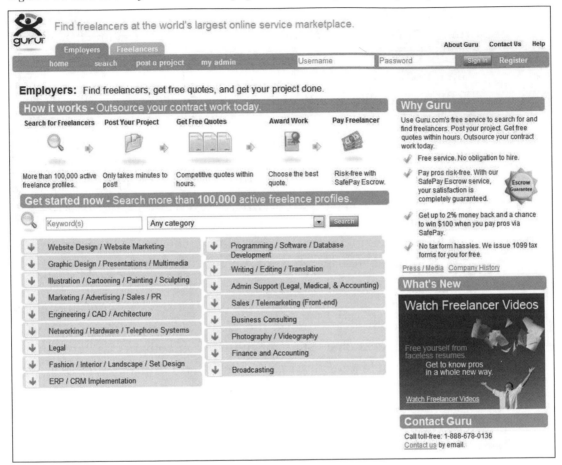

Working with Freelancers

Asking for bids and then working with a freelancer through a service like Guru can be intimidating at first. But there are safeguards built into its system (e.g., the funds you deposit can be put into an escrow account until you release them), so there's little to worry about if you choose your freelancer carefully.

Figure 9-10. GemAffair, operated by Michael Jansma, is a beautiful example of an independent WebStore

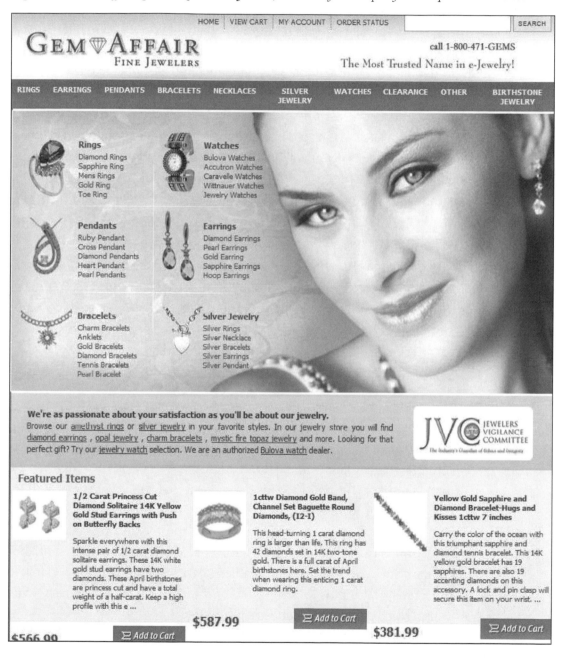

At one point, we were looking to take our own modest website up several notches. We posted the following ad on Guru:

> My wife and I are authors with a rather bland website. We'd like some-thing that better showcased our existing work, that made a stronger case for the services we offer clients, and that allowed us to include offers from affiliates. We would also like the ability to easily update the site ourselves. I'm sure you will have other ideas for how this could be improved. Right now it's based on a template from the Author's Guild. Finally, ideally, we'd keep the same URL.

> We wrote that when our project budget was between $1,000 and $2,500. (Remember, we were looking for more of an online brochure and not a full-featured e-commerce site.) Our ad drew 31 bids ranging from $800 to $2,500, and we definitely would have been comfortable choosing a freelancer from that pool. (Unfortunately, we never pursued that project since we got busy with other things, like writing the book you're holding.)

Once your store is up and running, you can start building your own customer base, and marketing your business as you see fit. Gary of Goggles and Glasses has added his own WebStore to his mix of venues. He likes the freedom his own corner of the Internet provides. Your own store does have its advantages. Gary, for example, enjoys living without the up-front fees to list or the closing fees at the end of the transaction. He can deal with customer service issues on his own without worrying that a problem can result in a poor feedback experience. As long as you're working hard to build a business, why not also have your own WebStore? he asks.

You control everything when the store is your own, setting your own policies, updating as you please, and acting as your own store manager, with no one above you to answer to. As Steve Jay of wholesalelaptopbattery told us, "We have a few websites, and they do very well. They are our best non–Amazon venue. We sell for a lot more on them, and we control everything and can make changes as needed."

Don't Forget to Make the Most of Your Amazon Association

"Having links to Amazon on our website helps to build trust, and some of our customers will buy from us through Amazon just because they like the Amazon payment system," Steve Jay noted.

Keep a Single E-Mail Domain

All of your customers' e-mail should funnel though to one e-mail domain, according to Gary Richardson, to make life easier for yourself. For example, you can set up various g-mail accounts through Google, each of which includes the selling venue as part of the address, so you'll know where the customer is coming from. These accounts would look something like amazonmerchant@gmail.com, ebaymerchant@gmail.com, websitemerchant@gmail.com. You can check them all at once just by reviewing your main g-mail account.

Other Ways to Market Your Expertise

Right now, you may not feel like much of an expert even as you've reached the last chapter of this book. But, don't sell yourself short. A year from now, you'll look back with astonishment at all you've learned and how far you've gone. The expertise you'll have gained along the way to becoming a successful e-merchant is something a lot of other people will want to have. Many sellers earn part of their income by sharing this expertise in ways that they find fulfilling.

Become a Consultant

The old joke used to be that anyone with a briefcase can call himself a consultant. Well briefcases aren't nearly as popular as they used to be, and, frankly, it always took a lot more than a briefcase to make money consulting. What you really need is a knowledge base in an area that people are interested in. Once you've been selling online successfully for at least two years, and have a network of other sellers with whom you share information, you have just such a knowledge base. Wall Street analysts, market research firms, and others will pay you for your time. They want to know your thoughts about selling online, what the climate currently is, what sellers are thinking and talking about, how sales are going for you, and a lot more. For this information you may be paid handsomely, say $200 an hour and up.

Of course you can also consult with others who'd like to follow in your footsteps and become e-merchants themselves. Any successful seller gets many e-mails from people wanting to know how they get started, where they get the merchandise they want to sell, and many other things related to their business. You shouldn't be expected to provide this hard-earned knowledge for nada, should you? Set a fair price for your services and offer to help for a fee. Some prospective sellers will just move on at that point, but others will gladly pay you.

Teach What You Know Well

Many community colleges offer classes about selling online. Right now, they're oriented toward eBay, as that's where the market has been. But as the idea of Amazon third-party selling grows, more and more colleges will want to hire teachers who can discuss Amazon as an opportunity, too. These classes offer you a way to get exposure for your own Amazon business, but also to establish yourself as an Amazon or e-commerce expert in your community. That can lead to more consulting work.

Write a Column About Selling Online

Most communities have local papers that are eager for copy. Offer your services as an e-commerce columnist and watch the offers come in. Obviously, you want to reach the most people you can so watch those circulation figures and arrange to retain the copyright on your articles. That way you can also post them on your blog, MySpace page, or a hundred other places on the Internet. It's all about grabbing mindshare and being perceived as an expert in your field. Think of yourself as an expert, market yourself as an expert, and people will think of you as one.

Looking Ahead

At the end of each chapter, we took it upon ourselves to give you a little glimpse of what was coming next. Sure, we wanted you to keep reading, but we also wanted to whet your appetite with temptations of more knowledge just around the turn of the next page. Well, as we end this last chapter, there is still more to come in this book. You'll find an appendix with details about using the Amazon Affiliates program. That's a fitting follow-up to this chapter, because it includes great information about making more money while actually selling other people's products. Yeah, we thought you'd like that at the end of the book!

But this time, the Looking Ahead section is yours to write. We've done our best to show you around Amazon, and we hope you've enjoyed it. We certainly enjoyed meeting and working with the fascinating sellers who have been so generous with their advice to all of us. Now, we'll look forward to the next sections of the story that you will write. You'll find your own corner here, and what you do with it will be as individual as you are. We hope you keep in touch, and let us know what you think, either through book reviews on Amazon or by contacting us through our website, www.bradanddeb.com. After all, it may be a vast Internet, but it's still a small world.

An Amazon Success Story

Tricia Records of Read_Rover_Books is quite familiar to you by now, since you've read her wise advice throughout the chapters of this book. It may come as no surprise to you that Tricia has been a longtime Amazon seller. She's been selling actively on the site for more than six years, which is forever in Internet time! Her Amazon adventure began "as a lark." She received an e-mail from Amazon inviting her to resell some of the books she'd purchased on the site. Her lark quickly turned into a successful full-time business. No wonder she has so many helpful things to share with newcomers.

All told, Tricia operates on 12 different selling venues. She finds diversity in sales outlets to be as important to her successful business as diversity in her product line is. Diversity is the key to maintaining profitability. "Reliance on any single platform to maintain profitability is folly, as too many factors beyond the merchant's control can cause sales slumps," she told us. To look at a basic example of this idea, just consider platform stability. If Amazon's payment processing centers are down, which can happen at times, it can be very challenging if not impossible to complete the checkout. The result, of course, is lost revenue for the merchant. If your other sites are still humming

along, a downturn on Amazon will still be a challenge, but it won't necessarily be a devastating loss. "By diversifying to other selling venues you spread out your inventory to the largest possible buying audience while also securing more 'up' time in which their stock is being exposed," Tricia explained.

Tricia agrees with many of the other sellers with whom we spoke that Amazon's discussion boards can be a valuable resource for new sellers. She also noted that there is a wealth of information in the archives of those boards, and searching them can be a valuable part of any newcomer's education. She is a member of the IMA and credits that group with sharing a great deal of knowledge and experience with her. She especially enjoys her interactions there, because they're not limited strictly to one venue. The group is "geared towards all manner of e-commerce businesses to include eBay as well as proprietary sites," Tricia notes. One of the most beneficial events Tricia has attended was the 2005 Annual Amazon Sellers Conference. This conference is hosted by independent sellers and focuses almost entirely on the issues involved with selling on Amazon. "As it is hosted in Seattle," Tricia said, "Amazon has always participated quite heavily to include a full-day event sponsored by Amazon headquarters. Jeff Bezos himself has historically always made an effort to make an appearance." You can get more information about this conference at http://www.sellerconference.com/joomla/index.php?option= com_frontpage&Itemid=1.

Perhaps not surprisingly, Tricia notes that the most important aspect of selling online is sourcing stock. She searches for unique stock that is already in short supply. "These titles tend to be out-of-print and of value to academics, researchers, and collectors," she said. "Because of their out-of-print nature, their value tends to increase over time rather than decrease." As such, they are much less susceptible to the "low-balling" practices of some other sellers.

To manage everything, Tricia uses the third-party inventory management provider FillZ (featured in Chapter 5). "They manage my inventory across 12 different sales venues with little additional effort on my part," she said. "Their service has been extremely reliable and robust and is constantly upgrading to meet the demands of the marketplace." Tricia noted they have been instrumental in helping her to add new venues and grow her sales across multiple venues.

Does Tricia have advice for those just starting out? "Don't make a big investment into an online sales venture without doing your homework," she says. She also recommends that you set yourself up legitimately with all the necessary tax ID numbers. (We told you so! You have done that by now, right?) Learn everything you can about your product line, and continually reinvest your earnings back into your business so you can expand. Finally, find ways to diversify. Remember, that's not coming just from us, but directly from an e-merchant who has been an Amazon success story for a long time now.

APPENDIX A

Amazon's Associates Program

Isn't it a wonderful dream to have a business set up to run itself? Unfailingly, it deposits money into our bank accounts even as we slumber. Just imagine the sound of gently ringing cash registers lolling you off to dreamland.

Affiliate programs pretty much do that. You agree to advertise someone else's product, for example, on your website. In exchange, you earn a commission on each sale that comes through your site. Amazon's own affiliate program, which you should definitely take advantage of, is called Amazon Associates. There's no charge to participate.

Amazon Associates was one of the first Internet affiliate programs, which explains why Amazon products are all over the Web. There are hundreds of thousands of participants—from large, well-known companies, to niche content sites and blogs, to comparison-shopping engines and search engines.

Why shouldn't you be among them? To get started, just click on the *Join Associates* hyperlink at the bottom of most Amazon pages. Sign up and you're an Amazon affiliate, able to add any of Amazon's millions of books, computers, digital cameras, whatever, to your blog or website. A click on an item takes the buyer to the Amazon site itself, where the sale is completed.

Adding Amazon products to your site is simple. You just copy and then paste the code Amazon gives you onto the appropriate page of your website or blog. That code will also identify you as the affiliate responsible for the sale when someone clicks on one of your links and buys something on Amazon. You can earn commissions of up to 10 percent for every purchase. (Figure A-1 shows some of the link options from which you can choose.)

About payment: You can sign up for either the *performance fee struc-ture* or the *classic fee structure*. Under the performance plan, the rate you earn increases from 4 percent to 10 percent as the volume of products you sell increases. Under the classic plan, you receive a fixed rate of 4 percent. Amazon recommends you sign up for the perfor-mance plan, and so do we. You deserve a higher rate as your performance increases!

As an affiliate, Amazon will send you a monthly statement show-ing what you earned. But more detailed performance reports, updat-ed every 24 hours, are available on the Amazon Associates website (as shown in Figure A-2). Be sure to review these carefully, as these reports are critical to your success. They show which links are and are not working, and from there you can adjust your inventory mix appropriately. Some of the details Amazon provides include traffic, revenue, earnings, conversion rates, and link types.

Of course, the more traffic your site or blog receives, the more products you're likely to sell, so develop those SEO skills! Affiliate money is free money that you can count on month after month.

Figure A-1. Here are some of the options Amazon gives you for promoting your affiliate business.

Omakase™ Links - Leave it up to us!

Omakase links uniquely combine information on each site visitor's taste, the site's content, and historical trends to dynamically generate relevant ads that Amazon serves to your site. With simple, yet powerful, customization options, Omakase lets you automatically provide personalized product ads to your site visitors that complement your site design. Omakase - Leave it up to us!

Product Previews - Enhance.Hover.Expand.

Product Previews let visitors to your site view valuable product information without having to click through to Amazon.com. When visitors hover over a Product Preview-enhanced text or image link, a small window appears that contains the product image, new and used prices, average customer review and availability. Visitors can either add the item directly to their Amazon.com shopping carts or click through to product details on Amazon from the product window. Product Previews allow you to offer your visitors a convenient, seamless option for adding products to their shopping cart while enjoying the content of your site. Product Previews - Enhance. Hover. Expand.

Recommended Product Links

Recommended Product Links are dynamic links in which Amazon automatically selects and serves the content. You enter the type of products you want displayed, and we will update them with the bestselling products based on your criteria. Since Amazon automatically updates these links with fresh content, there is less work on your part to keep your links and banners updated. For convenience and flexibility, you can build Recommended Product Links in two different ways--by category and by keyword--each in multiple sizes. And by changing their background color,

 TIP

Test Complementary Products Risk-Free!

Kathy of Element Jewelry & Accessories recently added purses and shoes to one of her WebStores (www.newelementjewelry.com). These

Figure A-2. Through the Amazon Associates website, you can track your performance as an affiliate.

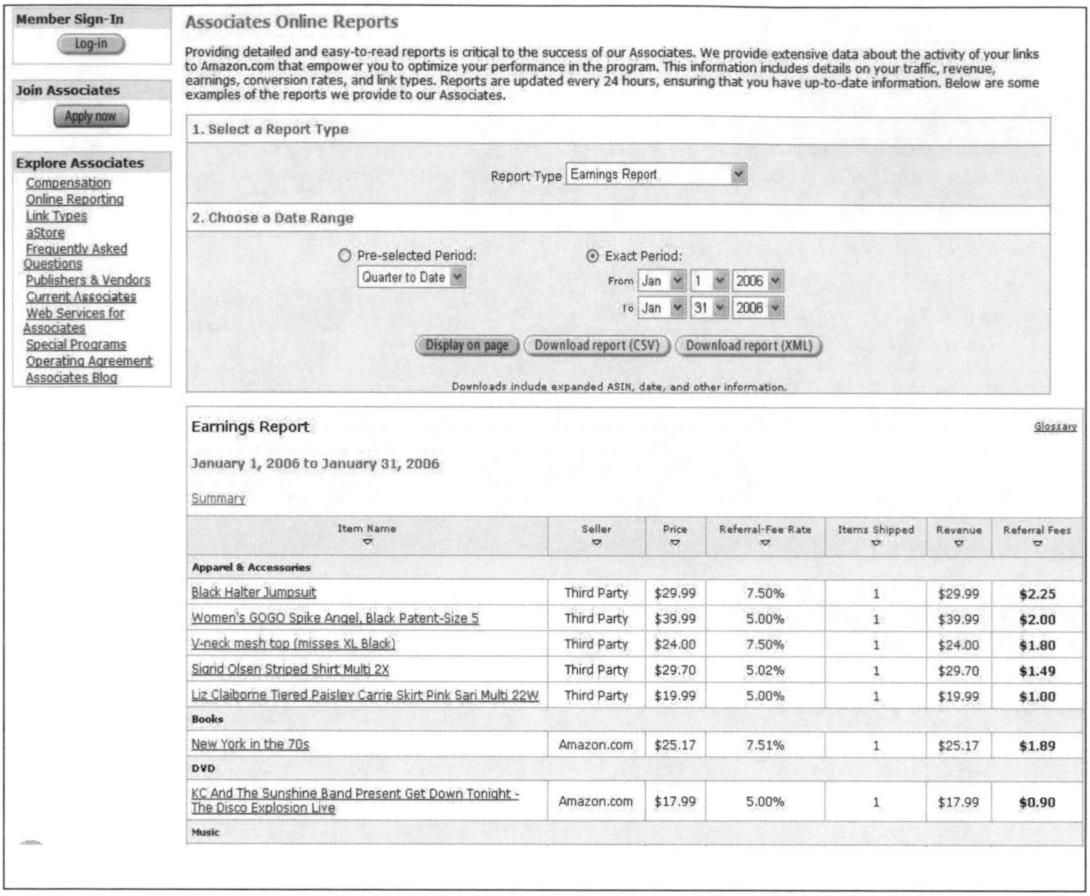
Member Sign-In
Log-in
Join Associates
Apply now
Explore Associates
Compensation
Online Reporting
Link Types
aStore
Frequently Asked Questions
Publishers & Vendors
Current Associates
Web Services for Associates
Special Programs
Operating Agreement
Associates Blog

Associates Online Reports

Providing detailed and easy-to-read reports is critical to the success of our Associates. We provide extensive data about the activity of your links to Amazon.com that empower you to optimize your performance in the program. This information includes details on your traffic, revenue, earnings, conversion rates, and link types. Reports are updated every 24 hours, ensuring that you have up-to-date information. Below are some examples of the reports we provide to our Associates.

1. Select a Report Type

Report Type Earnings Report

2. Choose a Date Range

Pre-selected Period: Quarter to Date

Exact Period: From Jan 1 2006 To Jan 31 2006

Display on page | Download report (CSV) | Download report (XML)

Downloads include expanded ASIN, date, and other information.

Earnings Report

Glossary

January 1, 2006 to January 31, 2006

Summary

Item Name	Seller	Price	Referral-Fee Rate	Items Shipped	Revenue	Referral Fees
Apparel & Accessories						
Black Halter Jumpsuit	Third Party	$29.99	7.50%	1	$29.99	**$2.25**
Women's GOGO Spike Angel, Black Patent-Size 5	Third Party	$39.99	5.00%	1	$39.99	**$2.00**
V-neck mesh top (misses XL Black)	Third Party	$24.00	7.50%	1	$24.00	**$1.80**
Sigrid Olsen Striped Shirt Multi 2X	Third Party	$29.70	5.02%	1	$29.70	**$1.49**
Liz Claiborne Tiered Paisley Carrie Skirt Pink Sari Multi 22W	Third Party	$19.99	5.00%	1	$19.99	**$1.00**
Books						
New York in the 70s	Amazon.com	$25.17	7.51%	1	$25.17	**$1.89**
DVD						
KC And The Sunshine Band Present Get Down Tonight - The Disco Explosion Live	Amazon.com	$17.99	5.00%	1	$17.99	**$0.90**
Music						

were actually Associate products that she was testing through the holidays to see if this is a direction she should grow her business.

If you sign up for the program, be sure to read Amazon's Associates Blog, which announces the latest promotions. When we checked, Amazon was running shoe promotions just in time for spring. There were other promotions for baby items, and videos from Amazon's Unbox Collection of movies and TV shows that you can rent or buy.

Earn with Amazon's Virtual Products

Amazon's Unbox videos, Kindle e-book products, and Amazonmp3s generally earn you some of the highest commissions.

We were surprised to learn that the majority of sellers we interviewed for this book did not participate in the Associates program. Some were too busy to look into it, and at least one seller was worried about quality control issues, in that if she carried another company's products on her site, she would be vulnerable to that company's quality control. But many other sellers planned to look into the program. Once you fill out the registration form, you will have access to Associates Central—the Amazon area that lets you link to almost any page in the Amazon catalog through the *Build Links* section.

The 18 Best Resources for Researching Anything Amazon

One of the best parts of writing a book, for Brad anyway, is the chance to research and learn about the best ways to do new things. Amazon sellers are, of course, the best sources of information about how to sell on the site. But they're also busy, meaning you have to learn a lot of these things for yourself. That said, here are the resources we recommend based on our research and interviews with some of Amazon's most successful sellers. We've mentioned some of these before but here they are all in one place.

These are all great, but listed in no particular order.

25 Vital Things to Know for New Sellers aka THIS AIN'T EBAY (http://www.amazonsellercommunity.com/ forums/thread.jspa?threadID=148872&tstart=0). This is one of the most popular posts to the Amazon Seller Community Boards. It's been read many thousands of times. As we were writing this book it had just been updated, so the information should be fairly current. We highly recommend you take a look at it!

AuctionBytes (http://www.auctionbytes.com/). Many e-merchants say that now that they are up to speed they're too busy running their businesses to read newsletters and magazines. But many still make time to read *AuctionBytes*. What's *AuctionBytes*? It's a website, newsletter, and source of podcasts and videos all having to do with e-commerce. Although it has an eBay slant—hence, the name *AuctionBytes*—Ina and David Steiner have been covering Amazon more and more as their audience migrates there as well.

Amazon's Click-to-Call Service. As a new seller, you're going to need help, a lot of it. Fortunately, Amazon has made getting that help easy. Just call a number and an Amazon rep, who is actually helpful, calls you back within minutes. We've found that even experienced sellers use this service. To get to this screen, click the *Help* link at the far right of any Amazon page, then look for the *Contact Us* button along the right-hand margin.

Here are Amazon's instructions for using this invaluable feature:

1. Log in to your seller account.
2. Choose the *Seller Help* link in the upper-right corner of the home page.
3. Choose the *By phone* link in the Contact Us box on the right side of the page.

4. Wait for the *Call back* request pop-up, or select the *Call Me* option.

5. Fill out the short Request call back form and click *Submit*. We'll call you back to assist with your questions.

Scot Wingo's Blog (http://ebaystrategies.blogs.com/). Scot is the president of ChannelAdvisor, a company that helps other companies sell things online. In fact, it will handle all aspects of this process for you—for a price, of course. It's more geared to the really large sellers than smaller- to medium-size ones. Scot also publishes a blog called Comparison Shopping Engine Strategies (http://www.csestrategies.com/) that's a great source for the latest thinking about comparison-shopping engines such as Shopping.com. Although Scot's main blog is eBay focused, many merchants read it no matter where they sell, just for Scot's insights into the e-commerce business. For example, Scot's analysis of whether eBay's new price and feedback changes from February 2008 were working generated lots of controversy. Scot is one of the go-to guys for reporters when they need a quote about e-commerce. Make him one of your resources as well.

Warehousedeals.com (warehousedeals.com). Speaking of Scot Wingo, he's the one who first brought our attention to this site. It's from Amazon, and he said at the time it was a "mostly unknown liquidation site." As journalists, we like it when things are mostly unknown, but we also like good deals. Check this one out.

Amazon Strategies Blog http://www.amazonstrategies.com/. This was a new blog when we came across it, but given that it's written by a ChannelAdvisor employee, we think it's definitely worth checking out.

Amazon's Seller Boards. Online coffee klatches (message boards) are popular all over the Net. On Amazon, they're a way for sellers of all sorts to chat with one another and get their questions answered. A lot of information is available on these boards, and not all of it is relevant to what you are doing at the time. So be sure to use the search function a lot rather than sift through too many messages to find what you need. But definitely put this on your list of top resources to check. The most popular board is the Amazon seller success board. (http://www.amazonsellercommunity.com/forums/forum.jspa?forumID=25). The Amazon announcements board is one you'll want to check as well for news and updates on any system glitches. You can get to either board by clicking the help hyperlink at the top right-hand corner of most pages, and then entering its name in the search box on the left. Dan Morrill of Alternating Reality found the "Amazon success and sellers boards have been great. We were able to remove many annoyance points right off the bat."

Amazon's Annual Sellers Conference. For Tricia Records of Read_Rover_Books, this was "one of the most beneficial events that I have attended." We had not heard much about it, but Tricia says it's a conference hosted by independent sellers, focusing almost entirely on Amazon selling. It's always in Seattle, so Amazon has participated quite heavily. In the past, the conference has included a full-day event sponsored at Amazon's headquarters. Sometimes Jeff Bezos himself is there! Here is the website: http://www.sellerconference.com/joomla/index.php?option=com_frontpage&Itemid=1

Your Own Customers. Eric Lau of Visiondecor believes that when it comes to market research, you should start with your own customers. "The best resources we used were our customers and their direct feedback to our service, quality, and performance. We communicate with our customers so that any experience turns out to be a positive one for both the customers and our ability to improve and meet their expectations." At times, Eric will actually solicit his customers' input. "We e-mail customers and ask them what they thought about our service, and we read every single one of those feedbacks to make improvements on our mishaps."

Internet Retailer (http://www.internetretailer.com/). This is a print magazine and online newsletter. They charge for some of their stuff (e.g., their annual list of the top Internet Retailers), but much of it gives you a bird's-eye perspective on the industry you're a part of. We find it's one of the few sources we regularly check.

Amazon (http://www.amazon.com/). Asad Bangash of Beachcombers! is one of the many fans of the Amazon site itself for seller help; he says he finds almost all of the information he needs right there. It's no wonder Asad doesn't have to venture far. Consider Amazon with its bestseller lists, Listmania lists, reviews, profiles, and feedback pages. Amazon has tons of information about the products you're thinking of selling and the other people now selling them. For example, spend some time looking at the feedback your competitors have received. Dan Morrill found that when Alternating Reality was doing its customer research, the comments the customers left for his competition were the most valuable research. "We spent days reading what ticked customers off, and came up with a top five list of things never to do with our store." Of course, there are also the Amazon FAQ and Help guides. And don't forget about the Help search bar either!

Seller Central (https://sellercentral.amazon.com/gp/homepage.html). Kathy Wojtczak of Element Jewelry & Accessories is a big Seller Central fan. "Amazon provides seller-related news and an in-depth Help section within Seller Central. The home page of Seller Central has regular Announcements and Headlines that keep sellers informed on selling tips, account changes, scheduled maintenance, etc.

The Help section has every topic imaginable and even provides tutorial videos for some issues."

Of course, once you're a big-time Amazon Seller, you will be on Seller Central a lot, too. Seller Central is also a great source of market intelligence about your own business. Just click the *reports* tab.

Amazon Business Services (http://www.amazonservices .com/businesssolutions/). Recommended to us by Amazon itself, this is the landing page for anyone who wants to partner with Amazon to make money. That includes sellers, advertisers, WebStore by Amazon owners, drop shippers, and those who represent corporate accounts. This is definitely one page you will want to bookmark.

Steve Weber (http://www.weberbooks.com/selling/ selling.htm). We recommend any of Steve's books, his blog, his website, whatever; this guy knows Amazon. His marketing ideas are fresh, and as fellow writers, we're in awe of the ground he's paved. His book (*Plug Your Book!*) about "plugging" books you sell online, applies to plugging all sorts of things, not just books.

The Internet Merchants Association (http://imamerchant .org/), the **E-Commerce Merchants Trade Association** (http://www.ecmta.org/index.cfm), and the **Professional eBay Sellers Alliance** (http://www.gopesa.org/). These are trade groups consisting of professional e-merchants. Join one of these groups and soon you'll have access to some of the best minds in the business. (Just be sure to reciprocate when you can!) They can suggest "best practices" and through their message boards answer almost any question. Besides the membership, these groups offer conferences where you can go and mingle with your fellow members and hear from industry experts about what's new and perhaps what will be new real soon.

We definitely think you should join at least one of these groups and see which one best suits your personality and budget. Be sure to attend one of their conferences, too.

Your Amazon Rep. Once you reach a certain level you will qualify for your own "Top Seller Account Manager" (TAM). Use her! Call her with any related questions you may have. If you don't yet have your own rep you can always call Technical Support or the most recent Amazon employee who's contacted you about an Amazon product, such as Fulfillment by Amazon (FBA).

LifeHacker (http://lifehacker.com/). This is a blog, pure and simple. It usually has nothing to do with e-commerce. But as an e-merchant you already use a computer, so you may as well have fun doing it. The point of this blog is to help computer users make their lives easier, but without having to study programming to do it. We don't have the time to check it out too often when we're under deadline, but we're always glad when we do. Another blog we recommend is boingboing (http://www.boingboing.net/).

Amazon's Seller Support Blog (http://sellersupport .typepad.com/). Amazon's own blog helps Amazon's third-party sellers gain valuable information and respond to topics discussed. Amazon.com's Seller Support staff writes for the blog as do guest bloggers. Both comments and topic suggestions are welcome. "Our motivation is simple," says Mackenzie Smith, Amazon's Director, Seller Support. "If our Sellers are successful, then so are we."

INDEX